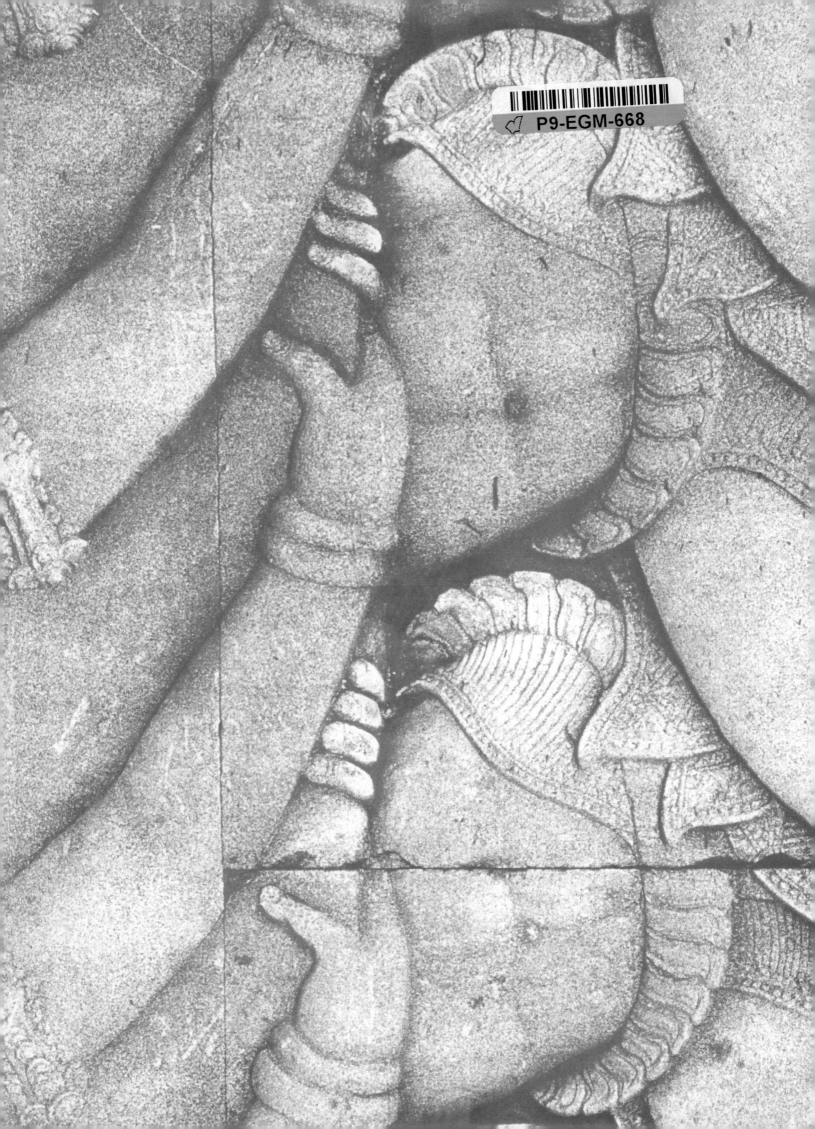

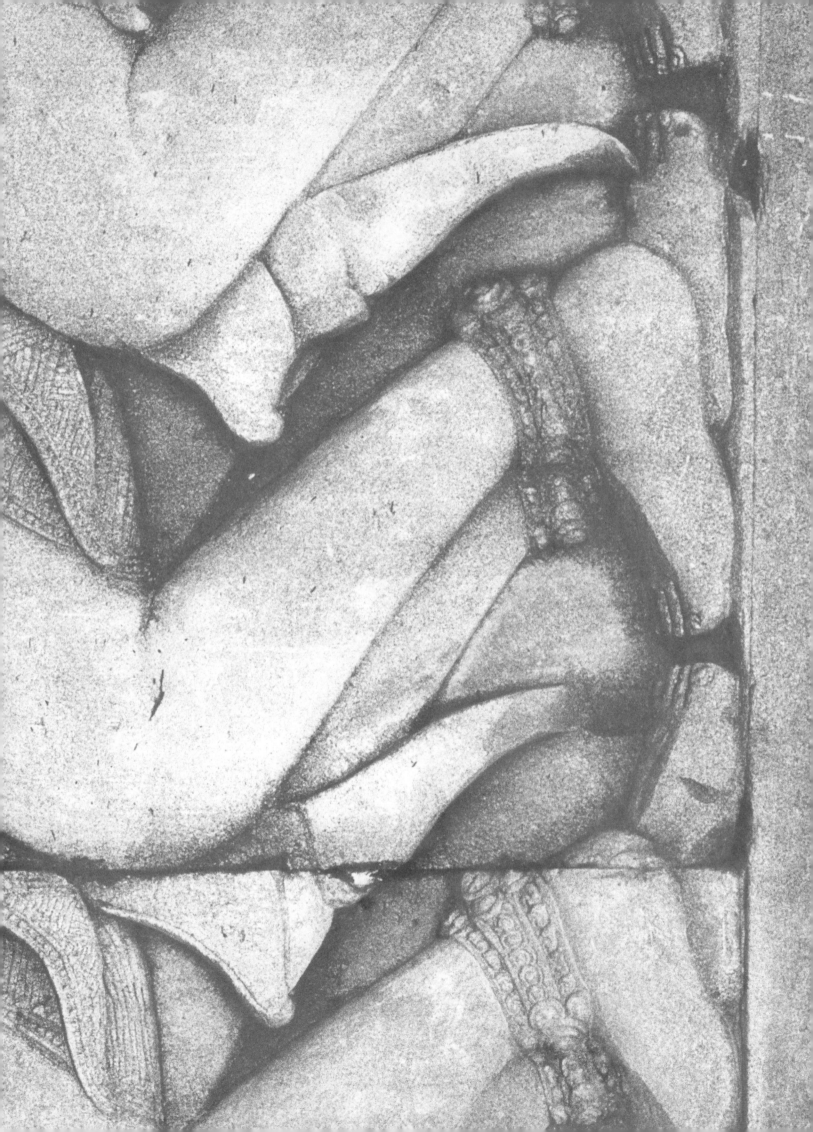

# THE HISTORY OF
# ARCHAEOLOGY

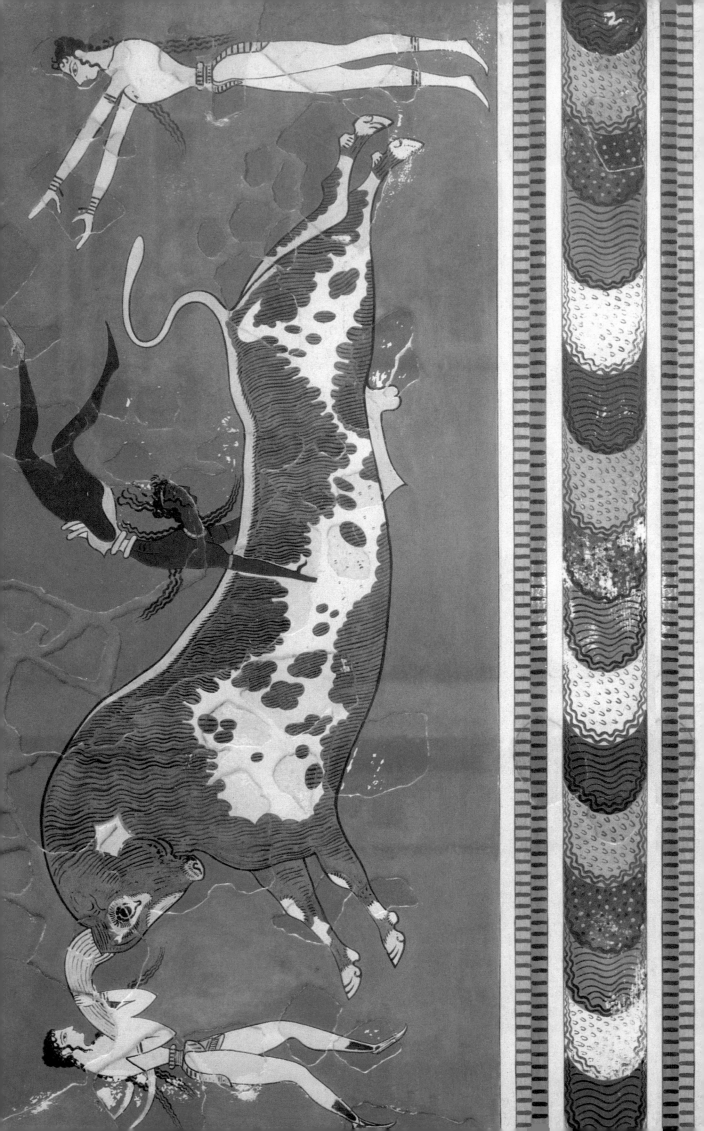

# THE HISTORY OF
# ARCHAEOLOGY

### MAEV KENNEDY

# CONTENTS

TIMELINE....................................................6
SITE MAP ...............................................8
INTRODUCTION ..........................................10

## 1 Ancient Ancestors     12

Before the Flood: The Stone Age ...................14
The Painted Hunt ...........................................16
Out of Africa, Into Australia.......................18
Old Bones and the Leakeys...........................20
Living in the Bones:
Ukrainian Mammoth Bone Houses ................22

## 2 The Bronze Age     24

Worshipping the Sun and Astonishing
the Neighbours: The Bronze Age....................26
Merlin's Calendar: Stonehenge .....................28
The Sun Also Rises: The Boyne Valley ...........30
The Marching Stones: Carnac .......................32
Immortal Furniture: Scara Brae.....................34
The Romans Arrive: Maiden Castle ...............36
Eye Witnesses from the Past: The Bog
People, The Ice Man, The Ice Maiden ...........38
The Inuit Ice Baby .........................................40

## 3 The Middle East     42

History is Invented:
The Archaeology of Writing ......................44
Nineveh .......................................................46
Ur: Leonard Wooley's Society Dig.................48
Bogazkoy: The Hittites Uncovered ................50
The Dead Sea Scrolls ....................................52
Mohenjo-Daro ...............................................54

## 4 Egypt 56

Egypt Finds its Voice Again:
The Rosetta Stone............................................58
Napoleon's Donkeys Struggle
into the Desert..................................................60
Tutankhamun: The Most Famous
Question and Answer in Archaeology............62
Where the Workers Lived: Deir....................64
The Rescue of Abu Simbel ...........................66
Ramesses, An Immortal Hero .......................68
Hatshepsut: Terrorism Among the Tombs......70
Faces From a Crossroads:
The Hawara Mummies ...................................72

## 5 China and The Far East 74

The Greatest Wall:
China and the Far East...................................76
The Divine Bronze Age: Shang Bronzes..........78
The Emperor's Army .......................................80
Immortality in Jade Pyjamas .........................82
The Silk Road: Curiosity Lures the
Chinese Out .....................................................84
Japan: The Mirror in the Keyhole .................86
Borobudar: A Mountain of Stone
Rises Again ......................................................88
Angkor Wat: A World Heritage Site on
the Black Market.............................................90

## 6 Greece 92

Digging for Homer: Greece ...........................94
Troy...................................................................96
Mycenae ...........................................................98
Evans and Knossos .......................................100
Elgin ...............................................................102
The School of Athens ...................................104
Delphi: The End of the Gods.......................106

## 7 Rome 108

The Scholar Cuckold: William Hamilton......110
Petra: One Immortal Line of Poetry.............112
The Painted Peace: The Happy Etruscans.....114
Rome: The Renaissance Treasure
Hunter's Larder .............................................116
An Eyewitness to Archaeology:
Pliny and Pompeii.........................................118
Bath: Minerva in a Sewer .............................120
Lepcis Magna: The Triumph of the
Local Boy Made Good ..................................122
Hadrian's Wall: Cold Feet on the
Border of Empire ..........................................124

## 8 Biblical Archaeology 126

Christianity and the Archaeology of Faith.....128
The Walls Fall Down: Jericho ......................130
The Queen of Sheba and
Great Zimbabwe.............................................132
Jerusalem: Archaeology Under a
Shower of Stones ..........................................134
Celtic Asceticism on the Rim of Ireland........136
Coptic Christians: A Living Link to
Ancient Egypt.................................................138
The Ark: The Search Continues...................140

## 9 Americas 142

Yearning for Vikings: The Kensington
Stone and American Archaeology.................144
L'Anse Aux Meadows and the
Missing Vineyard ..........................................146
Jefferson, The 'Father' of American
Archaeology, Digs Up His Own Back Yard...148
Great Serpent Mound, A Puzzling
Monument.......................................................150
Jamestown, The Colony That Failed............152
Mesa Verde, The Cattle Rancher's
Treasury..........................................................154
The Bloody Ball Game:
The Mayans at Copan ...................................156
The Aztecs Under Mexico ...........................158
Sipan: The Unlooked For Royal Tombs ........160
Machu Picchu, The Misinterpreted City
in the Clouds .................................................162
El Plomo, Chile: The Saddest Sacrifices........164

## 10 Modern Times 166

The Ancient History of Modern Times ........168
Archaeology Gets its Feet Wet.....................170
Bringing Up the Boats: The Mary Rose
and the Vasa ...................................................172
Palaces Under the Sea:
Cleopatra's Alexandria..................................174
Cooking Pots and the Industrial
Revolution ......................................................176
Any Old Iron? The Archaeology of
Yesterday's Redundancies .............................178
And Did Those Feet? A Retired
Chiropodist Looks Down..............................180
More Science, Less Digging, and Still
the Water Rises: Conclusion ........................182

GLOSSARY .....................................................184
BOOK LIST .....................................................186
INDEX ..............................................................187
ACKNOWLEDGEMENTS...........................192

This edition published in 1999 by CLB,
an imprint of Quadrillion Publishing Limited,
Godalming Business Centre, Woolsack Way,
Godalming, Surrey, GU7 1XW, England.

Distributed in the US by Quadrillion Publishing Inc.,
230 Fifth Avenue, New York, NY 10001.

First published in the UK 1998 as
Hamlyn History of Archaeology
by Hamlyn, a division of Octopus Publishing Group Ltd

Copyright © 1998 Octopus Publishing Group Limited

ISBN 1–84100–311–5

Printed and bound in China

# TIMELINE

It is difficult to gain a perspective on archaeology unless you begin with an overview. Here, using major archaeological (above) and historical (below) events, is a chronological rough guide to what was going on in history. throughout the ages.

Old Stone Age (Paleolithic) from the earliest human times to the end of the last Ice Age, around 10,000 B.C.

Middle Stone Age (Mesolithic) 10,000–4500 B.C.

New Stone Age (Neolithic) 4500–2300 B.C.

Bronze Age 2300–800 B.C.

Iron Age 800 B.C.–A.D. 400

Dark Ages A.D. 500–1100

Middle Ages 1100–1453

Modern Ages 1500–present day

Eruption of Mount Vesuvius

## ARCHAEOLOGICAL EVENTS

Neolithic stone pick

**550 B.C.** Nabonidus, last native king of Babylon, keenly interested in archaeology, establishes first museum of excavated objects in his palace.

**1586** William Camden publishes Britannia, his study of British antiquities.

**1649** John Aubrey (1625–1697), wit, gossip and antiquarian, identifies Bronze Age stone circle and henge of Avebury, Wiltshire.

**1662** Olof Verelius appointed Professor of the first Chair of Antiquities, at the University of Upsala.

**1674** The coining of the word Archaeology is credited to Jacob Spon, 17th-century German physician.

**1744** First published excavation, of megalithic passage grave, in first issue of Danish Royal Society journal.

**1764** J. J. Winckelmann, father of modern archaeology, publishes History of the Art of Antiquity.

## HISTORICAL EVENTS

**1.5 million years B.C.** Development of earliest hunter gatherer societies.

**9000 B.C.** Origins of agriculture in the Middle East.

**5500 B.C.** Settled farmers in the fertile Nile valley, Egypt.

**3300 B.C.** Sumerians develop writing.

**3100 B.C.** Newgrange, Boyne Valley, Ireland, megalithic passage tomb.

**3000 B.C.** First ditch and bank at Stonehenge.

**2700 B.C.** Earliest Egyptian pyramids.

**2200–1450 B.C.** Rise of Minoan civilization and their palaces on Crete.

**2000–1,000 B.C.** First Greek mainland culture, the Mycenaean.

**1750–1050 B.C.** First Chinese dynasty, the Shang, develops superb bronze working skills.

**753 B.C.** Traditional date for the foundation of Rome.

**323 B.C.** Death of Alexander the Great—his body preserved in honey.

**44 B.C.** Murder in Rome of Julius Caesar.

**27 B.C.** Octavian becomes Augustus, first Roman Emperor.

**0** Christian dating begins the Anno Domini, the "years of the Lord," from the birth of Jesus Christ.

**A.D. 79** Pompeii and its port, Herculaneum, buried in the eruption of Mount Vesuvius.

**A.D. 600** Height of the Mayan Empire.

**A.D. 632** Death of the prophet Muhammad, founder of Islam.

**A.D. 986** Vikings, from Iceland colony establish settlement at L'Anse Aux Meadows, Newfoundland, only confirmed site in North America.

**1119** Decree in Rome warning against looting stone from victory columns of Trajan and Marcus Aurelius.

**1572** Spanish kill the last Inca Emperor.

**1709** Abraham Darby succeeds in smelting iron using coke instead of charcoal, at Ironbridge Gorge, England, enabling mass iron production and the Industrial Revolution.

1803 — Lord Elgin begins to ship the Parthenon Marbles from Athens to the British Museum in London.

1812 — Swiss traveler Johann Ludwig Burckhardt (1784–1817) walks into Petra, disguised in Arab robes.

1819 — Christian J. Thomsen, sorts objects for new museum displays at Copenhagen into the Stone, Bronze and Iron Ages.

1822 — Jean François Champollion (1790–1832) publishes his translation of part of the Rosetta Stone, carved in about 196 B.C.

1849 — Austen Henry Layard (1817–1894) publishes world bestseller on his excavations, Nineveh and Its Remains.

1859 — Charles Darwin publishes On the Origin of Species by Means of Natural Selection.

1865 — Sir John Lubbock, Lord Avebury, politician, banker, and archaeologist, publishes Prehistoric Times, suggesting division of Stone Age into Paleolithic and Neolithic.

1870 — Heinrich Schliemann (1822–1890) begins to dig at Troy.

1871 — Karl Mauch (1837–1875) German explorer, finds the ruins of Great Zimbabwe—mistakenly identified as the palace of the Queen of Sheba.

1873 — First use of photographs in excavation reports, in Alexander Corze's publication of his work at Samothrace.

1873 — Schliemann finds "Priam's Treasure."

1887 — General Pitt Rivers (1827–1900) publishes the first of four highly influential volumes of excavation at Cranborne Chase, Wiltshire.

1888 — Flinders Petrie (1853–1942) discovers the Hawara mummy portraits in Roman cemetery in the Fayum, Egypt

1900 — Arthur Evans (1851–1941) begins excavating Knossos.

1911 — Machu Picchu, Peru, "the Lost City in the Clouds" of the Incas, found by American explorer Hiram Bingham (1878–1956).

1914–1918 World War I in Europe.

1922 — Leonard Wooley (1880–1960) begins excavating Ur.

1922 — Howard Carter (1873–1939) finds the first almost intact Egyptian royal tomb, of the insignificant boy pharaoh Tutankhamen.

1924 — Flinders Petrie publishes Methods and Aims in Archaeology.

1939–1945 World War II in Europe.

1940 — Two schoolboys find the painted caves, France.

1947 — Bedouin boy looking for a lost goat finds the Dead Sea Scrolls, in a cave at Qumran, now in Jordan.

1950 — Tollund Man, most famous bog body, found by peat cutters in Denmark.

1950s — Sir Mortimer Wheeler (1890–1976) becomes first archaeologist television star, on B.B.C. panel game "Animal, Vegetable, Mineral?"

1952 — Dame Kathleen Kenyon begins four year dig at Jericho, finds some of the world's earliest farmers.

1952 — Linear B, Minoan script, deciphered by Michael Ventris.

1960 — Largest archaeological rescue project in history begins, to move Abu Simbel and other monuments to higher ground.

1968 — Lewis Binford's New Perspectives in Archaeology launches "the New Archaeology" in the United States.

1974 — "Lucy," oldest most complete hominid skeleton found in Ethiopia, three-million-year-old female adolescent, named after Beatles song "Lucy In The Sky With Diamonds."

1974 — The Emperor's Terracotta Army found in Shaanxi Province, China, by farmers digging a well.

1982 — The Uluburun Ship, Bronze Age trader with all her cargo intact, found off the Turkish Coast.

1996 — The School of Athens, where Aristotle taught philosophy in 320 B.C., found under a car park in the Greek capital.

Hawara mummy

The Terracotta Army

# SITE MAP

A world view of some of the most significant archaeological sites and discoveries throughout the world.

**1** Lascaux  PAGE 17

**2** Australian rock paintings  PAGE 18

**3** Olduvai Gorge  PAGE 20

**4** Kiev mammoth bone houses  PAGE 22

**5** Avebury, Stonehenge, Bath, Stanton Drew  PAGES 26, 28, 120, 182

**6** Newgrange  PAGE 30

**7** Carnac  PAGE 32

**8** Scara Brae  PAGE 35

**9** Tollund Man  PAGE 38

**10** The Ice Maiden  PAGE 38

**11** Ice Baby  PAGE 41

**12** Nineveh  PAGE 46

**13** Ur  PAGE 48

**14** The Dead Sea Scrolls  PAGE 52

**15** Mohenjo-Daro  PAGE 54

**16** Tombs of Tutenkhamen, Deir El Medina, Ramses II, Hatshepsut,  PAGES 62, 64, 68, 70

**17** Hawara mummy portraits  PAGE 72

**18** The Great Wall  PAGE 76

**19** The Terracotta Army  PAGE 80

**20** Imperial tombs  PAGE 86

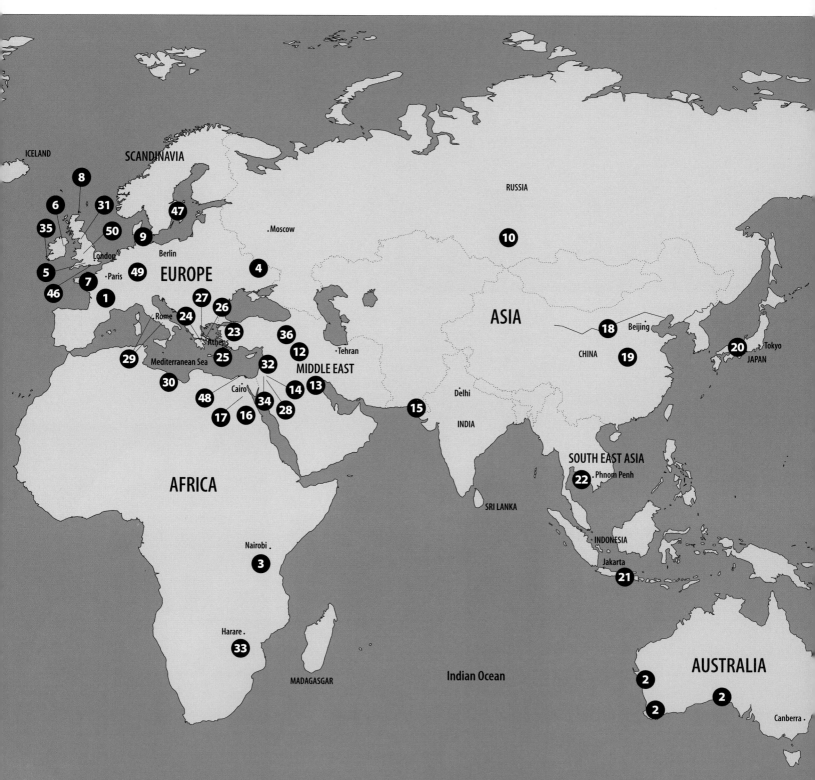

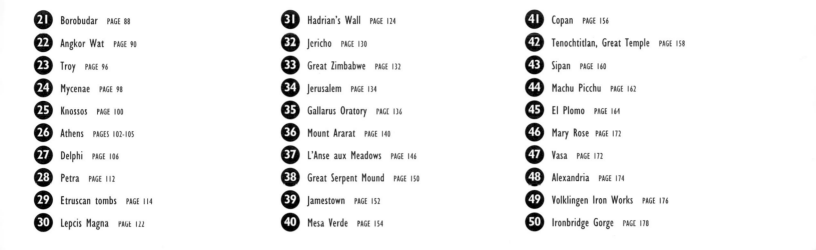

21 Borobudar PAGE 88
22 Angkor Wat PAGE 90
23 Troy PAGE 96
24 Mycenae PAGE 98
25 Knossos PAGE 100
26 Athens PAGES 102-105
27 Delphi PAGE 106
28 Petra PAGE 112
29 Etruscan tombs PAGE 114
30 Lepcis Magna PAGE 122

31 Hadrian's Wall PAGE 124
32 Jericho PAGE 130
33 Great Zimbabwe PAGE 132
34 Jerusalem PAGE 134
35 Gallarus Oratory PAGE 136
36 Mount Ararat PAGE 140
37 L'Anse aux Meadows PAGE 146
38 Great Serpent Mound PAGE 150
39 Jamestown PAGE 152
40 Mesa Verde PAGE 154

41 Copan PAGE 156
42 Tenochtitlan, Great Temple PAGE 158
43 Sipan PAGE 160
44 Machu Picchu PAGE 162
45 El Plomo PAGE 164
46 Mary Rose PAGE 172
47 Vasa PAGE 172
48 Alexandria PAGE 174
49 Volklingen Iron Works PAGE 176
50 Ironbridge Gorge PAGE 178

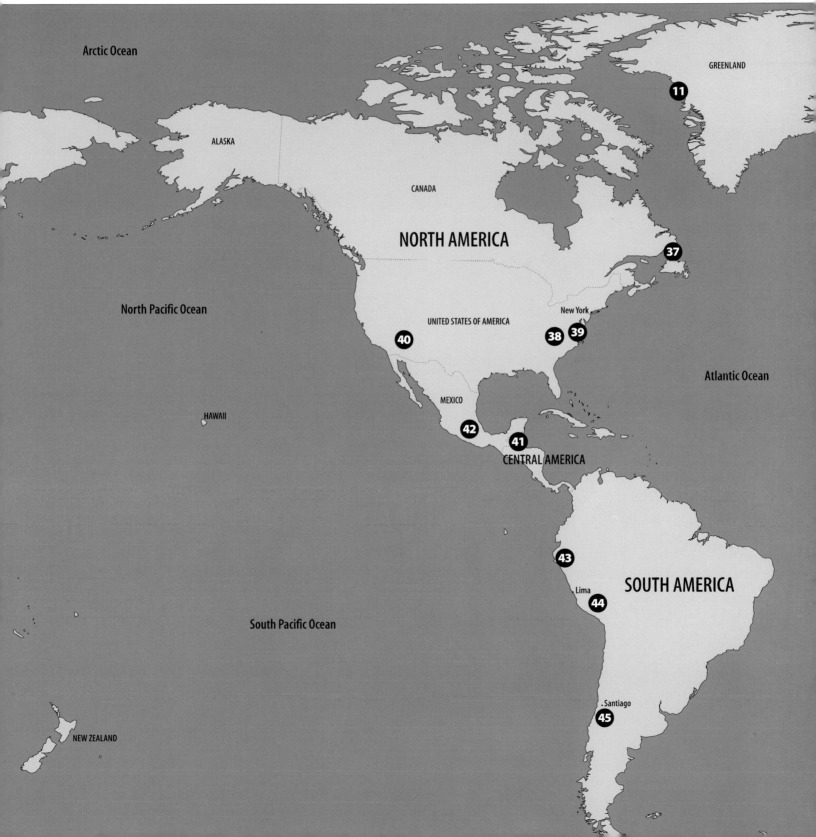

# THE SLEEPERS UNDER THE HILL

Once, there was a man walking home from the fair on a dark night. He missed his lift with a neighbor, and the road was long. When he could walk no further he lay down under a furze bush to rest. He woke to find a tall woman bending over him. "Come and take shelter with my people, stranger," she said, "the night is bitter." Be sure he did not need to be invited twice. She led him through a great stone doorway into a noble hall, where there was firelight and song, drink that never ran dry, and plates heaped with food for every guest. After the food and the drink, the singing and the dancing, he fell asleep on a pile of sheepskins. He woke, too stiff to rise and too cold to speak, under his furze bush, and however he looked he could find nothing nearby but a green hill. That man never married, and to the end of his life he was always looking in every place for the great stone door into the noble hall.

That story exists in innumerable versions in Ireland, and all over the world as the legend of the sleepers under the hill.

There came a time for most people when the world shrank again to the size of a village, and the highest roof shrank to the size of the longest plank you could cut from a tree. But the people were surrounded by evidence that giants had walked on the earth before them.

There were roads and palaces, bridges and towers, and flights of stone steps leading nowhere. Plows turned up fragments of carved marble, gold, bone, and the tesserae from mosaics. The man who, as a child, found the superb gold collar, the Gleninsheen Gorget dating from 2000 B.C, told me it was "folded under a stone the way you'd put away a collar in a drawer." When he brought it home he was told it was a coffin handle, and unlucky, so it was thrown out into a nettle patch where it lay for years until somebody recognized it.

It has become customary to date archaeology primly to the mid-19th century, when geological science and the theory of evolution supplied a framework for the relics of ancient days. Everything before that is treasure hunting and superstition.

While waiting for the scientists, ordinary people came up with the best explanation they could. From America to China there are legends of the sleepers under the hill, kings and knights, horses and carriages, who went away into the earth and remain there, waiting to be called again in time of need.

There was a lot of archaeology being done while people were waiting for archaeology to be invented. Nabonidus, last native king of Babylon in 555–539 B.C., is credited with the first museum and the first archaeological excavation to provide exhibits for it.

The Renaissance collectors, who rolled back green sheep pastures in the center of Rome looking for classical sculptures, are now dismissed as treasure-hunters. But it was not quite that simple—they were also looking for the book of rules for the classical world, the formula for the golden mean.

The conventional wisdom is that it took Darwin and Evolution to explode Archbishop Ussher's precise date for the world, based on

the Bible: God made the world in 4004 B.C.

But the division of the pre-classical world into Stone, Bronze, and Iron is itself precisely dated, and it was already 40 years old when Darwin published *On the Origin Of Species* in 1859. It was devised by an exceptionally orderly minded museum keeper, Christian J. Thomesen, struggling to come up with a sensible way to organize displays at his museum in Copenhagen. And 50 years before that an English country gentleman, John Frene, was looking at stone axes buried layers deep in Suffolk soil, and wondering. And 200 years earlier when John Aubrey was out hunting at Christmas in Wiltshire, England, he became the first man to spot that the huge stones in Avebury were not random monoliths but part of a structure even vaster than nearby Stonehenge.

It is not fair to dismiss these early efforts as archaeological dinosaurs, doomed to flap their rudimentary wings and be extinguished by the next asteroid collision. The germ of modern archaeology is surely in that spark of curiosity which got Aubrey down off his horse, and in his plight to answer the questions it provoked.

And when the scientists did come along, it turned out that the storytellers, from Homer to the anonymous author of "Jimmy Patsy Murphy's" traumatic trip home, were quite right.

There were indeed warriors under the hill, and fair ladies who lay down in golden ribbons fit for a ballroom under the great mound at Ur; there were ships under mounds far from the sea and palaces under the sea itself; under a plowed field in China there were not just kings in gold crowns, but an emperor in a jade suit, and a whole army of knights and horses.

If there's no sensible agreement on when archaeology began, there's no hint of when it will end. Around the world, the history of the 19th-century Industrial Revolution is being treated as archaeology, which already feels like ancient history. In the month I began researching this book, a major archaeological survey of the Cold War, that grim background to my childhood, was announced. In the same month a field worker fell into a hole near a Scottish airstrip, and dropped into a perfectly preserved Iron Age hut. Like the poor man coming home from the fair, it's best to keep looking.

**CHARLES DARWIN**
Charles Darwin (1809–1882) knew what turmoil his life's work would cause. He agonized for years, and finally published *On The Origin Of Species By Means Of Natural Selection* in November 1859, on learning to his dismay that a much younger, utterly obscure colleague was about to publish an identical theory. The storm he dreaded broke around his head: newspaper editorials, bishops, and cartoonists denounced him. His book changed the world, and helped establish the scientific framework for archaeology.

The giant oxen of Lascaux were
left sealed up in the darkness for
millennia, until schoolboys
stumbled into their cave in 1940.

# 1

# ANCIENT ANCESTORS

In Hollywood movies Stone Age man grunts and lumbers through a brutish life, scarcely more human than the animals he hunts. It is possible to look casually at a 100,000-year-old flint tool and dismiss it as a crude lump of rock, missing the skill involved in using one stone to shape another into a cutting edge as sharp as a modern knife. Stone Age paintings, however, whether interpreted as art or magic, shout a different message, that of developed human intelligence.

# BEFORE THE FLOOD:
# THE STONE AGE

Long before Darwin took a deep breath and published *On the Origin of Species* in 1859, antiquaries were having great difficulty fitting their finds into the 6,000 or so years which was all the time in the world.

Archbishop Ussher had given a great deal of attention to the matter, and announced that God had made the world in 4004 B.C.—or rather, taking into account Kepler's calculations, for Ussher was nothing if not scientific in his approach, 4,003 years, 70 days, and six temporary hours B.C. In the afternoon.

It was bad enough trying to work out where the mammoth bones fitted. In Scandinavia, where government-sponsored archaeological excavations began centuries before they did in southern Europe, they had to assign all such finds to an Age of Giants, which was some nebulous time before the Great Flood.

It became really difficult when what looked like man-made artifacts started to turn up among the mammoth bones.

Around the 1830s, a Roman Catholic priest in the west of England, and a customs officer in northern France, were both wrestling with the perplexing problem.

Father James MacEnery was a priest in Torquay, Devon (then a fishing village), and a passionate part-time fossil-hunter. In a cave called Kent's Cavern he found fossilized bones of extinct animals, and what appeared to be ancient flint tools. He tried, but he found it impossible not to conclude both must be contemporary, since he found them together under an undisturbed floor of stalagmites.

MacEnery wrote to William Buckland, who was the first professor of geology at Oxford University and went on to become Dean of Westminster Abbey in London, and got rebuked for his pains. Buckland refused to come and examine the finds himself, and said that primitive man must have tunneled into the bones layer. MacEnery would find the evidence of this if he just kept looking. Most importantly, Buckland said, there was "no reason for not considering them post-diluvian." Poor MacEnery persevered, but found it impossible to change Buckland's mind.

Jacques Boucher de Crèvecoeur de Perthes suffered from being extremely boring. It is clear from the accounts of people who waded through his reports—which invariably contained a lament about his previous report being ignored—or sat through his speeches, that his audience had nodded off long before he got to the point. There can't be many people who read all five volumes of his *De la Création*.

He was a somewhat underemployed customs official at Abbeville, in the Somme valley, France, who spent all his spare time chipping ancient bones and ancient flint implements out of riverbeds near his home, until every spare inch of his house was stuffed with flint and bone. Like Father MacEnery, he became convinced that since the two types of finds were clearly in the same undisturbed layer, they must be contemporary, and come from before the Flood.

Within a few decades of their deaths, more and more ancient implements would be found, along with human bones, and cave paintings of their fossilized animals alive and galloping. In the 20th century, finds of human and humanoid skulls, in Africa (as Darwin expected), Java, and China would push the

**ARCHBISHOP JAMES USSHER**
Archbishop James Ussher (1581–1656) was a graduate of Trinity College, Dublin, and became bishop of Armagh in Ireland in 1625. In 1640 he gave the full weight of his scholarly mind and his theological training to a problem troubling scientists and philosophers alike: when, exactly, did God make the world? His answer was precise: on October 23, 4004 B.C., though he fine-tuned the date to reflect the astronomer Kepler's calculations.

William Buckland was a grandee of his day, the first professor of geology at Oxford University and later Dean of Westminster Abbey, England. He used this awesome authority to crush the helpless doubts of Father MacEnery, a humble parish priest and amateur fossil hunter, about the date of Creation.

date of earliest man even further back, further than either man would have dared to imagine.

Poor Father MacEnery died without managing to resolve his conundrum, and his work was only vindicated by more work in Kent's Cavern and other caves in the area, long after his death.

Jacques Boucher de Crèvecoeur de Perthes arrived at an elegant and generous solution of his own:

"These shellfish, this elephant, this axe, or the person who made it, were, therefore, witnesses to the cataclysm that gave our country its present configuration. Perhaps the shell, the elephant, and the axe were already fossilized at this time; could they be the debris surviving from an earlier deluge, the souvenirs of another age? Who can put limits on the past? Is it not infinite, as is the future? Where, then, is the man who has seen the beginning of any one thing? Where is he who will see it end? Let us not bargain over the duration of ages; let us believe that the days of creation, those days that began before our sun, were the days of God, the interminable days of the world."

Nobody paid any notice, but he was more or less right all the same.

# THE PAINTED HUNT

Above: Are the man and the animal in this vivid painting from Tanzania, part of the same composition or simply sharing the same rock? A hunter spearing an elephant? A Shaman in a trance conjuring a vision of the animal with his wand?

Writing is the infant sibling of painting. Written language isn't much more than 5,000 years old, but before the wheel, before pottery, before iron, there was painting. The dates keep being pushed back: 15,000 years, 20,000, 40,000 . . .

The paintings are startling, because they are often the only evidence not just for the physical presence of ancient ancestors, but for how they thought and what they believed in.

The rock of ages endures, outlasting flesh and bone. The hand prints stenciled on cave walls in France and Spain often have one or two fingers or a thumb missing, sometimes all of them: fertile ground for argument as to whether they are evidence of ritual mutilation, disease, clumsiness with flint axes, or prints made with the fingers folded as some kind of sign language.

Rock art has been found wherever there is rock, all over Europe, all over Africa, in Australia, China, and the Americas. In Europe most has been found within caves, but where desert air preserves external rock faces, there is more in the open air than underground. This rock art ranges from the simplest stencils of hands and objects, such as children make in nursery school, to stick figures of human hunters and animals scraped with a sharp stone, to ravishingly painted animals demonstrating refined use of color and the natural texture of the surface.

The first attempt to explain the cantering bisons and antelopes was simple: what else would man do, in the long dull nights of the Stone Age, but scribble on the walls?

There were a few problems with this explanation, apart from the quality of the art. It fitted drawings on overhanging rocks at settlement sites, but many of the caves where art was found showed no sign of habitation. Man, this argument would imply, had whiled away the long, dull nights by crawling into pitch-dark underground caverns to paint walls, and in some cases, as at Lascaux where post holes have been found in the walls, had to build a form of scaffolding to get at roofs.

The next explanation, which prevailed for most of the 20th century, was "sympathetic magic," the painted hunt: man painted the animals to give him the power to kill them in the flesh. Again, there were problems: where the bones of eaten animals were found associated with paintings, they didn't match—man ate antelopes, but not lions, and some of the most common food species, smaller easily killed animals such as primitive sheep, were never portrayed at all.

The next theory, that the paintings are connected with magic ritual, often portraying a shamanistic trance dance, fits some rock art very well. The strange and sinister figures etched into the rock at Monte Pellegrino were found during World War II when the Allies blew up a munitions dump in a cave. The explosion brought down a stalactite wall, and behind it, therefore unquestionably ancient, there were startling images. They were beautifully drawn with a cool modern elegance. They appear to be dancers, and bird-beaked masked figures, circling and watching two figures, backs violently arched, tumescent, apparently bound from neck to ankle, and strangling to death. Other interpretations have been suggested for the figures, but that some sort of ritual is portrayed seems undeniable.

The Lascaux caves in France are probably the single most famous prehistoric artwork, but by no means the oldest at an estimated 17000 B.C., nor the largest or most elaborate.

The discovery of the Lascaux caves was a sensation, partly because it was a joyful story in the darkest days of the World War II. Four schoolboys scrambled into a cave they had discovered in the Dordogne, and found that the walls were rippling with huge animals. The cave had evidently been sealed for millennia. The colors sparkled, the condition of the paintings was immaculate, including the largest paleolithic painted figures ever found, the huge and beautifully painted over-life-size bulls. So many people came to see them that within 20 years the beautiful ochers and russets started to cloud with algae. The caves are now closed to the general public, although a replica Lascaux is almost as popular.

The tragedy was that they were found half a century too late to save the reputation of Don Marcel Sanz de Sautuola, a landowner in Santander in Spain, who found some splendid painted bison on the walls of a cave at Altamira.

Señor de Sautuola had been greatly impressed by the small and very old carvings he had seen the previous year at the Paris Universal Exposition of 1878. He made a huge, startling, and entirely correct leap of the imagination, and concluded that the painted bulls he was looking at were from the same period.

For his pains he was mocked for the rest of his life—which was less than ten years—by every expert on early man. He was accused of stupidity by some and even fraud by others. By the end of the century he was vindicated when similar paintings were found, associated with Paleolithic artifacts.

In a few cases it has been possible to interview ancient artists, and ask what they were doing. The Bushmen of the Drakensberg, in South Africa, had been painting and chipping people and animals on rocks for thousands of years. Their last works, at the end of the 19th century, showed Europeans on horseback, with guns: the white settlers who were to wipe out their art, their civilization, and most of their people.

A. R. Wilcox, who spent half a lifetime recording the art of these ancient people, wrote: "The Bushmen held on until about 1890, and at last perished, regretted then by none but now by every serious student of anthropology, psychology, and art, for they were the last of the Paleolithic."

The sophistication, elegance, and the vivid color and refined use of the rock surface of the Lascaux caves astonished the art world, while archaeologists continued to argue about what they meant.

# OUT OF AFRICA, INTO AUSTRALIA

Dating in archaeology is not a neutral science: from Schliemann shoveling aside centuries of evidence in search of Homer's one true Troy, to biblical fundamentalists looking for the day the rain started the Great Flood, *when* things happened can be as passionately disputed as what happened.

In Australia, prehistoric art has become entwined with politics, specifically with the issue of Aboriginal rights.

There are hundreds of thousands of sites of rock art in Australia. Unlike the caves of Europe, most of the Australian sites are on sheltered rock faces in the open, so perfectly preserved by bone-dry desert air that scientists have been able to analyse the human blood mixed with some red pigments. In the central Queensland sandstone belt alone, Grahame Walsh has identified 10,000 sites, including stencils of hands, and outlines of implements and weapons, such as sharp-edged stone "killing" boomerangs.

In northern Australia, archaeologists have used the changing images in rock art to date the rising sea levels of the paleolithic age, as the land mammals vanish from the drawings, replaced by fish and salt-water crocodiles.

The age of 13,000 years for art at Early Man Shelter in Queensland is regarded as remarkable, the age of 40,000 years in South Australia questionable, and an isolated age of 100,000 years announced in the 1990s is now considered a freak of wishful thinking.

Some of the earliest dates have come from a technique which is still the subject of much debate, pioneered by American scientist Ronald Dorn. This analyses the "varnish," a crust of mineral deposits and microscopic plant spores and organic materials, which bakes on to rock surfaces in desert conditions.

The earliest dates suggested for Australian art have given a new lease of life to the "Out-of-Africa" argument about human evolution, the alternative view that the earliest hominids may have evolved simultaneously into early man in different parts of the world, including Australia. Instead of man arriving no earlier than 15,000 years ago, this theory suggests that not only were the Aborigines there first, but they are among the ancient ancestors of the white settlers and all other modern men.

Australia is another place where the rock-art traditions survive into modern times. X-ray fish, a style of drawing fish with the bones revealed, are found at very ancient sites. The last man known to have drawn X-ray fish in Arnhem Land is not only identified, but he was interviewed and filmed. Najombolmi was still drawing in 1964, and only died in 1967, a living link with an ancient time—the jury is still out on just how ancient.

Opposite: The etched dancers and hunters, fish and animals of Australian rock art, an artistic tradition that has survived into modern times, have become embroiled in modern political arguments about land rights.

In the bone-dry conditions of the Australian desert, thousands of rock art sites survive superbly preserved. Controversial new techniques are now being developed in attempts to date them.

# OLD BONES
# AND THE LEAKEYS

"Old-bones people" are slightly mad. They can spend half a lifetime at the bottom of some quarry, knowing that their chances of finding what may or may not be there are no better than a lottery. When Mary Leakey found "Nutcracker Man" her husband Louis leaped, yelping in excitement, from his sickbed. When Donald Johanson and Tom Gray found "Lucy," they held hands and whooped and pranced, until they realized they might be trampling more of the precious skeleton into dust.

Mary Leakey, like the other members of her family, has the happy ability to breathe life into the very old bones which two generations of Leakeys have been prizing from the African soil.

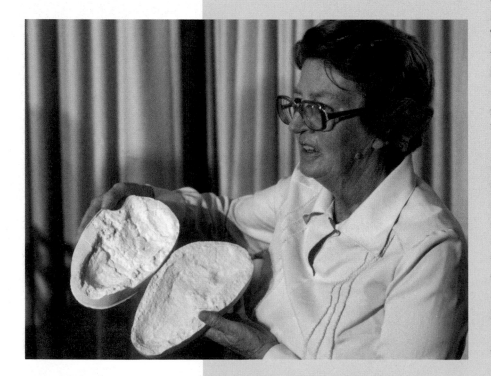

Charles Darwin, when he upset the biblical apple cart in the 19th century, thought that the origins of man lay in Africa. In the 20th century, finds in South and East Africa have proved him right.

Olduvai Gorge, Tanzania, has all the conditions to cheer the heart of the geologist, anthropologist, or archaeologist: two million years of sedimentary deposits neatly stacked up on the sides of the gorge, sandwiched between layers of volcanic ash; a silted-up lake full of fossils; and thousands of sites of human and hominid activity spanning millions of years. The volcanic ash is a particular bonus, since it can now be dated by potassium argon dating, which, like carbon 14, measures the rate of decay of a radioactive isotope.

The first European to take an interest in the site, in what was then German East Africa, was a German butterfly hunter called Kattwinkel. The fossils he brought back along with his butterflies inspired another expedition in 1913 by Hans Reck. His specimens inspired a young anthropologist, Louis Leakey, Kenyan born of missionary parents and educated at Cambridge University, England, to study the site himself.

Two generations of the Leakey family, Mary and Louis, and their son Richard, have spent decades picking out the animal bones, stone artifacts, including the axes used to kill and chop the animals, and the fossils of our most ancient ancestors who made the axes and ate the animals—though the evidence suggests they usually waited for them to fall over a cliff, or be killed by other predators, rather than killing them themselves.

The site obviously offered so many advantages—water, shelter, and prey animals—that

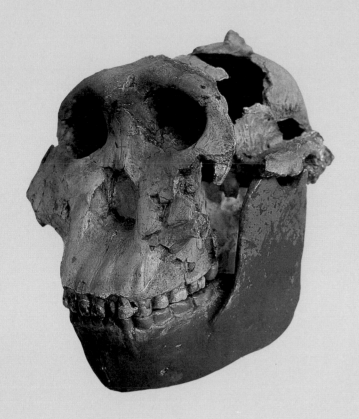

His scientific name is Australopithecus, meaning Southern ape-human. This one was a new type, and Louis Leakey formally named him Zinjanthropus Boisei, from an Arab word for East Africa, and their patron Charles Boise. The media dubbed him "Nutcracker Man," for his huge jaws and teeth. The Leakeys, to whom he brought not just fame but research funds, called him "Dear Boy." When he was dated at 1.75 million years B.C., doubling the age of human origins, the news went round the world.

the record of human settlement covers millions of years. Mary Leakey, who has recorded over 37,000 stone tools, divided the sites into butchery sites, where the animal carcases were cut with stone axes and the bones smashed for their marrow, and living sites.

The oldest hand axes, large pebbles or flakes of stone chipped away to give a point and a cutting edge, are over 1.5 million years old; 2.5-million-year-old stone implements have since been found in Ethiopia. The sites where they were made, leaving a distinctive scattering of fragments, have also been found.

The first hominid fossils were discovered in South Africa in 1925 by Raymond Dart, who named them *Australopithecus*, the southern ape.

In 1959 Mary Leakey found an *Australopithecus* skull with massive jaws. By happy chance there was a film crew in the camp, and film went round the world of the 1.75-million-year-old skull being prized gently out of the soil. The articulate, charming Leakeys became media stars as much as the bones, and offers of sponsorship poured in. The press dubbed the skull "Nutcracker Man," while the Leakeys affectionately called him "Dear boy."

The suggestion now is that *Australopithecus* was a dead-end rather than a true modern human ancestor.

In 1975 the American paleontologist Don Johanson, and his student Tom Gray, working in the Hadar region of northern Ethiopia, were walking back to camp for lunch when they spotted a half-buried thigh bone. Other fossil bones were scattered nearby. They had found "Lucy," named for the Beatles' song "Lucy in the Sky with Diamonds," estimated at over three million years old, the most complete skeleton ever found. In 1984 a Kenyan fossil-hunter, Kamoya Kimeu, found "Turkana Boy," by the shores of Lake Turkana in northern Kenya. This was an almost complete skeleton, apart from the feet, of a boy of about nine years old, who died some 1.6 million years ago. His body closely resembled modern physiques, and science suggests he would have grown to about six feet tall.

The dates, as in so many areas of archaeology—farming, painting, religion—keep being pushed further back.

In 1976, south of Olduvai at Laetoli, Mary Leakey's team found the oldest hominid footprints in the world. Two adults and a child, walking upright like modern man, crossed a wet patch of volcanic ash; the sun then baked their footprints into clay, and another fall of ash preserved them. They are estimated at more than 3.5 million years old.

**LOUIS AND MARY LEAKEY**
Louis Leakey (1903-1972) was the son of missionaries and trained as an anthropologist before turning to archaeology. He spent his working life in Olduvai Gorge, in Tanzania, beside his wife Mary (b. 1913). Their small children were trained up to help sort and clean finds, until their son Richard joined the team permanently. They worked for decades with little recognition and even less funding, until 1959, when a film crew happened to be on site when they found the oldest hominid skull ever. They have since become the First Family of palaeolithic archaeology.

# LIVING IN THE BONES: UKRAINIAN MAMMOTH BONE HOUSES

The houses at Mezhirich look like the wildest imaginings of science-fiction. It took archaeologists a long time to recognize that they were houses, not the graveyards of mammoths.

Human ingenuity and necessity often combine to extraordinary effect. The bone houses of the Ukraine exploited the largest building components available, the huge skulls, ribs, and leg bones of mammoths. The resulting structures are as beautiful as sculptures.

Once he came down from the trees and out of the caves, man used whatever his environment provided for shelter. Houses were made of stone, wood, mudbrick, turf, even snow if there was nothing else.

There was no timber in the area some 20,000 years ago. It was the last grip of the Ice Age on parts of Russia, the Ukraine, and Poland, and so cold that trees got no higher than scrubby shrubs. But there was a ready supply of very large prefabricated building units: mammoth bones.

The dumps of bones had been spotted at Kiev around the turn of the 19th century, but were taken as evidence of kill sites. More were found at Iron Age camps near the River Don in the 1920s, but most of the site had been washed away by floods. Farmers took some to grind up for fertilizer.

In the 1960s the archaeologist and paleontologist Ivan Pidoplichko began a careful study of several of these clumps of mammoth bones, at Mezhirich near Kiev.

There were several large dumps, each consisting of hundreds of bones. They were very oddly arranged if they really were the remains of kills, and could not possibly be where an animal had died naturally.

They were found in pits, and the huge bones had been very carefully sorted and arranged. They were first thought to be some ritual offering, but then evidence was found of hearths in the center. Eventually the evidence was conclusive: they were the remains of circular houses made of bones and tusks, with massive skulls for foundations, ribs and spines used

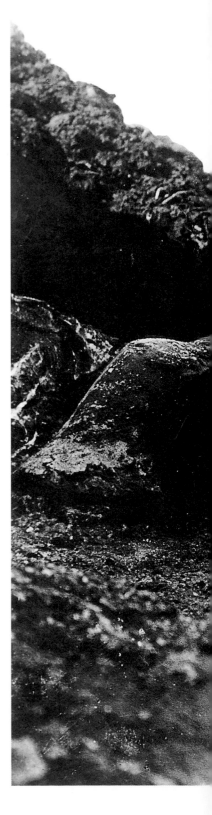

for curved walls, and straight leg bones for doors and openings. The gaps and crevices were presumably filled with mud, and possibly covered with animal skins.

The houses have been claimed as the earliest evidence of man as architect. One has been reconstructed, and is as beautiful as an art installation. It is so impressive, and it would have required such skill and organized effort to move the huge heavy sections of bone—the heaviest weigh up to a quarter ton—that archaeologists have wondered if the houses denoted high social status, and represented a kind of palace of the Ice Age.

When this Ukrainian peasant was uncovering bones taller than himself in the 1920s, it was still believed they belonged to slaughtered mammoths. Farmers were grinding the bones for use as fertilizer.

Archaeologists, tourists,
modern-day Druids, and New
Age Travelers all claim
Stonehenge as their own.

Megalithic just means "big stones." Across a swathe of Europe, from Malta to Scandinavia, Bronze Age people dragged such stones miles across the land and raised them up into imperishable monuments. Modern science can explain how they were raised by men using stone tools and timber rollers and wedges, without in any way diminishing their power to awe.

# THE BRONZE AGE

# WORSHIPING THE SUN AND ASTONISHING THE NEIGHBORS: THE BRONZE AGE

John Aubrey was interested in pigs, stained-glass windows, books, rocks, sex, history, gossip, scandal, metalwork, church architecture —Aubrey was interested in everything. He had the greatest difficulty in finishing any sentence on paper, because every line he wrote reminded him of six other things that interested him.

The 17th century was a splendid time for gentleman scholars like Aubrey, before the lines got fixed and mathematicians realized they weren't supposed to be interested in art or musicians in science. All over western Europe the fabulous Neolithic and Bronze Age monuments, the henges, mounds, artificial hills, passage graves, and megalithic stones, were suddenly catching the eye of such scholars. No excavation was necessary: they reared up out of the landscape. A gentleman could go for a day's ride across his own land and inspect half a dozen of them.

Aubrey was born in Wiltshire, England, and he walked, measured, and drew Stonehenge, but seemed just as interested in the Marquesse of Hamilton's unsuccessful attempts to transport live carp to Scotland: "their noses did still gangrene, being bobb'd against the barrell."

He had a good sharp eye. Inigo Jones's *Stonehenge Restored* was published in 1655, in which the classically minded architect tidied up the stones into a perfectly regular symmetrical temple. Aubrey read it with delight. "But having compared his Scheme with the Monument it self, I found he had not dealt fairly," he wrote. "That is, he framed the monument to his own Hypothesis, which is much differing from the Thing it self."

Aubrey's great discovery was another Wiltshire monument, which he said exceeded Stonehenge as a cathedral does a parish church.

He spent the Christmas of 1648 with friends, and they all cantered out on an amusing Twelfth Night hunt. Aubrey suddenly spotted that the stones were not random monoliths, but part of a great complex: Avebury. "One might fancy it to have been the Scene where the Giants fought with stones against the Gods," he wrote.

Opposite: Scholars have studied the great stone monuments of the Bronze Age for centuries. Their construction methods are now better understood than the traditional explanation that they must have been the work of giants. Their symbolism and purpose remain as obscure as ever.

**JOHN AUBREY**
John Aubrey (1625–1697), English gentleman, scholar, gossip, and antiquary, scarcely managed to finish any work he started in his lifetime, so many interests competed for his attention. His combination of sound, educated common sense, and rapturous child-like enthusiasm for all the works of man and nature, still blazes from every line he wrote.

"I was wonderfully surprised at the sight of those vast stones, of which I had never heard before; as also at the mighty bank and

The monuments were built over three millennia, in the Neolithic and Bronze Ages, from about 4500 B.C. to 800 B.C. The gentleman scholars of the 17th century were often just in time to record them before they were destroyed. In Denmark, Professor Peter Glob has described how the burial mounds were particularly prized as good, fertile soil to spread on poor fields. The barrows were leveled for plowed fields or in the hope of gold, the stones smashed for building or from superstition.

grass ditch about it. I observed in the Inclosures some segments of rude circles, made with these stones, whence I concluded they had been in old time complete."

In Wiltshire, Aubrey was followed by William Stukeley, who was a sensible, shrewd man when not distracted by Druids. Stukeley was racing against the stone-breakers to record the stones. He could not stop the destruction, but he could record their villainy so we still know the guilty men: Green and Griffin, John of the Whitehouse Alehouse at Kennet, Richard at the Hare and Hounds at Beckhampton, and Mr Smith, a lawyer.

And Mr Ayloff, who got his just retribution. The punishment of Mr Ayloff must stand as revenge for all the wreckers across Europe. He smashed up a huge stone to use as a millstone, and brought a cart yoked with 20 oxen to drag it away. "Yet so great was its weight that it repeatedly broke all his tackle to pieces, and he was forc't to leave it."

# MERLIN'S CALENDAR: STONEHENGE

Every year or so an engineer or an archaeologist sets up pulleys and wooden rollers to demonstrate how the huge Sarsens of Stonehenge were erected.

Geoffrey of Monmouth explained them in 1136: the stones had been flown through the air from Ireland to Wales, and from Wales to Salisbury Plain in England by Merlin the Magician. Today a low-loader and crane could do the job in a morning. None of the explanations diminishes the wonder of the stones.

When a British government committee described the setting of the stones as "a national disgrace" in the late 1980s, my newspaper sent me to solicit tourist opinions. It was impossible to get them to complain. Trampling around in the mud, traffic roaring past on the road which nudges the circle, kept 165 feet back from the stones by a rope barrier, the

tourists from all over the world stubbornly described the stones as wonderful, awesome.

Whatever other purpose the stones served, they were built to awe. Like the Taj Mahal or the *Mona Lisa*, Stonehenge has genuine iconic status: modeled as an elaborate cake, or a henge of wrecked cars at a rock concert, it is still instantly recognized all over the world.

The truth about the stones was scarcely less startling than Geoffrey's explanation. The oldest stone circle—Stonehenge III, coming after the bank-and-ditch and timber circles—was made from bluestones, which were brought, probably by land and water, from the Preseli Mountains in southwest Wales. These were

Above: There are regular automobile accidents on the road near Stonehenge, as drivers come over the hill and get their first glimpse of the astonishing 5,000-year-old monument.

rearranged several times before and after the enormous blocks of Sarsen stone, a very hard sandstone, were brought a mere 18½ miles, then shaped and fitted together with "mortice-and-tenon" joints, and so engineered that the tops of stones of different sizes, standing on an irregular site, are virtually level.

While there are still arguments about whether the circle is primarily a calendar or a ritual site, its orientation toward the summer solstice sunrise is clear, and it is also aligned with other monuments, often older, in the landscape.

Carbon dating of some scraps of bone and timber, including antler picks certainly used to dig the ditch, has pushed the date of the earliest Stonehenge back almost 500 years, to 3000 B.C. Between the first earth-bank and ditch circle, to the final setting of the huge stones, the Stone Age farmers spent over 1,000 years modeling and remodeling the monument.

It was never lost—it still dominates the wide shallow saucer of Salisbury Plain—and because it was so visible it was one of the first monuments to be studied seriously by antiquaries.

The witty and shrewd 17th-century John Aubrey typically noted not the stones, but a ring of barely discernible depressions inside the ditch, still known as the Aubrey Holes, which originally held timber posts.

The splendid William Stukeley came next, and though he did the stones a lasting disservice in associating them with the Druids, he is particularly useful to current archaeologists because he recorded many features, such as the mysterious long parallel ditches of the Cursus—so-called because Stukeley thought it must have been used for Celtic chariot racing—which have now almost disappeared above ground.

Hundreds of the surrounding barrows were opened in the early 19th century by a pair of gentleman-landowning antiquaries, William Cunningham and Colt Hoare, but unlike most of their peers they carefully recorded what they found, including the rich grave goods from Bush Barrow, beautifully worked gold plaques, a gold decorated staff, copper and bronze daggers, and flint tools.

After World War I—when the British Air Ministry insisted the stones were a traffic hazard and wanted them demolished —Stone-henge was given to the state. Archaeologists have been working there ever since, particularly on its relationship to the monuments in the landscape around it. Even in a landscape studied continuously for 500 years, surprises emerge: the post holes of the very oldest structure on the site, vast totem-pole-like timbers, carbon dated to 8000–7000 B.C., were found under the visitors' car park in the 1990s. In 1978 bones poked through the edge of a rather dull trench, and proved to be those of a skeleton riddled with arrowheads, wearing his own stone archer's wrist guard. Ritual sacrifice or a warrior buried with honor? The archaeologists still do not agree.

The archaeologist Jacquetta Hawkes famously said that every generation got its own Stonehenge. Inigo Jones, the 17th-century architect, recreated the stones as a geometrically regular Roman temple, which in turn directly influenced the design of the famous Royal Crescent in Bath a century later. The painter Turner saw it as a romantic desolation, the stones shuddering under wild and blazing skies. In the shadow of the Millennium every shade of New Age believer has been drawn toward them, and theories as wild as Geoffrey of Monmouth's are spiraling around the stones again.

Every generation gets its own Stonehenge, Jacquetta Hawkes said. This 19th-century version borrows from the visions of Inigo Jones and William Stukeley, reconstructing the monument as a perfectly symmetrical temple of sternly planed blocks, filled with hordes of decorative and wholly fictitious Druids (priests).

# THE SUN ALSO RISES:
# THE BOYNE VALLEY

The great mound of the Newgrange passage tomb so dominates its landscape, the lush water meadows of the River Boyne, Ireland, that it's hard to imagine that it could ever have been lost.

A photograph dating from the turn of the 19th century shows a scruffy hillock no more imposing than its neighbors. It has now been scoured back to its smooth bald outline, and controversially refaced with its presumed original brilliant white quartz stones. It is again visible from many miles away, as it was built to be 5,000 years ago.

Knowth and Dowth, each covering more than one acre, are in sight. Their construction—Newgrange took some 200,000 tons of stone and rock—tells archaeologists of a prosperous and ordered society, with the leisure, skill, and wealth to build such huge shelters for their cremated dead. Bru na Boinne, the bend in the Boyne, has been claimed as the greatest architectural achievement in Europe of Neolithic man, and is now a United Nations Educational and Cultural Organization (UNESCO) World Heritage Site.

Newgrange was found accidentally in 1699, by laborers—according to legend it was the lost cow that they were following which found the entrance. It created a sensation.

Among the antiquaries who made the long journey by land and sea was the Keeper of the Ashmolean in Oxford, Edward Llwyd. At a time when any ruin bigger than a cowshed was credited to the Romans, he insisted it was far earlier. He suggested that the Roman coin found on one of the stones was lost or offered up by a traveler from the empire when the monument was already ancient; more Roman finds, discovered later, proved his thesis.

The Neolithic farmers built monuments out of huge stones across a swathe of Europe, from Malta to the Orkneys, with clear artistic and trading links between many of the sites. Sir William Wilde, father of Oscar, argued in 1849 that the Boyne monument must be a royal cemetery, because of the enormous size of the stones, their sophisticated construction—the corbeled roof of the Newgrange chamber is 20 feet high, and still watertight—and, above all, their magnificent carved stones, found within the passages and chambers, or as curbstones around the mounds. One of the largest and most famous, with its triple-spiral pattern, was found still in position defending the Newgrange entrance.

Hundreds of stones are believed lost, looted or still buried, but hundreds remain, the greatest concentration of Megalithic art in Ireland and one of the largest in the world.

Archaeologists still argue about the significance of the geometric shapes, triangles, lozenges, spirals, circles, and zigzags, often applied with elegant and artistic regard for the contours of the stones. They were carved into the stones or left in relief by chipping away all the rest of the surface.

Newgrange kept its greatest secret for 300 years after it was rediscovered. The first comprehensive archaeological survey was only carried out in the 1960s, by Professor M. J. O'Kelly. He was interested in local oral tradition connecting the mound with the rising sun. He wondered if this was confusion with Stonehenge, as the orientation made a midsummer connection impossible.

Archaeologists had long puzzled over a second carved lintel stone, set into the mound like an eyebrow above the entrance. It was only when Professor O'Kelly reconstructed the "roof box," a slot above the entrance, that the legend was vindicated. At the winter solstice, an even more important date than the summer solstice for ancient farmers who needed to know when the worst of the weather was over, the rising sun shines through the slot, on to the rising 80-foot passage floor, until it pierces to the back wall of the innermost chamber. The sight has been known to leave somber, objective scientists speechless, and the handful of places for non-archaeologists are booked out well into the next Millennium—and if it's a rainy dawn when the sun never shines, as so often in Ireland, the witnesses must go to the back of the line and wait their turn again.

Opposite: Newgrange held a 5,000-year-old secret, only revealed when archaeologists reconstructed the slot over the entrance. On the winter solstice the rising sun shines through that slot, until it lights the back wall of the chamber.

Below: The great stone guarding the entrance is still in its original position: contemporary archaeologists, art historians, and New Age travelers argue over the significance of the double and triple spirals: a plan of the three burial mounds in the Boyne Valley, light and dark, winter and summer, water and wind, or just a beautiful decoration exploiting the shape of the stone?

# THE MARCHING STONES: CARNAC

It's hard not to feel that Bronze Age farmers who built Carnac, on the storm-battered Atlantic coast of Brittany in France, just didn't know when to stop.

They built a stone circle, and some passage graves, and a stone avenue, and a stone circle, and some passage graves, and an avenue—and they kept on going.

The greatest of the stones fell centuries, perhaps millennia, ago. *Le Grand Menhir Brise* originally stood 70 feet tall, as high as a medieval cathedral. The tallest stone at Stonehenge is just under 30 feet tall.

One of the first people to survey the Carnac stones in the 18th century was the Marquis de Robien, a local landowner, who observed drily: "All one can say is that this work represents a prodigious amount of labor, and it must have needed an incredible multitude of people to carry it out."

In 1880 French antiquaries calculated that there were 6,192 standing stones in France, 4,747 of them in the Carnac region.

There are four groups of uprights, arranged in parallel lines, each group running on a slightly different alignment from the west toward the northeast. The stones are most carefully arranged: at the eastern end they are only about a yard or so high, but they increase in size, as the avenues run for up to two miles, over hills and through woodland, to the monsters at the western end.

The stones at Carnac were turned into a patriotic symbol of revolutionary French glory by a passionate nationalist, Jacques de Cambry. As a present to Napoleon, he sent his 1805 *Monument Celtiques*, in which he proclaimed Bretons, Celts, Druids, Gauls, and Franks as all the same people and one of the world's master races at that.

However, he also complained bitterly that if the stones were in Britain the English government would have found the money to care for them, publish scholarly works about them, and pay poets and painters to celebrate them—a singular, if not unique, view of the official British attitude to contemporary and prehistoric culture.

Cambry was one of the first to claim astrological significance for the stones, and his work

did have the effect of attracting much wider interest in the stones.

Detailed drawings were made of the stones by many antiquaries, including several English scholars, which are extremely useful to archaeologists now trying to correct the enthusiasm of the late 19th century. A campaign to restore the stones was led by Zacharie le Rouzie, who devoted most of his life to research on Carnac, and founded a museum there.

Le Rouzie and his teams re-erected thousands of stones—most of those now standing. Despite his passion and scholarship, it is not certain that they all went back in exactly the

same place. In particular, archaeologists are trying to determine whether the occasional sinuous wriggles in the straight lines are modern mistakes or original, and if so what meaning they might have.

Le Rouzie marked all the stones he re-erected, but there is a suggestion that he may also have marked stones he believed to have been re-erected previously—and his records do not make clear which is which.

The entire monument was resurveyed in the 1970s by Alexander Thom, aided by plans made by bored German army surveyors during World War II, which helped locate stones now buried in undergrowth. Thom concluded that the lines were originally straight or in geometrically planned arcs, and that the stones were separated by a unit he labeled the "Megalithic rod." The arguments continue.

The Catholic farmers and fishermen did their best to tame the pagan monsters left among their fields. Iron crucifixes were set on top of them, or crosses were scored into their sides, or the tops were carved into crosses. The side wall of Le Mans cathedral is actually built up against a 20-foot menhir, as if the cathedral builders, in the end, did not quite have the affrontery to destroy it. The stones still exist in a fog of folklore: the 30-foot menhir at Champ-Dolent, topped with a cross, is said to be sinking into the earth at the rate of one inch per year, and when it disappears completely the world will end.

From the 19th century, as artists and photographers began to descend on the stones of Carnac, Breton farmers and villagers became adept at posing in traditional costume beside the stones they had earlier ignored, broken up, or attempted to Christianize.

Opposite: Agriculture and roads shoved aside hundreds of stones but the survivors, marching for miles across the fields at Carnac, remain incredibly impressive. The largest stone, now fallen and broken, was the size of a railroad car.

# IMMORTAL FURNITURE: SCARA BRAE

There is usually much better evidence for the interiors of the ancient tomb-homes of the dead than of the homes of the living in times past. Tombs are frequently uncovered appointed with all the luxuries of life, while the archaeologist working on house sites is left with the foundations of walls, the marks of long-cold hearths, and, if exceptionally lucky, good, rich trash dumps and dunghills.

This elegantly incised stone pick is one of many examples of fine stone-working skills, excavated from the Scara Brae site.

The palaces of the wealthy survive to some extent, in painted walls and marble floors, but the interiors of the houses where the poor lived have rotted back into the earth.

In one Stone Age settlement, however, out on the windy edge of the world, at Scara Brae in Orkney, it really was the stone age. There was nothing but stone.

The settlement lasted from about 3000 B.C. until 2500 B.C. The houses of the dead were imposing. Maes Howe, the most splendid of them, is still the highest point in its landscape, an artificial hill 100 feet in diameter, containing a passage grave leading to a high corbeled chamber. When it was opened in the 19th cen-

tury, the archaeologists found that the tomb was empty because the Vikings had got there first in the 12th century, and left one of the largest collections of runic graffiti ever discovered, boasting of how they had removed a great treasure from the tomb.

The Vikings probably came in to shelter from the eternal gale. Their graffiti may have been saga-making to pass the time rather than "journalism," since they also left drawings of a great serpent and a dragon.

Uniquely, however, the houses of the living also survived. The wind blew the sand to bury and protect them, and in the 19th century a great storm scoured them bare again.

In the late 1920s Vere Gordon Child excavated the site of what must, by necessity, have been a very self-sufficient community.

The eight substantial drystone houses were connected by a covered passage. The houses were built half buried in pits to protect them from the everlasting wind, with one small door and walls over three feet thick, and a central stone fireplace.

The interiors were remarkable because they were found complete with their fitted furniture. This survived because it was built, like everything else, out of flags of the local stone. Each house had two stone beds, benches, closets, and "dressers"—so-called because the arrangement of shallow shelves and deep closets so closely resembled the wooden dressers of the typical British cottage interior of 4,000 years later.

One cottage even had a fireside stool, still standing by its hearth. Excavation uncovered evidence of how important fishing was, but there were also sheep and cattle bones, so there would have been furs and skins, with heather and bracken, to fill up the bed-frames and cover the cold benches.

The houses may have been roofed with whale ribs for roof timbers, and skin and turf covering. Reroofed they would be perfectly habitable today, and far better insulated than many modern houses on the islands.

Wind-blown sand buried the Scara Brae houses, and in the late 19th century the wind of a great storm scoured them bare again, with all their stone furniture still in place.

# THE ROMANS ARRIVE: MAIDEN CASTLE

Maiden Castle, a vast Iron Age fort in Dorset, high on a ridge of the Downs in southwest England, made a powerful impression on the novelist and poet Thomas Hardy. "At one's every step it rises higher against the sky, with an obstrusive personality that compels the senses to regard it and consider."

During the 1930s hundreds of people came to consider, either to help dig or to watch, as Mortimer Wheeler conducted a famous excavation which trained a whole generation of field archaeologists. He recorded that wherever in the world he went, for the rest of his long working life, he was sure to meet somebody who had worked with him at Maiden Castle.

It was an exciting site and produced exciting finds, but there was a glamor about the dig which had more to do with Wheeler's personality: film crews, Lawrence of Arabia, Hardy himself, who lived nearby in the ugly redbrick house he designed, all came to look.

It was scholarship with jokes: among the more memorable was the "Iron Age Crocodile," a small crocodile skeleton liberated from a university museum store, and stealthily buried under cover of darkness in the section marked out for the following day's work. Mortimer Wheeler solemnly recorded the find.

Maiden Castle is just outside the market town of Dorchester, a Roman town still visibly sitting on its Roman grid. It is not the largest hillfort, but it is one of the most impressive with its complex of sinuous ditches and the labyrinthine defences at the main entrance.

It was built on a monumental scale from the start. One of the earliest monuments was the longest Neolithic barrow ever measured, almost one-third of a mile, dating from about 3500 B.C. The first Iron Age site was on one end of the hill, but its ditches were expanded to surround the entire hilltop, and then there are two more ditches outside that.

Finds within the enclosure indicate periods of occupation and cattle enclosure, possibly seasonal, and long periods when it was abandoned. So many flint implements were found it suggested they were being manufactured in the fort, possibly for export and trade.

From the ramparts of Maiden Castle you can see for miles. The defenders would have seen trouble coming a long way off. They were expecting it: among the finds were huge caches of slingshot stones, up to 10,000 in each, brought from Chesil Beach which is 10 miles away.

Above: The stranded whale bulk of Maiden Castle, where a hilltop already studded with older monuments was enclosed as an Iron Age fort, dominates the landscape. From its ramparts the defenders could have watched their attackers marching toward them from a long way off.

The most striking, and controversial, finds were made at the entrance, the "war cemetery." Suetonius's life of Vespasian says he led the Second Legion into southwest England in A.D. 43–44, where they defeated "two very formidable tribes." Wheeler believed one to be the last defender of the hillfort, and that the cemetery represents the buried dead of the last, lost, battle against the Romans.

In addition to these finds, there were other burials on the site, including a single Saxon burial, up at the sky line, long after the fort had been abandoned.

The graves in front of the entrance were different. They were all adult males, buried with some grave goods, including mugs and weapons, and many had clear marks of violence: smashed bones and sword cuts. The cause of death of the most famous was clear: he had a Roman iron arrowhead sunk deep between two vertebrae in his spine.

Mortimer Wheeler wrote:

"That night, when the fires of the legion shone out (we may imagine) in orderly lines across the valley, the survivors crept forth from their broken stronghold and, in the darkness, buried their dead as nearly as might be outside their tumbled gates in that place where the ashes of their burned huts lay warm and thick upon the ground. The task was carried out anxiously and hastily and without order, but even so, from few graves were omitted those tributes of food and drink which were the proper and traditional perquisites of the dead. At daylight on the morrow, the legion moved westward to fresh conquest, doubtless taking with it the usual levy of hostages from the vanquished."

There are signs of later occupation, including the foundations of a small Roman temple built almost 300 years after the battle at the gate, but after the foundation of Dorchester the strategic importance of the fort quickly started to decline.

Modern archaeology mistrusts dramatic stories. Since more work was done at the site in the 1980s, other interpretations have been offered. None is as persuasive as Wheeler's leap of the imagination across the centuries.

**Mortimer Wheeler interpreted the skeletons at the gate as the fallen warriors of the last battle, against the Romans. The Romans won.**

# EYE WITNESSES FROM THE PAST: THE BOG PEOPLE, THE ICE MAN, THE ICE MAIDEN

'Tollund Man," "Lindow Man," "the Ice Maiden," and "the Ice Man" are among the handful of individuals who have come straight from the ancient past, not swaddled in bandages like the Egyptians, but bare before us in their own leathery skin. They are touching unlike anything else in archaeology.

People may have lined up around the block to see the treasures of Tutankhamen when they came to the West, but they didn't weep over his smooth golden mask, as visitors regularly do over the wrinkled face and clenched hands of Lindow Man, nicknamed "Pete Marsh," curled in a bed of peat in the British Museum.

The bog bodies and the ice mummies have been preserved by freaks of climate: the bog bodies tanned, the ice bodies deep frozen, with eyelashes, tattoos, and toenails all intact. They also have in common the fact that police were often called in to investigate supposed recent murder when their bodies were found.

Tollund Man is the most famous because of his tranquil smile. Professor Peter Glob's book about him and his peers, *The Bog People*, is as much a literary as an archaeological work.

Worship of water, without which no life is possible, is as old as life itself. Man threw offerings into lakes, springs, wells, and rivers: sometimes jewelry or weapons, sometimes other human beings. The Iron Age bog people, found wherever the right conditions exist, across Scandinavia, northern Germany, Fenland Britain, and Ireland, were preserved just as they were sent to the gods.

Most were found by turf cutters—Lindow Man was sliced in half by a blade. Tollund Man was found in 1950 by two men who were aghast to see the smiling human face emerge from the bog. They called the police, and the police called Professor Glob: it was murder, but the murder was 2,000 years old.

It has been suggested that the bog bodies represent no more than the execution of common criminals, but there seem to be too many elements of ritual in their deaths. They were strangled, stabbed, or bludgeoned, sometimes all three. Sometimes there is evidence that the bodies were staked down in shallow water. Often there is a ligature around the neck, even if not the cause of death. And many had a last meal of a sort of porridge of grains and wild herbs, which some archaeologists believe had magical significance—Lindow Man's contained the

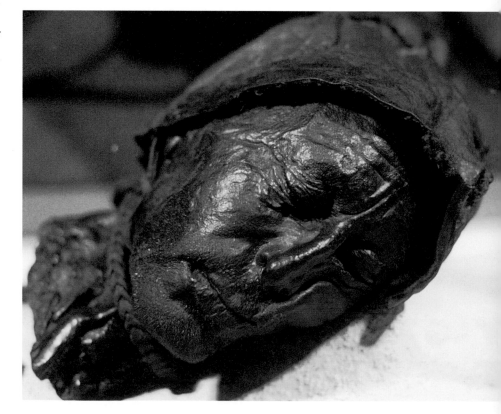

magic berry, mistletoe. The porridge was analysed and recreated for a panel of experts in the 1950s: the irrepressible Mortimer Wheeler tried some and pronounced it inedibly foul.

The Ice Maiden was not murdered but buried with high honors and all her finest possessions.

The Altai Mountains of Siberia have revealed amazing burials, dating from around 400 B.C. The most famous are from Pazyryk, where the Russian archaeologist Sergei Rudenko excavated a man in 1949. He was buried with his horses, all their harness and a four-wheeled wagon, all his clothes in perfect condition, and his greatest treasure, a magnificent set of tattoos of real and mythical animals, coiling all over both arms, a shoulder and one leg.

The burials must have been in summer, when the ground had thawed enough to dig. The bodies were in log coffins, within a log-lined enclosure. Any moisture in the grave froze the bodies into an ice sheath, and the log insulation maintained the temperature.

Most of the graves had been robbed centuries ago. In 1993 another Russian archaeologist, Natalya Polosmak, working higher and further east at Ukok on the Chinese border, found an undisturbed grave with the delicately tattooed body of a young woman. She has become a focus of feminist theory about the role of women in such societies, because she was buried with goods as rich as any man, including beautiful textiles, her silver mirror, and six horses. It has been suggested that she may have been a wise woman or priestess.

The Ice Man was not murdered; he slipped. He was found high in the Tyrol in September 1991, by some German trekkers, and sparked the usual police hunt for missing tourists. The body had been in perfect condition, but was damaged by the frantic efforts of rescuers who mistakenly thought they were recovering a recent corpse.

He had fallen into a crevice, perhaps because of the arthritis revealed in his neck, back, and hips, and had frozen to death; he suffered worse injuries from the jackhammer used to prize him from the ice than from his original fall. All his possessions were found with him, including a quiver of partly finished arrows, leading to

speculation that he may have been a fletcher, and a neat larchwood-framed backpack.

The first scientific suggestions were that he was probably medieval. His axe was then thought to be bronze, making him a Bronze Age man from about 2000 B.C. The axe was copper. He turned out, to general astonishment, to be very, very old indeed: from 3300 B.C. by radio-carbon dating. He is the oldest fully preserved human body in the world.

In the spring of 1998 the Ice Man was transferred to a specially built refrigeration unit in a museum in Bolzano, on the Italian side of the Tyrol border, despite protests from the Austrian scientists who had studied and conserved the body. It took an international mediation committee to resolve the dispute about his nationality: the conclusion was that 5,000 years earlier, the Ice Man had slid 260 feet inside the Italian border, and was therefore an Italian.

Ordinary people have been troubled about the ultimate fate of all of these bodies. They are of great interest to scientists, but many lay people are disturbed that these ancient humans, buried with reverence or overtaken by tragedy, should end up as peep shows in a tourist attraction.

The Ice Maiden is now in a museum, and likely to bring unprecedented tourist revenue to her remote region. Yet many of the local people, who believe they are her descendants, feel she should have been reburied and left to rest in peace.

Lindow Man was sliced in half by the peat cutting machine which uncovered him. He was nicknamed "Pete Marsh" and, like many of the bog people, provoked a murder inquiry which is still rumbling on.

Opposite: Tollund Man, the most famous of all the bog people because of his sweet, accepting smile, also sparked a murder inquiry. The braided, leather noose around his neck belied the tranquil face. He was indeed murdered but the case was 2,000 years old, beyond the remit of the Danish police.

# THE INUIT ICE BABY

There was a briefly fashionable theory that love for children as unique individuals is a modern phenomenom. The argument went that infant mortality was so high for so many primitive societies, and for Western societies until relatively modern times, that children were not much regarded as individuals until it was clear they were going to live.

The delicate tattoos on the faces of the Inuit women, made with a sooty thread drawn under the skin, marked their status and their families, as well as making them more beautiful in the eyes of their people.

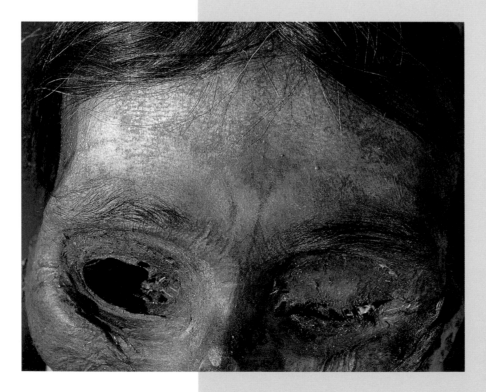

The evidence of ancient graves often seems to bear out this theory, with tiny bodies packed into any available space in adult coffins, and their own grave goods usually only found with much older children.

"The Ice Baby" was found by hunters in 1972. He died about 500 years ago in a society where death, from starvation, injury, animal attack, drowning, or disease, was never far away. The chances of babies, human or animal, living through their first year were low.

He was only six months old when he died in about 1475, at Qilakitsoq, an abandoned Inuit settlement on the west coast of Greenland.

He was so small that he didn't really need a complete set of tailor-made clothes, particularly when he would have been growing out of them in weeks—he could just have been swaddled. Instead his garments must rank among the most beautiful and lovingly made baby clothing ever found. They were buried with him instead of being salvaged for the next baby to come along.

The Aleut people, fishers and hunters on the islands along the Alaskan coast, did have a technique for mummifying, which very sensibly treated human bodies as raw meat to be preserved and dried. They removed the organs and pegged the bodies out in a stream which scoured them inside and out and washed away much of the fat. The remaining sack of bones, skin, and muscle was then dried in the open air, and finally hung up like a ham from hooks in the ceiling of a dry cave, or placed on racks. The technique was extremely effective: archaeologists found over 50 bodies, spanning almost three centuries, in one cave.

The Greenland baby was naturally mummified. He was among eight bodies in two graves, in a shallow cave under an overhanging rock, where they were mummified by the extreme cold and dryness.

All the baby's tiny garments, fur and leather tailored with minute stitches, survived in perfect condition. They testify to the status this small human being already had in his community.

The condition of the bodies allowed scientists to retrieve their lives in astonishing detail: they were well fed, on reindeer meat, arctic hare, and various plants and herbs, as well as fish, but their lives were clearly extremely hard.

Several showed signs of congenital disease, including the four-year-old boy. He had a distorted pelvis and may never have been able to walk. A woman in her fifties had a broken collarbone, fractured years earlier, which had never set properly and must have been extremely painful. She also had early stages of cancer. She had gone through a period of starvation, or serious illness, as a child, but at the time of their death they were all well fed. They all had soot in their lungs, even the women in their teens and early twenties, from living in small spaces lit by seal-blubber lamps. The women had tattoos on their faces, two identical and presumably by the same artist, one so different that archaeologists assume she had married in from another region.

The baby was the best preserved body, laid across the lap of a woman, in a grave with three other women who may have been his mother and aunts.

All his clothes were perfectly preserved, and they showed that this tiny person was already very much a member of the society, worth dressing in beautifully made-to-measure garments, sewn with as much skill and care as the adult clothes. Altogether, 78 garments were found, mostly of seal skin, but also using the down and feathers of geese and ducks, each meticulously selected for its task.

The baby's clothes included a leather shirt, and leather over-pants, made out of the finest supplest skins, fur shorts, and a fur parka, and boots.

It was not clear what killed any of them, but it was clear that the baby's small life was as valued as that of any of the adults.

# THE MIDDLE EAST

In the lost kingdoms of the Middle East, archaeologists were to find the history of the earliest farmers and city dwellers, and the invention of writing, which is defined as the beginning of history itself.

3

# HISTORY IS INVENTED:
# THE ARCHAEOLOGY OF WRITING

**W**hat could be drabber than spending years deciphering a dead language? And what could be more glamorous than Colonel Sir Henry Rawlinson, sweeping through the streets of Baghdad, his pet mongoose and baby leopard at his heels, on his way home to wrestle with cuneiform by the cooling side of his artificial waterfall.

Archaeologists are very grateful to the Assyrians, who had the useful habit of burying dated clay cylinders in the foundations of their buildings, like this from 686 B.C., boasting of the glorious deeds of King Sennacherib.

The history of writing is the history of history: archaeologists class pre-literate societies as pre-historic, though that does lead to logical absurdities—the brilliant Incas, by that standard, never entered history at all.

Rawlinson is only one of the more glamorous of the soldier/scholar/diplomat/spies who crop up all over the archaeology of ancient writing. The same sort of mind was attracted to the labyrinth of diplomacy and the crossword puzzle of reed-pen strokes on a crumbling clay tablet.

Clay tablets inscribed with cuneiform (named for the wedge-shaped characters) had been turning up on Mesopotamian and Egyptian sites for centuries, but unfortunately nobody could read them.

Rawlinson was a career soldier with the British East India Company, on an exercise in Persia in 1835, when he heard about some interesting carvings near a small town called Behistun, in present-day Iran.

He went to take a look, and found himself cricking his neck, staring up at a huge carving over 300 feet up a sheer cliff. It showed Darius, king of the Persians, treating some barbarian rabble unsympathetically.

There were carved inscriptions, line upon close-packed line, all around the images. Rawlinson was only twenty-five. It was not the sort of challenge he could resist. "I certainly do not consider it any great feat in climbing to ascend to the spot where the inscriptions occur," he wrote later.

He admitted that when you got up there it was a bit tricky: the top lines were too high to see except on a ladder, but the ledge was only 18 inches deep so the ladders tended to topple back into the ravine. He tried crossing from a nearby ledge hanging by his hands from the lower edge of the ladder wedged sideways, but found that the ladder would keep dropping to pieces in an annoying way.

The inscriptions were a cuneiform kind of Rosetta Stone, in three languages, so it was essential to copy the entire thing. He did this by drawing them, and by pressing sheets of wet paper on to the rock, which then dried in the sun to preserve a perfect image of the carvings.

The task was urgent, because he could see that the most vital parts of the carving were being eroded by trickling water.

"A wild Kurdish boy, who had come from a distance" proved the hero of the hour. Rawlinson promised a hefty reward, and the boy shinned up cracks in the rock, hammered in wooden pegs and fixed ropes. "It then only remained for him to cross over the cleft by hanging on with his toes and fingers to the slight inequalities of the bare face of the precipice."

Rawlinson and the Kurdish boy were well matched. One wonders what became of the boy after he had finished rigging "a swinging seat like a painter's cradle" 300 feet up the cliff, and had taken the impressions for the mad Englishman.

Rawlinson retired to the quiet life of a consul in Baghdad, aged thirty-three, and set to work. Over the next ten years he translated the Old Persian, Elamite, and Babylonian texts, encouraged a flock of followers into ancient languages, including George Smith who found the Deluge Tablets, salvaged the priceless archive of Assyrian texts from Austen Henry Layard's cavalier excavation at Nineveh, and, if absolutely necessary, even went out into the desert and did some digging himself.

The paper pressings he took, at such danger to life and limb, were given to the British Museum, where they were eaten by rats.

The dismal conclusion from all the earliest writing, everywhere in the world, is that the function of literacy is not literature, poetry, or religion: it is political propaganda and taxes.

The translators are in no immediate danger of running out of work: they are still working through the archive of 15,000 clay tablets found at Ebla in Syria in the 1970s, another unknown language, another unknown state, of 5,000 years ago.

**SIR HENRY RAWLINSON**
This photograph of Colonel Sir Henry Creswicke Rawlinson (1810-1895), as silver haired scholar, "the Father of Cuneiform," indicates little of his glamorous youth, when as a young soldier with the East India Company he scaled a sheer rock face to transcribe the boastful inscription of King Darius. He worked on cuneiform for the rest of his long life. Occasionally he left his calm study to return to the field: in 1853 he found cylinders recording how the great Nebuchadnezzar, King of Babylon, had rebuilt the ancient temple at Borsippa.

# NINEVEH

There must have been a time when there was traffic congestion on the Tigris, of rafts buoyed up with inflated goat skins, carrying away winged bulls and lions with stern human faces.

The grim kingdoms of the ancient Mesopotamians, the Assyrians, and the Babylonians, forever locked in battle, got a powerful grip on the 19th-century imagination. The names boomed with biblical resonance: Nimrod and Nineveh, Sennacherib, the Assyrian who "came down like a wolf on the fold, And his cohorts were gleaming in purple and gold," Nebuchadnezzar, and the famous hanging gardens of Babylon.

A typical panel of Assyrian carving, from the palace at Nimrod, now in the British Museum, shows rows of warriors defeating, humiliating, and slaughtering the Elamites. At the bottom of the panel the Tigris flows by, choked with headless bodies, hacked limbs, torsos, and fish clustering eagerly for their supper. Even in their sunnier scenes, of music in the palace gardens, the court officials look as if they are marching out to skewer the singing birds on their wands of office.

Paul Emile Botta, the French diplomat and explorer—he sent a crowing cable to Paris proclaiming "*Nineveh est trouvé*" but was wrong—got his raftloads back to Europe first in 1846. Nothing like them had ever been seen: they created a sensation, and launched not just a new science, Assyriology, but fashions in dress and furniture.

The British Museum in London had been wrong-footed by Paris. Soon its own agent, the glamorous figure of Austen Henry Layard, lawyer turned antiquity-hunter and possibly spy, was digging furiously.

Layard had started to work immediately, and even before his permit from the Ottoman authorities arrived had uncovered the remains of two palaces.

The competition between the French and British antiquaries was fierce and occasionally farcical, as when they ended up digging furiously into opposite sides of the same mound. It did not make for conscientous record-keeping, particularly since most of the buildings were of mudbrick, which crumbled away as the slabs of decorated stone were wrenched out.

Layard excavated hundreds of yards of carvings from the ancient palace of Nimrud, and shiploads of stone began to arrive back in London amid unending disputes about money, the British Museum being notoriously mean.

The museum, Layard himself, and Henry Rawlinson, were worried about whether the sculptures would interest the public. All agreed that to an eye trained on the sculpture of Greece and Rome, they were strange and savage. The huge pieces of stone were fitted in wherever room could be found and, as in Paris, the public flocked in to look.

Layard was probably most pleased when he succeeded in shipping two vast winged bulls from Khorsabad, which Botta had excavated but abandoned as too vast to move: Layard pragmatically chopped them into four.

Austen Henry Layard's book, *Nineveh And Its Remains*, was a world bestseller, with romantic illustrations such as this one of the young archaeologist directing the removal of a colossal winged figure for shipping to the British Museum. The figures were carved with six legs, to be viewed either straight on or in profile, but viewed at an angle, as here, they strike a most uncommon Assyrian note of low comedy.

In 1847 Layard turned to another project abandoned by Botta. He had begun, but gave up on, a hill called Kuyunjik. One of the first of the scholar diplomats, Claudius James Rich, the first British consul in Mesopotamia, had looked at it 20 years earlier. Botta found nothing exciting, and moved on to Khorsabad. Layard dug deeper and found Nineveh and the palace of Sennacherib.

His account of his work, *Nineveh and its Remains*, with romantic illustrations of huge stone heads being hauled out of the desert, became a much imitated best-seller.

He found enough of Nineveh to hint at its magnificence: the seven-mile walls, the huge gates, the courtyards and fountains, and the sophisticated plumbing, heating, and ventilation systems.

But his most valuable contribution to history was when he found a room which was the first known library, collected in the early 17th century B.C. by Sennacherib's grandson, who brought together rare cuneiform tablets from all over his empire.

Layard sent back 24,000 tablets, enough to keep the scholars busy for years.

The first cuneiform tablets came to Europe in the early 17th century. The last survivor of the 1765 scientific expedition sent to Mesopotamia by the King of Denmark published his transcriptions of more cuneiform from Persepolis. Still more came to the British Museum in 1820 when the widow of Claudius James Rich sold his collection. It was a French scholar, Jules Oppert, who suggested that the oldest written language was not Babylonian, but Sumerian, from Sumer in southern Mesopotamia, dating from 3000 B.C.

Among the scholars wading through the mounds of tablets in the British Museum, most of them literally as-dry-as-dust inventories of stores, was a very junior member of the staff, George Smith. One day he found a document which was far more exciting, the sort of thing Victorian archaeologists craved: it appeared to be an account of the biblical flood, complete with the one just man building a wooden boat, and loading it with his family and animals—and there the narrative broke off.

If Smith had found a signed photograph of God, the newspapers couldn't have been more excited. *The Daily Telegraph* paid for him to go off to Nineveh, and hunt for the rest of the story. In a coincidence, which even a tabloid newspaper would hesitate to invent, he found the other half of the broken tablet within a week of arriving.

The rest of the story is sadder—the missing piece added only a few lines of text, which unfortunately did not reveal anything new, and Smith himself died of dysentery, still digging, only two years later.

This watercolor, based on Layard's own conjectural reconstruction of the palace of Nineveh, epitomizes everything the Victorians saw as romantic and exotic about the past: shining marble, sumptuous gardens, midday langour in the shade of a palm tree. The vision is rather belied by the Assyrians' own bloodthirsty carvings of their world.

# UR: LEONARD WOOLEY'S SOCIETY DIG

It became quite the society thing, to drop in on Ur and see how Leonard was getting on.

Like Sir Mortimer Wheeler, Sir Leonard Wooley lived into the television age as one of the century's great media archaeologists—dashing, articulate, and scholarly, but witty too. He was also a pioneer of scientific archaeology, and renowned for training and inspiring the people he worked with.

He was in military intelligence during—and probably before—World War I, was blown up at sea, and spent two years in a Turkish prisoner-of-war camp. Instead of fleeing the Middle East for ever, he was back within a couple of years, leading what was dubbed the "dig of the century:" the joint British Museum/University of Philadelphia excavation of the enormous mound of Ur, in southern Iraq.

It really was the dig of the century. Between the wars the Middle East briefly became a colonial playground again, and everyone who was anyone came to see the Ur dig. Agatha Christie came with her archaeologist husband, Max Mallowan, and used it as a setting for *Murder in Mesopotamia*, published in 1936.

Her suburban London nurse was, however, less than impressed:

"The whole excavation looked like nothing but mud to me—no marble or gold or anything handsome—my aunt's house in Cricklewood would have made a much more imposing ruin! And those old Assyrians, or whatever they were, called themselves KINGS."

Ur was an archaeologist's dream city: it had a beginning some 7,000 years ago, a glamorous middle, and an end, when the Euphrates river changed course leaving the port city high and dry, in about 400 B.C. It had an alluring biblical connection, as the birthplace of the prophet Abraham, and it had an imposing temple, magnificent royal graves, and an irresistibly blood-curdling tale of human sacrifice to tell.

This was the site of one of the first recorded archaeological excavations, when the Babylonian king Nabonidus burrowed into the foundations of the mound, looking for interesting inscriptions, and partly rebuilt the great ziggurat temple.

The port and trade were what made the Sumerians rich, so rich in fact that they had to invent writing to keep track of their wealth and the number of temple offerings to their many gods. Archaeologists agree that Sumerian is the oldest written language, dating from about 3500 B.C., and their cuneiform script, written on clay tablets with a reed pen, became the basis of the written version of the later languages of Mesopotamia.

It was writing which identified the mound as Ur, capital of the Sumerians: the Sumerians, Assyrians, and Babylonians had the very useful habit of burying inscribed drums in their foundations, identifying the building and the builder. Rawlinson deciphered one found in a cursory dig in 1854 as the site of the royal capital of Ur.

Wooley started digging at Ur in 1922, and after excavating the 80-foot ziggurat and training his huge work force, he turned his attention to the cemetery. Eventually he excavated over 1,800 graves, the shaft graves of ordinary citizens, and 16 vaulted royal tombs, dating from Ur's glory days, around 2500 B.C.

All the royal tombs he found first had been

**LEONARD WOOLEY**
Leonard Wooley (1880–1960) combined scholarship with an ability to use plain English to communicate the glamor of archaeology. By the age of 25, he was assistant director of the Ashmolean Museum at Oxford. In World War I he worked in military intelligence—a trade he had evidently combined with archaeology several years earlier —and spent two years in a Turkish prisoner-of-war camp. His fame rests on one of the most spectacular excavations of the 20th century, the Royal Tombs at Ur. His flair for publicity insured that every celebrity passing through the Middle East in the 1920s dropped in to see how he was getting on.

"The whole excavation looked like nothing but mud to me—no marble or gold or anything handsome—my aunt's house in Cricklewood would have made a much more imposing ruin!"

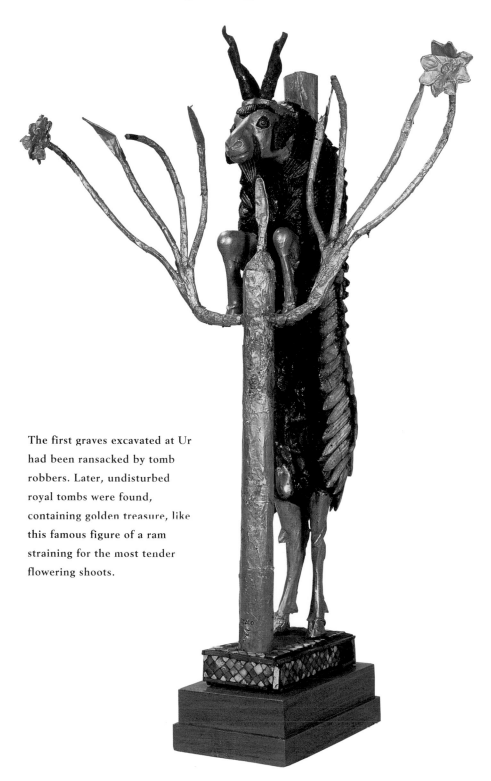

The first graves excavated at Ur had been ransacked by tomb robbers. Later, undisturbed royal tombs were found, containing golden treasure, like this famous figure of a ram straining for the most tender flowering shoots.

robbed, centuries earlier. The evidence suggested to Wooley that one tomb of a king could only have been robbed by the grave-diggers making the later tomb for his queen. Her tomb was intact and astonishing: not just gold, cornelian, and lapiz-lazuli jewelry, weapons, and bowls, but exquisite inlaid musical instruments and furniture, with scenes of banquets and hunts, domesticated animals and furniture. One of the most famous pieces from the Middle East, a golden ram standing on its hind legs to nibble the tender shoots from the top of a bush, came from these tombs.

The most remarkable feature lay not in, but just outside, the chambers: the oxen, carts, and dozens of people who had walked down into the tombs to go with the king and queen into the next world.

They reposed in what Wooley called death pits. From their dress and jewelry they were not slaves but wealthy courtiers, perhaps nobles. The women wore exquisite headdresses, made for a frivolous ball, of ribbons and beech leaves beaten out of thin gold. Some were packed so closely that they died with their heads pillowed on the feet of the next row. There was no sign of violent death: Wooley surmised that they drank poison and lay down quietly, voluntarily, to die.

"It is most probable that the victims walked to their places, took some kind of drug—opium or hashish would serve—and lay down in order. After the drug had worked, whether it produced sleep or death, the last touches were given to their bodies and the pit was filled in. There does not seem to have been anything brutal in the manner of their deaths."

Wooley thought that one of his most valuable finds was made not of bronze or gold, but of mud. Down at one of the earliest levels, he found a 10-foot thick stripe of clean silt.

He telegrammed London: "We have found the Flood."

It was, he was convinced, evidence of the biblical flood. However, scientists have not found the same flood evidence in other Mesopotamian sites of the same date, so either Wooley was wrong, or the Bible exaggerated and God drowned only Ur and all its citizens.

# BOGAZKOY: THE HITTITES UNCOVERED

I t took most of the 19th century to lure the Hittites out of the shadows. They were glimpsed occasionally in the gaps of other peoples' histories, the clues being put together like a jigsaw with the corner pieces missing. It was a crotchety German scholar, sitting under a tree on a hill in Turkey, who finally identified the suspects by their handwriting.

After 150 years of digging, there are now tons of Hittite writings, still being translated: 25,000 cuneiform tablets recovered from their capital, Hattusha, 3,000 found in one cache alone in the 1960s.

Hugo Winckler, a German scholar who could read Babylonian cuneiform as easily as reading a newspaper, eventually ran the Hittites to ground in 1905.

One gets the impression from his journals that he would have been far happier staying in his university library in Berlin. They are full of grumbles about heat, dust, flies, uncomfortable tents, uncomfortable companions. His field archaeology techniques were straightforward in the extreme: he went to the site in Turkey which was producing most of the tablets, hired some workmen and set them digging, and then sat under a tree in the shade reading whatever they brought him.

There had been no great mystery about locating the city. In 1834 villagers at the small Turkish village of Bogazkoy led the French antiquary Charles Felix-Marie Texier to the ruins of a gated stone-walled city. They then led him further up the hills to a place where the sheer faces of rocks were carved with processions of giant kings and queens.

Texier was so astonished he was almost angry. Like many other antiquaries he regarded Anatolia as a treasure trove of unexcavated

Greek and Roman remains. He was looking for a small Roman colony, and he could see immediately that these weren't Roman. They were clearly extremely old, but there was no record in history of a major civilization in the region before the classical period. He was an excellent artist, and sketched and published his drawings of strange ruins, carvings, and inscriptions, to general puzzlement.

It took nearly 40 years before another scholar put these together with some carved stones recovered from Syria by an Irish missionary, William Wright. Some of the symbols were identical, raising the startling possibility that there had been a forgotten empire stretching from the Mediterranean coast of Turkey right down into southern Syria. Wright had already suspected it, and he even suggested an identification: the Bible's mysterious Hittites.

More references to the Hittites and their way of life started to turn up in Egyptian and Babylonian inscriptions.

Clay tablets, in cuneiform writing but in an unknown language, began to appear at Bogazkoy, and at other sites, and eventually found their way to Winckler in Berlin.

Grumbling as usual, he set out to find the source. He seems to have had virtually no interest in the ruins, and didn't bother keeping detailed site records, which has caused the usual subsequent muddle.

Eventually the workers brought him a document which he could not only read at a glance, but realized that he had read before. The Hittites had for centuries been a thorn in the side of Egypt. This was the Hittite copy of a peace treaty between the pharaoh, Ramses II, and the Hittite king, Hattushili III, made in 1270 B.C. Winckler already knew the Egyptian version, inscribed in hieroglypics on the wall of the temple at Karnak.

The Hittite language wasn't translated until 1915, after Winckler's death, by the Czech scholar Bedrich Hrozny. The Hittites emerge from their own words as a more interesting people than the prejudiced Egyptian view of a bellicose nuisance. They had a sophisticated law code, and the stately queens in Texier's drawings had rights, of property and authority, unrivaled in their day.

German excavations continued at the site throughout the 20th century, but there are still puzzles about the Hittites. Their first king, Hattushili, took his name in 1640 B.C. from the city which was already an ancient place. It is not clear how the Hittites had suddenly emerged as a major power, nor what scattered them after 500 years.

Opposite: The Hittites, a lost people and a lost empire which once stretched from modern Turkey to Syria, emerged from the shadows of other people's histories—for example, as a constant irritation to the Egyptians—throughout the 19th century.

Below: It took decades longer before their cuneiform writing was translated, and revealed a sophisticated people with an advanced law code. Thousands of their inscribed tablets have been excavated and are still being translated.

# THE DEAD SEA SCROLLS

In the winter of 1947 three Bedouin shepherds, moving herds along a steep slope on the northwestern shore of the Dead Sea, found what must have looked most unlike treasure to them. Half buried in a bone-dry cave, were some pottery jars containing manuscripts written on papyrus or leather. It was, in the frequently abused cliché, one of the "finds of the century."

In archaeological, in historical, and in biblical-study terms, the contents of the cave were nothing short of sensational.

The Dead Sea Scrolls dated from around the first century B.C., almost 1,000 years older than the oldest known Hebrew version of the Old Testament, the *Aleppo Codex*. The first find included seven almost complete manuscripts, including two copies of the *Book of Isaiah*, and a scroll of hymns.

The scrolls attracted conspiracy theories like ants to honey, greatly fueled by the fact that the first find included *The Manual of Discipline*, a set of detailed rules and rituals of an unknown community, evidently devoted to strict religious discipline, living in imminent expectation of the end of the world, in which they alone would be seen as the chosen people.

Later finds included a copper plaque detailing where the temple treasure had been hidden.

The first seven scrolls were passed among dealers in Hebron and Jerusalem, and some were smuggled into the United States, but they were eventually brought together again and are kept at the Shrine of the Book in Jerusalem.

It took two years before the archaeologists managed to get to the caves, and by then priceless context material had been destroyed. Excavation continued, complicated by the endless political upheavals in the area, which left the scrolls in Israel and the site in Jordan.

More caves and thousands more pieces of manuscript were found. In Cave Four alone, over 15,000 fragments were found. It was an entire library, deliberately hidden to be retrieved at the time of final apolcalypse.

Above: Almost the only undisputed fact about one of the greatest discoveries in 20th-century archaeology, is that many of the Dead Sea Scrolls were found in this cave at Qumran, high on the slope of a cliff overlooking a ruined Roman fort.

Above: Some of the manuscripts were intact, but many were crumbling into fragments. It was years after their discovery before any proper work was carried out. Scholars are still poring over every fragment.

many it was obvious: the Essenes wrote, studied, and hid the scrolls.

There is an even more romantic twist to this interpretation. The settlement or monastery died out in the first century after Christ, and was briefly reoccupied as a small Roman fort, about the time the manuscripts were hidden.

Similar—though not, as some have claimed, identical—manuscripts were found at Masada. The excavation of this site was one of the achievements of the young Israeli state. Masada was where legend insists the first Jewish rising against the Romans, of A.D. 66, ended in the mass suicide of the besieged inhabitants. The suggestion is that the monks of Qumran first hid their greatest treasure, their library, then went to join the besieged in Masada and perished to the last man. The fact that archaeologists have found only 30 human remains in the ruins doesn't affect what is a matter of faith rather than history.

One eminent British archaeologist has described deliberate non-publication of archaeological finds as "a form of theft." In the case of the Dead Sea Scrolls, it provoked a major international outcry.

It also left a scholarly void in which conspiracy theories flourished: that the texts were fakes, had been stolen, or were being suppressed by whichever set of powers suited the argument, from the Israeli government to the C.I.A., because their subject matter was so explosive.

An editorial team had been set up to study and publish the texts as early as 1953, and while they worked all outside access was refused. By 1991, when only a fraction of the material had been released, the clamor was irresistible. The complete text, deciphered and raw, published and unpublished, was finally made available on microfilm.

Work is continuing on the texts, and more have been found at other sites, but their content has not shattered the foundations of either Christianity or Judaism. They contain major textual variations from the accepted Old Testament, and fascinating additions to the apocrypha; there are additions and omissions, but generally, given the huge gap in time, the similarities between the two are more striking than the differences.

Between 1952 and 1956 archaeologists turned to the problem of who had hidden the manuscripts. Below the caves there was a stump of a small Roman fort, Khirbet Qumran, which was a logical place to start digging. They uncovered a complex of buildings, built about 125 B.C. around a reused Iron Age fort, as well as a large cemetery. Not all scholars agree—there is in fact no aspect of the Dead Sea Scrolls on which all scholars do agree—but given that the cemetery contained a disproportionate number of adult male burials, one persuasive interpretation is that this was a monastery of the Essene cult, a forgotten sect once ranked with the Pharisees and the Philistines in influence. The finds included a solid gypsum table, and some inkpots, and pottery identical to the pottery in the caves. For

# MOHENJO-DARO

It is over 70 years since the head of the Indian Archaeological Survey announced they had discovered a new Bronze Age civilization, the Harappan, the earliest in the Indian subcontinent.

Archaeologists, including Sir Mortimer Wheeler, have been excavating at Mohenjo-Daro on and off ever since, with long breaks for war and politics, yet in many ways the Harappans, their way of life, and their cities remain as mysterious today.

The great mudbrick mound of Mohenjo-Daro is now in Pakistan. In 2,300 B.C. the city may have had up to 40,000 people living in a neat grid of wide streets, with the best sanitation in the Middle East, baths in many houses, and drains from most.

The city of Harappa itself, over 400 miles northeast, was on the same scale; there were several other major cities, and dozens of town and village sites. The state stretched as far in the opposite direction, to the port of Lothal, and the style of building and of artifacts is absolutely uniform across the whole region.

They traded widely, in semi-precious stones such as lapiz lazuli and cornelian, and made fine sculptures, including a refined portrait of a priestly figure, and a famous little bronze of a dancing girl, hand on hip, wearing only an armful of bangles and a necklace. They even had jokes: a happy little pottery pig, trotters over its eyes, also found at Mohenjo-Daro, must have been a child's toy.

But the cities seem to have come from nowhere, and disappeared for no reason. There are none of the expected primitive village settlements before they appear; there are huge buildings but nothing that looks like a palace; there is no sign of invasion or earthquake to explain the end of Mohenjo-Daro; and there is no reference to it in later Indian writings.

Before Sir John Marshall's dramatic

The great bath and the other monumental buildings on top of the mound at Mohenjo-Daro are still relatively well-preserved. Down in the city streets, where up to 40,000 people lived 4,500 years ago, a conservation nightmare is developing, as the water table rises and the mudbrick starts to dissolve.

announcement in 1924, archaeologists believed there was no urban society in India before 1000 B.C., and they doubted the earliest dates suggested for the great brick platform, covering over 20 acres, for the "citadel," the upper town, of Mohenjo-Daro.

Then the distinctive Harappan seal plaques began to be found in Mesopotamian sites, and the earlier dates could no longer be doubted.

The Harappan writings were known long before their cities. The neat square plaques, with images, usually of animals, and short inscriptions, had turned up regularly in the 19th century—hundreds were found when mudbrick was dug out of the Mohenjo-Daro site to use as track ballast when the railway line came through.

The writing, despite regular announcements that experts were on the point of break-through, is still undeciphered.

The remains of one of the monumental buildings in the citadel, with hundreds of stumpy square columns dividing narrow passages, baffled Mortimer Wheeler, until he visited a modern granary. He immediately concluded that his puzzle was also a granary, on a vast scale; that a wooden barn would have stood on top of his maze-like drying platform, where priest-kings gathered in the taxes in stored grain. The other buildings of the upper city have been given impressive names, such as the College, the Assembly Hall, and the Great Bath, but these identifications have been challenged by other archaeologists.

The city now presents a huge conservation problem, which may be faced by many other archaeological sites if the grimmest warnings of global warming are correct. The water table is rising, carrying pollution and corrosive salts with it, and dissolving the mudbrick foundations. This is a problem being experienced by many mudbrick sites: it has been reported that Merv, once called the Queen of the World as capital of the Silk Road, and home of the 11th-century poet-mathematician Omar Khayan, is experiencing identical problems. At Mohenjo-Daro experts are still undecided on how to tackle it—indeed whether it should be attempted or whether to stand back and watch a civilization rediscovered only 70 years ago melt back into the sand.

Opposite: This lively little bronze dancing girl, naked apart from her jewelry, speaks for herself. The thousands of inscribed tablets found at Mohenjo-Daro and other Harappan sites have yet to be translated.

The Pharaohs, who had themselves portrayed as

# EGYPT

4

In many public libraries there are more books on Egyptian archaeology than all the other countries of the world together. Modern Egypt's multi-million dollar tourist trade is based entirely on its archaeological treasures.

# EGYPT FINDS ITS VOICE AGAIN: THE ROSETTA STONE

The Rosetta Stone, the lump of black basalt which unlocked the miles of inscriptions covering every monument of ancient Egypt, is in the British Museum in London, through the fortunes of war.

**Egypt was dumb until a French scholar unlocked the secrets of the hieroglyphics covering all its monuments.**

The great monuments of Egypt were never lost: they surged up all along the line of the Nile, the line both of life and of the tombs of the dead, running the whole length of the country. Travelers, traders, and soldiers had stopped and stared at them for centuries.

The meaning of the monuments was lost beyond recall, however. All had long inscriptions, beautiful as sculpture, explaining who made them and when and why. The mummies were coffined in inscriptions telling who they were and which gods they had gone to and the proper invocations to make to both. All the little stone figures, the jewels, the scarabs, and the gold necklaces ripped out of tombs by robbers and sold to insatiable Western collectors, had inscriptions stating who had owned them. The tomb-robbers could not read the fearsome warnings of eternal punishment on the tombs they violated.

The whole country—the most glamorous, the most romantic archaeological site in the world—was dumb. Every monument was covered in inscriptions, and nobody could read a word of them.

In 1799 Napoleon's soldiers had marched into Egypt, on what would prove a disastrous campaign—except for archaeology.

The Rosetta Stone was found by a French legionary, who was digging out stones near a little village called Rashid, for a small desert fort called St. Julien. He noticed that there were letters on one smooth black stone, and reported it to his superior, a Lieutenant Bouchard, another forgotten hero of archaeology, who spotted that the inscriptions appeared to be in three different languages, and instantly realized they might be significant.

When the military campaign collapsed and the French surrendered at Alexandria, the English captured the stone, with a treasury of other antiquities. The French, the English officer sent to collect it reported, maliciously tipped it out of the splendid carrying case they had made for it, so he had to drag it away on a cart.

The name forever linked to the stone in the popular imagination is the French boy-genius Jean François Champollion, who started translating ancient languages as a teenager, and gave most of his short life to the Rosetta.

The British Museum gives a lot of the credit back to a man Champollion never acknowledged publicly. Thomas Young, an English physician and scholar, 20 years older than Champollion, was already absorbed in hieroglyphics when Champollion started his career.

Young also noticed the recurring groups of symbols in the hieroglyphics which they could not read, and realized that they could be matched to recurring characters in the Greek which they could. He matched 86 groups of characters—many, though not all, correctly—and sent his notes to Champollion. Champollion finished and published the job, and took the glory.

Champollion eventually published his explanation of the symbols that had proved so indecipherable in 1822, his translation in 1824, and in 1828 went like a film star to Egypt, in a blaze of publicity, to become the first man to stand in front of the monuments and translate them aloud to crowds of admirers. Within another four years he was dead, aged forty-two.

The chipped black basalt stone, saved by a French officer's sharp eyes from becoming a foundation stone in a desert fort, passed to England through the fortunes of war, and ended up in the British Museum. It was worth more than its weight in gold to scholarship.

Napoleon famously believed that an army marched on its stomach, but he believed it needed spiritual nourishment too. When he marched his armies into Egypt, he swept an arm toward the monuments and cried: "Soldiers, forty centuries of history look down on you!"

# NAPOLEON'S DONKEYS STRUGGLE INTO THE DESERT

**GIOVANNI BELZONI**
Giovanni Belzoni (1778–1823)
The Patagonian Sampson, an
Italian-born circus strongman
turned professional Egyptian
tomb-robber, was an
irresistible villain. He wrote of
his adventures with ruthless
gusto. He complained of the
discomfort of having to
scramble over and under
disintegrating mummies:
"Fortunately I am destitute of
the sense of smelling, though
I could taste that the mummies
were rather unpleasant to
swallow." He died ignobly
of dysentery.

The Sphinx, smiling her battered enigmatic smile, was to look down on some more history, to see not only the great army scattered, but the end of the first major scientific archaeological expedition.

There was something peculiarly French about those unfortunate scholars rudely referred to as the "Donkeys." The British and American armies have taken war artists on recent expeditions, but one could not somehow imagine half the staff of the British Museum or the Smithsonian Institution, with a sprinkling of distinguished grey heads from the Society of Antiquaries, scurrying at the heels of the army into Kuwait or Sarajevo.

When Napoleon marched disastrously into Egypt, the Donkeys, grumbling, squabbling, catching fevers and dysentery, went in too, with the baggage train.

The Donkeys were 200 "savants," wise men. They included artists, historians, philosophers, antiquaries, and language experts. Their job was to map, record, and explain all the monuments in the path of the army. It was thanks to their presence that the Rosetta Stone didn't

simply end up as the foundations of a French desert fort, and the books and beautiful drawings that they published—for a far higher percentage of the scholars than of the soldiers got safely home to France—launched the science of Egyptology.

After Nelson battered his navy, Napoleon saw that the campaign was doomed. He returned to France long before the army and the scholars who still struggled on.

Major General Tomkyn Turner, himself an antiquary, was sent in 1810 to take the Rosetta Stone captive from the French forces who held it. He was informed "by the French scavans" that another inscribed stone had been found near the Rosetta, but they had left it behind because it was "obliterated, or nearly so, by the earthen jugs being put on it, as it stood near the water."

He acquired a long list of the French scholarly acquisitions, which included botanical specimens, carvings, and Arab manuscripts—the French claimed it all as private property, not war booty. After a lot of haggling it was agreed "that the care in preserving the insects and animals had made the property in some sort private" so the French kept them, but the antiquities had to be surrendered, which they did with very bad grace.

The first book published was a really good read, *Journeys in Lower and Upper Egypt*, by Vivant Denon, which included lyrical illustrations, and stirring travelers' tales of splendid monuments, dreadful living conditions, snakes, and sand; it was a runaway bestseller, in French and in English.

However, the main work was an academic sensation, *Description of Egypt*, which was published in 19 handsome volumes with stunning illustrations, between 1809 and 1822.

The last volume came out just in time for Champollion's translation of the Rosetta Stone, which meant that the hieroglyphics covering every monument in the illustrations could be read for the first time. Every scholar who saw the lovely books yearned to go and see the originals, and the rise of Egyptology launched the careers of professional antiquity pirates like Giovanni Belzoni.

The campaign also started a craze for the Egyptian style in the drawing rooms of Europe: obelisks on mantelpieces, sphinxes on sofa ends, and lotuses twining everywhere, a style considerably more successful and enduring than the military expedition had been.

The sumptuously illustrated volumes produced by the scholars who followed Napoleon into Egypt were the most successful part of an ill-starred enterprise. The volumes began to appear in 1809, and they brought scholars, tourists, and artists flocking to see the wonders for themselves.

David Roberts, R.A.

# TUTANKHAMEN: THE MOST FAMOUS QUESTION AND ANSWER IN ARCHAEOLOGY

"Can you see anything?"
"Wonderful things."

In November 1922 there was a distinct edge to the most famous question and answer in archaeology.

Howard Carter was a quick-tempered man, regularly falling out with his employers and patrons. Lord Carnarvon had bankrolled his excavations in Egypt for decades, and the search for Tutankhamen, the boy Pharaoh, for five years. Carter had found nothing really exciting, and Carnarvon was about to pull out.

Carter was now certain he had found the right site in the Valley of the Kings, but he had been convinced of that before. What he had discovered so far was a short flight of stone steps leading down to a sealed door. The seals were encouraging, but of all the thousands of tombs excavated by Egyptologists in the 19th century, every single one had been plundered by grave robbers, most soon after the burials. In fact, as it turned out, this one had been robbed but the robbers were apparently disturbed before they reached the chamber itself, and the door was sealed again.

On November 6 he sent a telegram summoning Carnarvon: "At last have made wonderful discovery in valley, a magnificent tomb with seals intact; recovered same for your arrival. Congratulations."

He waited impatiently, and on November 25, with Carnarvon watching, he broke through the sealed door. Beyond the door there was a short rubble-filled corridor, and when that was cleared they came to a second sealed door. Carter broke a small hole in the door, and held in a torch. Carnarvon asked his fateful question.

There were wonderful things, the like of which no Egyptologist had ever seen. There were four rooms stuffed with wonderful things, and they took years to clear: wine-jars, harps, beds, stools, daggers, the remains of four carts, jewelry, chests, spears . . . there was the chair he'd had as a little boy, and the throne he had as a near man, with a beautiful carved and inlaid back showing his queen gently massaging scented oils into his languid arm.

Within the great gold shrine which almost filled the burial chamber itself, there were three coffins, of increasing splendor, and then a solid gold mask, of great beauty, over the head and shoulders of the mummy.

This was an insignificant little pharaoh, who reigned for less than a decade. His tomb was second-hand; because he died so young, his own was not finished, and one of his coffins and some of the canopic jars for his organs were second-hand too, originally made for his older brother. The mummy was no master-piece of the art: the resins had glued it to the bottom of its coffin and rotted the bindings, and inside, when it was X-rayed, the body was shriveled and wasted. He left no heirs—his two stillborn babies were buried with him, and a lock of his grandmother's hair.

The whole collection has left Egyptologists wondering, awed, what has been lost to almost four millennia of grave-robbers, ransacking the really important tombs.

However, Lord Carnarvon never saw the face of the boy king, either the glorious gold mask or the shriveled flesh. He died before the inner coffins were opened, of an infected mosquito bite, and this gave birth to one of the most persistent and romantic legends of Egyptology: the curse placed on those who defiled the pharaoh's tomb.

All who were there on that fateful day died tragically and young, the legend insists, ignoring the fact that half the diggers lasted another 20 years or more, that Carter died crosser than ever and not particularly young in 1939, while the annals of Middle Eastern archaeology are spattered with names of scholars who did die young, of dysentery or fever, after blameless careers doing nothing more blasphemous than translating a few papyri.

Opposite: Every other royal tomb found had been plundered, many almost as soon as the High Priest fixed the seals on the doors. Robbers had broken into this tomb as well but had been disturbed, and it was sealed up again with its treasures. The contents made the world gasp and wonder what was lost in the really important tombs.

Above: Tutankhamen was one of the least significant of all the Pharaohs. He was little more than a boy when he died, so suddenly that he was buried in a borrowed tomb.

# WHERE THE WORKERS LIVED: DEIR

The great and the good of ancient Egypt left their mark as in few other cultures: temples, palaces and tombs, pyramids, obelisks and sphinxes, and colossal statues and cliffs of stone inscribed with their names and virtues.

But where are the ordinary people?

Thebes rose to its peak of prosperity, from around 1540 B.C., as the capital of the 18th dynasty of the New Kingdom. One dusty road led to the other side of tracks, to a mudbrick village on the edge of the desert, one mile from the nearest water source.

In the 19th century various archaeologists took a glancing look at the village, Deir El Medina, a tumble of mudbrick cottages turning back into desert. Great discoveries were beckoning them to the Valley of the Kings, the possibility that somebody some day might find a tomb the grave-robbers had missed, complete with its royal mummy and all the fabulous wealth he carried into the next world.

In the 1920s a French team took a proper look at Deir El Medina, then continued work for half a century. They disinterred a lost world, that of the skilled workers who built the magnificent tombs. The village lasted for 450 years, with generations of the same families working as stone-cutters, carvers, plasterers, and painters. They made and decorated the 62 tombs so far identified in the Valley of the Kings, some cut over 330 feet into the living rock.

There were over 100 houses inside and just outside the village wall. They were small, but compare favorably with the living conditions of most poor Egyptian laborers today, with four rooms and a kitchen courtyard. Later houses show signs of greater prosperity, with stone foundations and painted decoration.

The French found thousands of documents in the village, which showed the tomb-builders about their work in microscopic detail. There were some inscribed stones, and rolls of papyrus, but in a rubbish dump there were the discarded daily notes, written on the cheapest materials available—pieces of broken pot and flakes of stone.

They recorded every detail of the work: the foreman and deputy who ran the village and the work-gangs, the copper tools supplied to them, the right and left teams of 60 men who worked on either side of the tomb, the rest huts near the site, the eight-hour working day and days off for holy days and festivals, and the days off for sickness or scorpion bites.

The wages are carefully prescribed for each skill, in grain, oil, fish, vegetables, and cloth, but the wages were not always paid on time. There were records of the first strike in history, when payday was delayed not weeks but months, and the workers put down their tools and walked off work on the tomb of Ramses III —there is no record of the strike being settled, but the work was finished and the village survived another 200 years.

The workers of Deir El Medina didn't have the status of those with the highest skills, such as scribes, but their talents were valued, and figures of carvers and painters at work may sometimes be glimpsed in corners of frescos and carvings.

The villagers of Deir El Medina got enough time off to insure their own immortality. Their own rock-cut tombs, small but beautifully finished, have also been discovered.

Opposite: Often, only evidence of the lives of the rich survives. It was only after a century of Egyptian archaeology that the importance of a scruffy little mudbrick village near the Valley of the Kings was recognized. It was the village of the craftsmen who made the sumptuous royal tombs. Their work records survive and show that they worked long but defined hours. They devoted some of their free time to decorating their own rock-cut tombs.

At the edge of his empire, Ramses II left the clearest warning statement to anyone thinking of invading from the south: four vast statues, each big enough to be a building itself, and all of Ramses, gazing out into Nubia from his huge temple at Abu Simbel.

# THE RESCUE OF
# ABU SIMBEL

Above: The rescue of Abu Simbel from the rising waters of the Aswan Dam caught the imagination of the world. The work took four years and cost over U.S. $40 million.

He could not have foreseen that it was the divine Nile itself, the source of all life in Egypt, which would rise against his temple.

The first Aswan Dam, in 1902, flooded many monuments and temples. However, near panic spread among archaeologists in the late 1950s, as the scale of modernizing Egypt's plans for a new dam, capable of supplying hydroelectric power, became clear.

Nasser's new lake, completely obliterating the Nile Valley for almost 300 miles below the new Aswan High Dam, would drown hundreds of temples, tombs, and monuments. Apart from the ancient Egyptian monuments there were centuries of later buildings, Roman, Arab, and Byzantine, lining the river in the fertile valley.

The dam was going ahead whatever the archaeologists said. UNESCO mounted an extraordinary rescue operation.

Nothing like it had ever been attempted before. Archaeologists, art historians, architects, construction engineers, geologists—and funds—poured in from all over the world to deal with the problem.

Teams were formed to record every inch of what was to be moved and what could not be saved. International museums were offered the less important monuments.

The operation also became a huge international media event. The world watched, astonished, as the Temple of Amada was cut free from the rock, placed on a platform, and transported by railroad to its new site.

Abu Simbel was the most important monument and the most difficult problem: it had been designed so that the living rock of the cliff behind it was incorporated into the temple, and its orientation was a vital part of its significance and impact. Also, it was accessible only by boat or across the desert, with virtually no services available locally.

It took four years even to design a solution, and by the time the engineers had worked out how to do it the dam had been under construction since 1960 and the water level was already rising. Another dam had to be made to protect the site during the work.

The final answer was to carve out a new slot for the temple almost 200 feet higher up the

cliff, cut the temple and the cliff behind it into 1,042 blocks, haul it up to its new site, and rebuild the cliff around and above it. The work took another four years (1964–8), and cost over U.S. $40 million.

The monuments which were not moved, such as the Temple of Trajan on the island of Philae, show the scale of what happened. Belzoni cast covetous eyes on every block of carved stone on Philae: only the very tops of the monuments, which even he and UNESCO decided it was impracticable to move, now show above the flood waters.

It is extremely unlikely that any such operation would be mounted at the turn of the 20th century. The consensus of the international environmental movement is strongly against such heroic engineering, as the wrong answer to the wrong questions. Conservationists fighting Indonesia's Pergau Dam, or China's Yellow

River Dam, would have welcomed a monument of unquestioned world class, such as Abu Simbel, as the surest way of getting such projects knocked on the head.

Abu Simbel, back on dry land, became the first World Heritage Site. There are now over 600, with more being added every year; mankind's official register of the sites, natural and archaeological, considered most precious.

The World Heritage Council, which monitors their condition, is now deeply concerned about the threat of flooding at hundreds of sites. The cause this time is not engineering but global warming and rising sea levels. In the early 21st century the council believes agonizing decisions will have to be made, not just about individual monuments such as Abu Simbel, but about entire World Heritage villages and towns. The answer is likely to be: record everything, and leave them to the rising water.

**The colossal statues of Ramses II again gaze out across the water into Nubia; the entire cliff face has been reconstructed around and above them.**

# RAMSES, AN IMMORTAL HERO

"I met a traveller from an Antique land
Who said: two vast and trunkless legs of stone
Stand in the desert . . . Near them, on the sand
Half sunk, a shattered visage lies . . ."

Percy Shelley never visited Egypt, but the poet read a traveler's description, and produced one of the most haunting images of its ruined glories, marooned in the modern world.

And on the pedestal these words appear:
"My name is Ozymandias, king of kings:
   Look
On my works, ye mighty, and despair.
Nothing else remains. Round the Decay
Of that colossal wreck, boundless and bare
The lone and level sands stretch far away."

The epic tomb-robber, Giovanni Belzoni, saw the same image with his own eyes. It moved him to rather less spiritual transports. "I found it near the remains of its body and chair, with its face upward, and apparently smiling on me, at the thought of being taken to England."

Belzoni cheerfully adds that he had to smash the bases of two columns in order to extract the colossal wreck.

Ozymandias is the Hellenized version of Ramses. The colossal head was that of Ramses II, one of the most remarkable of the pharaohs, who crosses and recrosses the path of Egyptian and Middle Eastern archaeology.

It was Ramses II who made the peace with the eternally belligerent Hittites, and the fact that the peace treaty survived in Egyptian hieroglyphic and Hittite cuneiform versions enabled the Hittite language and cultures to be deciphered.

Ramses was indeed the king of kings. Other pharaohs are portrayed as enjoying intimate conversations with the gods. Only Ramses is shown as a god praying to himself.

He carved his name, literally, all over the Egyptian empire. He stamped his authority by building on an heroic scale, and everywhere he built he left his name. He completed his father Seti's temple at Karnak with the Hypostyle Hall, a forest of stone, and his inscriptions stretched all the way to Abu Simbel, further south in Nubia than any previous pharaoh had built before.

He reigned for 67 years, twice the life span of an ordinary man, and lived for 90. He had almost as many sons as years, and his daughters were uncounted. His beautiful queen, Nefertari, was buried in one of the most wonderfully painted tombs ever discovered.

Two men have been tracking the works of Ramses II for decades: one the French linguist and novelist, Dr Christian Jacq, and the other the noted American archaeologist, Professor Kent Weeks.

**Right: Ramses had himself portrayed as a man of war and peace, as a human praying to a god, and as the god himself. He lived for 90 years, twice the average life span, and ruled for 67.**

Left: Ramses II was the original of Shelley's Ozymandias, but it is not true that nothing else remains except one shattered statue: he left his name carved on monuments from one end of Egypt to the other.

In 1995 Professor Weeks and his team from the American University in Cairo, announced the discovery of a vast tomb in the Valley of the Kings, the largest ever found. Work had begun eight years earlier, because the site, regarded as of only marginal archaeological interest, was threatened by the proposal to widen a tourist road into the valley.

By 1995 the full scale of the tomb was revealed by sonar, because the chambers were choked with rubble. As in the nearby tomb of Ramses himself, flash floods centuries earlier had brought down clay and stone which then set like cement. The tomb was unique, a labyrinth of chambers and passages on five levels. The team has now identified 118 rooms, and is still working on the site.

Inscriptions say the tomb was built for the first-born and other sons of Ramses, and scientific tests are being carried out on skeletons to see if they can be matched with DNA from the mummy of Ramses himself. The first-born, according to the Old Testament, was one of those struck down at the time of Moses and the plagues of Egypt, when "it came to pass that at midnight the Lord smote all the first-born in the land of Egypt, from the first-born of Pharaoh that sat upon his throne."

Christian Jacq's novels about Ramses, thousands of pages in three volumes, have sold by the million all over the world. Their success is understandable in France, with its long tradition of Egyptology, but they have also been sensational bestsellers in countries such as Finland and Korea.

Dr. Jacq, who still deciphers particularly tricky hieroglyphics for relaxation between writing novels, has a simple explanation: "People need heroes, particularly now in the modern world, and Ramses is the greatest hero of all."

Ramses' own tomb and splendid sarcophagus are empty, but his mummy survived, rescued by priests and hidden in an undignified heap of other royal mummies.

One small intimate secret about the Pharaoh only emerged when his skull was X-rayed in Paris in the 1970s: a little animal bone in the nose, put in by the embalmer to support his splendid hawk-like beak in death as in life. It would have tickled Shelley.

# HATSHEPSUT: TERRORISM AMONG THE TOMBS

No tourist ever visited Egypt for the picturesque charm of modern Cairo or Alexandria. The country's extraordinary archaeological treasures have been a magnet to tourists for as long as tourism has existed. In the mid-19th century Thomas Cook had boatloads of tourists steaming along the Nile in specially chartered boats.

The danger of tourism was thought to be the gradual damage to the monuments of Egypt, until tourists themselves became the target of terrorist attacks in the 1990s.

By the last decade of the 1900s the tourist industry was worth billions of dollars, and its dangers were obvious: the risk to the monuments. They were threatened directly, by the lines of people scrambling over fragile carvings, shuffling through tombs and brushing against painted walls or clouding them with their breath, or indirectly in insensitive development of hotels and roads.

What nobody had predicted was that tourism, with all its overtones of westernizing influence and conspicuous consumption, would itself become a target for fundamentalist terrorists in the late 1990s.

Hatshepsut was the first recorded female monarch in history, and was presumably even more conscious of the need to present an image of impregnable, unquestionable authority. She reigned with her stepson, Tuthmosis III, who was a child when his father died. He remained in the shadows during her entire reign from 1473 to 1458.

Statues and carvings from her reign show her as a bearded sphinx, or as a bearded man being greeted as an equal by the god Amun, and she added gateways, obelisks, and statues to Amun's already vast temple at Karnak.

She may have died naturally. She may not. Certainly her splendid tomb wasn't finished, and her architect, companion, and possibly lover disappears from the records at the same time. During the reign of Tuthmosis III his stepmother's name was hacked out of inscriptions and official records, but he couldn't obliterate her vast mortuary temple at Luxor,

for which half a cliff had been carved away, approached by sweeping flights of broad steps.

One of Howard Carter's early jobs in Egypt, long before he found immortality himself by discovering Tutankhamen's tomb, was drawing the carvings and paintings of the temple for the Egypt Exploration Fund, which published his work in six handsome volumes.

The temple even has a little joke, though Carter was not really the man for such things. Instead of the usual lists of wars and conquests, Hatshepsut's carvings credit her with a trade mission, to Punt. The Queen of Punt is shown as a totteringly obese figure, and the donkey that has to carry her is even identified, with a snigger that can be heard down the millennia.

Hatshepsut is a magnet for tourists: her extraordinary history, the suggestion of foul play, and the splendor of her monument have provided material for several bestselling books.

Below: One of the most unusual monuments in Egypt, the broad terraces of the mortuary temple of Hatshepsut, the only female Pharaoh, became the scene of a massacre of tourists in November 1997. For months afterward, the Valley of the Kings was deserted, apart from security guards.

They created a sensation when they were discovered, and in 1997 visitors to the British Museum found the first major exhibition of the mummy portraits from the Fayum very disquieting. Some burst into tears, some had to leave, unable to bear the clear bright gaze of the living dead.

# FACES FROM A CROSSROADS: THE HAWARA MUMMIES

The portraits were made in the first centuries A.D., at a cultural crossroads: their subjects were Roman citizens, of Greek ethnic origin—their ancestors probably Macedonian soldiers paid off in land—living in the Fayum, one of the most fertile regions of northern Egypt.

They were embalmed according to the ancient techniques perfected for the pharaohs, but painted not as the stiff formal Egyptian mummy masks, but as living, breathing human beings. Some are painted in the latest fashions of the Roman empire, but shown on their shrouds being led into the presence of the Egyptian gods of the dead.

There are children, youths with the first down of beards, beautiful young women, strong tanned men in the prime of life, and a few haggard faces with the dragging lines of mortal illness. A few mummies bear the Greek valediction to the dead: Farewell! Be happy!

A few are named, in Greek, including "Hermione the school teacher," a slender, elegant pale woman. Flinders Petrie, the archaeologist who found many of them, described her as a "studious and meek school mistress without a trace of show or ornament." In fact she rather resembled his young wife, Hilda. He sent Hermione to Girton, the women's college at Cambridge University, England, to set a good example.

Most gaze just past the shoulder of the viewer, as if into eternity. There is nothing comparable in portraiture until the Renaissance, over a thousand years later.

The subjects must have been wealthy, because work of such quality would have been very expensive, but nothing is known of the artists, although several works by the same hand have been identified. It is not known whether the portraits were commissioned in life—plausible of subjects in middle age suffering from a long illness, but hard to imagine of the sudden death of children—or how the artists produced such a striking impression of the subjects in life if they were only called to the deathbed.

For art historians they provide an agonizing window into an entirely lost heritage, classical Greek painting, known from documentary references and scraps of color on sculpture.

The most striking were painted in encaustic, where the pigment was thickened with wax, and sometimes modeled with a tool, to give a three-dimensional effect. They were carefully shaped to be bound over the head of the mummy, which itself was stuffed and bound to give a lifelike shape. The effect is remarkable.

After the third century they stop. There are no more portraits, and no such sophisticated embalming. Remarkably they seem to have lost any power either as religious objects or works of art. Flinders Petrie found them tumbled in heaps, or piled into pits, thrown aside to make way for later burials.

Mummy portraits had occasionally been acquired by collectors since the Renaissance, and have since been found over a wide region. They remain associated with the Fayum because it was the source of the two major groups, both from cemeteries originally excavated by local people.

In 1887 an Austrian businessman, Theodor Graf, came upon portraits being dug up from a cemetery at er-Rubayat, and bought as many as could be uncovered. He did not bother with the mummies, or any details of where and how they were found. He exhibited and sold them across Europe and America.

The following year Flinders Petrie found a major Roman cemetery at Hawara, and kept careful records. He worked there for two seasons, and returned in 1911. He was able to preserve several mummies intact, took only the portraits from some too rotted to move, and kept the heads of other mummies.

Nobody who has seen them doubted that they were portraits, but there was debate as to whether they represented the subjects at an idealized time of life, or at the time of death. The mummy of the sober Hermione has been X-rayed and C.A.T.-scanned, and a computer image made of her head and face; it closely matches the portrait.

Before the exhibition, first seen at the British Museum, there was one of those coincidences that strike sparks in the history of archaeology. Paul Roberts, a curator from the museum, gave a lecture explaining that the skulls Petrie collected had long since been separated from the portraits, and lost. A postgraduate archaeology student in the audience, Meredith Thompson, said "No," on the contrary, she had several on her desk.

When they were reunited it was possible to call in a team which specializes in recreating ancient faces. Among the skulls Richard Neave and John Prag have worked on was one from a tomb in Vergina in northern Greece: the result matched the portraits, and the accounts of his being blinded in one eye in battle, of Philip of Macedon, father of Alexander the Great.

They modeled two heads from the skulls, without seeing the masks, and the results answered the question vividly. The match, of a sparky young woman nicknamed "Fatima," and a swarthy young man, was uncanny, though the 2,000-year-old painted portraits, on balance, have more life than the modeled heads.

Opposite: Like most of the Hawara mummy portraits, the grave young face of Artemidorus gazes unnervingly just over the shoulder of the viewer, into eternity. His stucco mummy case shows the ancient Egyptian rites of the dead, his name and dress are Romanized, and the inscription, "Farewell Artemidorus," is in slightly misspelled Greek.

# 5 CHINA AND THE FAR EAST

W hile the cultures of the West were trading merchandise, styles, materials, and craftsmen, China developed alone. The West, centuries later, struggled to reinvent such Chinese contributions to the arts of war and peace as gunpowder and porcelain.

Opposite: The First Emperor's terracotta army has been standing guard for 1,800 years. The thousands of faces are so distinct that some archaeologists believe they are individual portraits of real soldiers, carved by the sculptor to keep their lord company.

# THE GREATEST WALL:
# CHINA AND THE FAR EAST

The man in the moon can see only one scar made by man on the blue globe of the earth: the Great Wall of China, begun in the third century B.C., and continued over mountains and plains until it was 1,250 miles long.

The Great Wall was built to awe and impress as much as for the military purpose of defending China's northern frontier. It still fulfills that function. Visiting political leaders are invariably brought to one of the best preserved stretches, near Beijing, to be photographed as tiny figures in a huge landscape, dwarfed by the might of Chinese history.

China on ancient maps is rumor and guess-work. It keeps that quality of wonder even as neon signs and soft-drink vending machines spread across the People's Republic.

The refinement of the art and culture of the Far East makes nonsense of the Western archaeological chronologies. China had a Bronze Age, but in its bronze age was casting objects that wouldn't be matched until the Renaissance in the West. Strictly speaking, Japan was a prehistoric country until the seventh century A.D., when written records began.

The art and architecture of the Assyrians, the Babylonians, the Hittites, and the Sumerians can be hard to see distinctly, when they all lived in Mesopotamia, trading and raiding, exchanging and borrowing.

All that time China, which regarded itself as not just the center of the universe, but all that was worth knowing in that universe, was definitely off the edge of the map as far as the West was concerned.

When legend says that Alexander the Great wept because there were no more countries to conquer, it never occurred to him to head east over the Himalayas.

China had a huge influence on countries like Japan and Korea, but its influence stretched only as far as its shadow fell. The West had to struggle on, trying to invent paper and gunpowder by itself.

Everything in China seems on an epic scale. Some of the earliest human remains outside Africa were found in China, including Peking Man. In one cave outside Beijing, the remains of at least 40 *Homo erectus* individuals have been found, the largest concentration of these fossils in the world. The cave seems to have been inhabited, by early hominids and animals including hyenas, over a span of more than 250,000 years. By at least 5000 B.C. some of the hunter-gatherers had settled down and were growing the first cultivated rice in the world.

One of the most spectacular discoveries in the 20th century was not gold or jade, but baked mud: the thousands of terracotta soldiers of the First Emperor's Army.

The First Emperor is said to have taken control in Qin, his native province, at the age of thirteen. He started building his tomb immediately, as he went on to seize all China. He intended to have the largest tomb in the world: eventually there are said to have been 700,000 men working on his tomb and palace.

Chairman Mao took an erratic interest in archaeology, the past pointing morals for the present. Archaeology is now carefully controlled by the state, and whole divisions of the army are sent in to help out on big projects. The First Emperor's huge burial mound is still undisturbed, behind its 3-mile long wall. The old records speak of fairy-tale wonders: models of the world with running rivers and lakes of mercury. China plans to open it some time in the 21st century. The archaeological world is agog.

Japan's strong state religion has protected many monuments which would otherwise have been wiped out in its explosive development in the 20th century. As China and other Far Eastern economies struggle to catch up, there's a lot of archaeology in their path.

# THE DIVINE BRONZE AGE: SHANG BRONZES

The Shang made bronzes of such quality they were regarded not just as suitable offerings to the gods, but as sacred objects, having acquired divinity in the transformation of molten metal into immortal objects.

China had a Bronze Age, but it was worlds away from the spears, shields, and cups of the Bronze Age in the West. By 2000 B.C., under the Shang Dynasty, village metalworkers had mastered bronze casting, and were soon producing work of a quality hardly equaled since.

Even the smallest bronzes, such as an elephant wine pourer just nine inches tall, have a monumental quality and a powerful presence even in museum cases.

The bronzes must always have been extremely expensive objects. They were cast for ritual ancestor worship, and to mark major dates and events, and they were treasured. Many bear inscriptions such as: "Let sons and grandsons for a myriad years cherish and use."

Anyang, the last Shang capital, near the current Anyang, was found in the 1920s.

Pinyin Li Chi was the first internationally renowned archaeologist to emerge from China, despite a career which was storm-tossed by China's tumultuous 20th century. He was born in 1896, and completed his education at Harvard. When he began work, at a time when almost all archaeology in China was by foreign teams, the bronzes were known, but almost nothing of the culture that made them; while the city was known from literary references, it was regarded as semi-legendary.

The Chinese civil war stopped his work, and Chiang Kai-shek left a military guard on the site to protect it from bandits. When Pinyin Li Chi was able to resume work he found hundreds of tombs and four royal burials, with their burial chambers, surrounded by the skeletons of human sacrifices, containing some bronzes of astounding quality.

His work was scattered again during the Japapese invasion of 1937, and eventually he moved his team and all his records with the Chinese Academy to Taipei in Taiwan.

Far older cities, with foundations of great ceremonial platforms as well as foundations of large public buildings and houses, have since been found. Most of the tombs had been looted of their jade and bronzes, but undisturbed Shang tombs have since been discovered. Over 400 bronzes were found in the 1300 B.C. tomb of Fu Hao, including one of a tiger devouring a remarkably tranquil-faced human victim.

Divination was extremely important to the Shang, and thousands of their oracle bones have been found at the sites. The bones were known from the 19th century, when antiquaries started to save animal bones with intricate inscriptions from being ground up for Chinese medicine; 3,000 years after they were made, the bones had retained enough superstitious power to be regarded as having magical healing properties. The diviners appear to have cracked the bones by piercing them with red-hot metal rods, and then interpreting the cracks—any particularly auspicious ones were saved, inscribed with interpretions of their meaning, and buried in foundations or tombs.

Shang bronzes are both massive and intricately decorated, cast in heavy sections in clay molds, then embellished with applied and incised decoration. They often feature vivid animal decorations, such as the elephant, its trunk raised as a spout, or a square vessel decorated with rams' horns, each in turn decorated with coiling and twining snakes, birds, and spirals and plants.

Many of the most splendid found in tombs are wine holders, presumably buried full of wine. They were also buried as offerings on hilltops or thrown into springs and rivers. In later tombs there are massive four-legged cooking pots, for banquets for the dead.

The tradition of splendid metalwork continued, and stone molds were used for less intricately worked tools and weapons. A fifth-century B.C. tomb in Hubei province, which was excavated in 1978, the tomb not of an emperor but of a more lowly local ruler, had a wooden rack of 65 perfectly tuned bronze bells, the largest the size of a man and weighing almost 500 pounds, inscribed with musical scales and tunes. The inscriptions on the sides of the bells show that both the music and the metalwork itself were regarded as having divine attributes.

Even the smaller bronzes, such as this three-legged Shang pot, have a monumental quality and a powerful, almost threatening, presence.

# THE EMPEROR'S ARMY

In 1974 some Chinese peasants digging a well turned up the body of a soldier. It was superbly preserved after 2,000 years underground, in full armor, and made of terracotta.

The soldier's grave and the peasants' field were at Lintong, about one mile from the mound of the tomb of the First Chinese Emperor, Qui Shi Huangdi. Discovering antiquities was almost commonplace in the area, which was about 20 miles east of the ancient capital, Xianyang. The archaeologists came in to examine whether the soldier had left any traces behind in the soil.

What emerged over seasons of digging was an entire army. They were intended to live forever, and there is something about the combination of their frozen immobility and their realism which gripped the popular imagination. Groups of figures have toured the world and drawn huge crowds. A computer scientist has spent years modeling them in virtual reality: in her film they stir in the earth and wake from their sleep; one sees that his companion's head has tumbled off, stoops, and tenderly replaces it. The sheds covering their pits have become one of the most popular tourist destinations in China.

The flesh-and-blood army, of highly trained, highly disciplined, splendidly equipped, utterly loyal soldiers, was the basis of the First Emperor's power. In 256 B.C., having toppled a dozen of their small neighboring feudal states, they conquered the once mighty kingdom of Zhou. Qin Shi Huangdi proclaimed himself the First Emperor, announced that his dynasty would last for 10,000 years, and set about building. Roads, palaces, and administrative buildings went up to control the standardized weights, measures, currency, taxes—and punishments, including forced labor on the huge building program. He also started building his own tomb.

Opposite: Row upon row, thousands strong, the Emperor's terracotta army has been guarding him for over 2,000 years. So many tourists wanted to see the figures that the Chinese had to build a new airport—in building it, they found another army.

Earlier Chinese rulers had gone to their graves with dancing girls and musicians, gardeners and farmers, and a few soldier figures for a personal bodyguard. Often the bodies, of concubines, servants, and soldiers, of horses and oxen, were flesh and blood.

Qin Shi Huangdi's original soldier came from a complex of vast pits. Eventually there were 7,000 soldiers, all life size, many taller than the laborers uncovering them. There were archers kneeling to draw arrows from their quivers, foot soldiers, cavalry officers, and charioteers. The ties and buckles of their clothes and uniform, the decorations and hair styles of their rank had all been meticulously modeled. Their bodies are of standard types, but the heads are strikingly individual, and of different ages and ethnic types. Many are slab faced and impassive; others wear faint smiles or look on the point of speech. They are so distinct that some archaeologists have wondered if the figures are portraits of actual soldiers from the Emperor's real army.

Work continues. There were more extraordinary things under the fields. In 1980 they found a team of bronze horses, with gold-and-silver harness, pulling a chariot of bronze, the sort of closed carriage in which an emperor could live for days on the road, traveling through his territories.

Other armies, of other emperors, have since been found. In 1990, a crew working near Xi'an, while in the process of building a road to the new airport, specially to bring tourists to see the Terracotta Army, found the foot soldiers of the Fifth Han Emperor. Jingdi's defenses against the afterworld were numerous, but rather less intimidating than those of the First Emperor's.

There were thousands of soldiers, up to 400 packed into each of 24 pits, but they were only two feet tall. Their movable wooden arms had rotted and dropped out of the shoulder sockets, and they were naked—textile conservators are still struggling with the scraps of crumbling silk and embroidery, which show that the little soldiers went into the ground wearing individually tailored suits of sumptuous fabrics, almost good enough for an emperor himself.

# IMMORTALITY IN JADE PYJAMAS

Jade is a comparatively common stone, in colors through clear dark green to white, widely distributed across the world. Some of its value must come from its hardness, and from the fact that it can be carved in intricate detail. It will then last, under almost any conditions, as near to forever as archaeology can uncover.

It has certainly been traded and revered across a huge range of cultures, from China to South America, often valued more highly than gold, worth killing for and worth burying with the most illustrious dead.

China took this reverence for jade to great extremes. Jade carvings dating back to 5000 B.C. have been found. By the following millennium, in tombs from 4000 B.C. of the Hongshan culture, in north-east China, the artists mastered the art of carving the stone into three-dimensional rounded objects, seen as a variety of shapes, from animals, birds, clouds, and even evocations of the outline of a

sacred mountain in the Liaoning province. A temple site in the province has produced fragments of life-size and over-life-size statues, one with inlaid jade eyes.

Jade was both a proper material for ritual objects, for jewelry and dress ornaments for kings to wear during public events, for vessels for temple altars, for offerings to throw into rivers to appease the spirits, and it also had intrinsic spiritual and magical properties.

The poor would try to bury their dead with at least a bead of jade, since it preserved the body from putrefaction. The emperors, going to join their peers, the gods, needed to insure

Below: Work forces as large as armies worked on Chinese royal tombs. Hillsides were carved away to form the Han tombs, where the royal dead were laid among heaped treasures accumulated during their lives or offered to them in death.

the preservation of their entire bodies, and so were buried in jade pyjamas.

In 1968, archaeologists found the tomb of Prince Liu Sheng, who died in 113 B.C., in the Early Han Dynasty. He was buried with his wife Dou Wan, at Mangcheng, in Heibei province.

The tombs themselves were spectacular. A hillside was gouged out to form the tomb. Thousands of artifacts went with the royal couple, including many objects they had owned themselves in life, such as a pair of bronze leopards inlaid with gold and gems, and images of musicians, dancers, gardeners, and warriors; there were lacquer vessels, a lamp modeled as a young servant girl, and a wonderful incense burner in the shape of a mountain with a myriad of wild animals pursued by hunters. At least six carriages and horses were among the tomb treasure.

The most spectacular find, however, was the bodies themselves. Their heads resting on bronze pillows, the royal couple were completely lapped in jade, from head to toe: jade jackets and pants, hoods and face masks, gauntlets and boots. Each suit is estimated to have taken 2,500 jade plaques, stitched together at the corners with over 30,000 pieces of gold wire. Archaeologists believe they would have taken years to make, so presumably one was measured for a funeral suit long before death.

The tradition continued for centuries: Prince Liu Yn, half brother of the Han emperor, Mingdi, was buried in A.D. 90, again in a jade suit, with a much more sophisticatedly fashioned hood which follows the contours of the head as closely as a ski-mask.

The belief was that the jade served two useful purposes: it not only preserved the dead but it made them so comfortable that they would rest quietly in their tombs, and not wander out to trouble the living.

It may have kept them in their tombs, but it didn't keep them uncorrupted. The jade suits were found in a chaos of pieces of jade and scraps of gold wire: the bodies had inevitably rotted away entirely.

In 1968 the archaeologists found thousands of little jade plaques and fragments of gold wire. It took almost as long to reconstruct the last splendid outfit of Princess Dou Wan as it had taken craftsmen to fashion it originally. The jade suit, covering the body from head to toe, with helmet, gauntlets, and boots, all stitched with gold wire, was designed to preserve her for all time, body and soul.

# THE SILK ROAD: CURIOSITY LURES THE CHINESE OUT

It can't have been complete ignorance: some nomads galloped their horses or followed their herds over the mountain borders, some fishermen and traders washed up on their shores. But China was vast, with every type of climate and agricultural condition, from the northern deserts to the southern rice fields; the oldest rice grains in the world, from 5000 B.C., have been found baked into pottery in Hangzhoe, in marshland near the mouth of the Yangtze. It found it had no need to expand, no real fear of attack except at the very margins in the shifting borderlands where a rebellious tribe had to be forcibly put down occasionally, and no economic imperative toward curiosity about what lay beyond.

For thousands of years China lived inside its own huge territories, apparently quite incurious about the rest of the world.

Under the 400-year reign of the Han emperors the walls began to crumble. The nomads on the borders were being particularly obstreperous, and captured prisoners had strange stories that there were civilized wealthy lands, not just contemptible savages, beyond the edge of the known world.

Much of the Silk Road was already in position, a trading route for silk, spices, precious metals—and knowledge—from India and Persia through Samarkand and Merv and further afield into the West.

The Chinese completed the link by eventually becoming curious enough to send their emissaries over their mountain walls.

The Han emperor, Wudi, sent Zhang Chien to investigate in about 138 B.C. He was gone for half a lifetime, having spent years in prison, but he came back with amazing stories, manuscripts in incomprehensible scripts, and some goods which even the Chinese found interesting, including grape seeds.

Within decades regular caravans of camels were following in his footsteps, out from the ancient capital of Xi'an, through the frontier town of Dunhuang, and into the pass in the mountains called the Jade Gate.

Thousands must have died on the journey—the road is studded with their tombs, and the monasteries and temples where monks prayed to protect later travelers from their ghosts. The dangers were real enough, not just the bandits likely to canter their fast horses down on the plodding caravans, but disease to which they had no resistence, hunger, thirst, snake bite, and sunstroke.

The traveler had to decide whether to take the route north or south of the utter desolation of the Takla Makan Desert, which still claims a regular toll of travelers' lives today.

The archaeology of the route is the archaeology of cultures repelled and fascinated by one another. The Chinese found the Westerners crude, red faced, and vulgar, but admitted the barbaric power of their music and art. There were Hindu priests exchanging poems with Confucian philosophers; there were inns and brothels, shops and stables, blacksmiths and musicians—a piece of Tang pottery, found in a tomb, shows a camel understandably

Above: The sites along the Silk Road—inns and monasteries, villages and towns, stables and brothels—reflect the clashing of many cultures. This settlement at Bezeklik was not just a refuge for travelers, but one of many religious centers devoted to the translation and study of Buddhist texts which came along the Silk Road from India.

Opposite: Marco Polo was the most famous traveler on the Silk Road. He came from a wealthy Venetian family, and went as an ambassador from the Pope to Kublai, the Grand Khan, with his father and uncle in 1271. He got all the way to China, and eventually returned to Venice by sea after 24 years away. This beautiful Catalan atlas, showing his weary party, was made in 1375, just 50 years after his death.

roaring in protest, carrying an entire troupe of Chinese musicians on its back. Collections of archaeologists every bit as motley, from East and West, are now working at numerous sites all along its route.

For centuries it seems to have been Chinese travelers coming into the West and then going back again. It took the Mongol Yuan empire, which began to spread and dominate central Asia in the 13th century, to smash open the isolation from the other side of the wall. Paper and paper money, printing and gunpowder, porcelain and, of course, silk came out; Arab numerals and Islamic religion went in.

A 14th-century Spanish map shows one of the most famous travelers ever to have made the journey: Marco Polo and his party, crossing a terrain of rough stones, figures on foot, and heavily laden pack camels and riding horses, one with a man slumped in utter exhaustion on its neck.

Marco Polo's account of his journeys are as vivid as a novel, so much so that they are now being doubted. He seems to have seen many things that nobody else did, and to have missed things he might have been expected to note, such as the bound feet of women. The jury is out, but archaeologists are still looking for evidence that he was ever there at all.

# JAPAN: THE MIRROR IN THE KEYHOLE

**N**ear the modern city of Osaka in Japan there is a vast keyhole-shaped mound, surrounded by a moat, surrounded by a park.

It is almost 500 yards long, and is believed to be the burial place of the Nintoku Emperor, the largest earth tomb in the world. Its contents may well be magnificent, but although the Emperor died over 1,000 years ago, it is still regarded as a shrine of the dead, and the archaeologists may not touch it.

Many of the Kofun, the huge mound and rectangle—therefore keyhole-shaped—burial mounds, dating from the third to the seventh centuries A.D., are similarly out of bounds. They are of great historical significance, since they mark the rise of the Yamato, the first centralized state in Japan, in the Kyoto, Nara, and Osaka regions.

However, in 1953 another burial mound literally spilled out its contents, and the archaeologists had to be sent for. Part of the Otsukayama Kofun, one of the earliest third-century mounds, was cut through by a railway line in 1895. When the line was widened in 1953 ancient metal objects began to cascade out of the hillside.

It was another huge mound, over 600 feet long, built on rising ground around a natural hillock. It dominated the whole surrounding district.

Archaeologist Takayasu Higuchi found a stone burial chamber at the heart of the mound, made of massive unmortared slabs— the ceiling slabs in other Kofun chambers weigh over 70 tons—and not a trace of coffin or corpse. The ground had been carefully covered in gravel and drainage chanels dug, but the wooden coffin and its contents had completely rotted away.

The contents included a mass of ancient metalwork: iron helmets, pierced metal plates from a long since rotted mail-shirt, spearheads and swords, knives and sickles.

There were also Haniwa, ceramic offering figures, in the form of houses, warriors, and women. Other tombs contained thousands of them, made by specialist ceramic works, in sets such as a dozen warriors, a dozen courtiers, and a dozen dancing women, as well as gardeners, farmers, falconers, and deerkeepers. In later tombs the figures become very large, almost as large as the Chinese terracotta armies which clearly influenced them, and were used to ornament the outside instead of being buried.

The most unusual items in the Otsukayama Kofun were 40 bronze Chinese mirrors, which were clearly highly valued objects. They were set very carefully, on edge, around the sides and end of the burial chamber.

Strictly speaking the Kofun are prehistoric, since there were no Japanese written records until the end of their era in the seventh century. There are references to Japan, however, in Chinese and Korean documents.

Another Japanese archaeologist, Tatsuo Koboyashi, set out like a detective on the trail

Unlike their Chinese cousins, many of the Japanese terracotta soldiers were not buried, but stood guard above ground, around the walls, or on top of the tomb mounds. There may be legions more below ground, but the tombs are still regarded as sacred shrines, and only a handful has been excavated.

For archaeologists the greatest treasures in the
Japanese Imperial tombs are the Chinese bronze
mirrors, with their vital date stamps.

of the Chinese mirrors. These usually, usefully,
had dated inscriptions. He found they had
been imported in bulk directly from China,
and that duplicates from the same molds
turned up in different sites, and so he could
trace patterns of trade and gifts by the Yamato
rulers across the distant, scattered provinces of
Japan. Of the 40 in the tomb, he found 19
duplicated elsewhere.

Another tomb, Koganezuka Kofun, south of
Osaka, was known locally as "Gold Hill" and
was said to be the burial place of a great
princess. Again there was no body—and no
gold—but of the three burials one was believed
to be a woman. There were no weapons in the
chamber, but a quantity of jewelry, and
another mirror.

In Chinese records, Koboyashi found an
account of the Emperor Wei, who was clearly
quite impressed by the splendid gifts and cour-
teous emissaries sent to him by the Japanese
Princess Himoko. He resolved to send her a gift
of some bronze mirrors. That was in A.D. 238.
The mirror in the Gold Hill tomb was dated
239; it is at least conceivable that the archaeologists found both the recipient and the final
resting place of the gift.

**The tombs that have been excavated have yielded
a wide variety of figures, made in sets by
specialist workshops: dancing girls, gardeners,
farmers, falconers, as well as soldiers. Some of
the tombs can be dated, from the third to the
seventh centuries A.D., by the date stamps on the
highly-prized imported Chinese bronze mirrors.**

# BOROBUDAR: A MOUNTAIN OF STONE RISES AGAIN

The great Buddhist temple of Borobudar, the most spectacular in Indonesia, is a stone mountain set among wide, flat expanses of brilliant green—the fertile rice fields which were the source of Java's wealth when the temple rose between the eighth and eleventh centuries A.D.

Indian traders had been operating across a great swathe of southeast Asia since the first century A.D., and where they went Indian missionaries and culture followed. The local rulers welcomed the Brahmans into their courts: they frequently adopted the religion, but they also sought the knowledge of science, astronomy, mathematics, literature, and the arts which the Brahmans brought.

As the Asian kingdoms grew wealthier they too began to build huge Buddhist and later Hindu temples, often importing stone-carvers, wood-carvers and craftsmen.

Java was one of the most fertile, and therefore became one of the richest, of these kingdoms. In the eighth century the rulers began to build a temple which took 80 years and over two million blocks of volcanic stones to complete.

At Borobudar there was originally a small village shrine on a low hill. The entire hill was gradually entirely encased in carved stone, and at some point the whole thing must have started to slip, because the temple stands on a stone platform which is actually a retaining collar for the entire mound.

It is decorated with over 1,300 panels of delicate stone carvings of gods, men, and animals, scenes of saints, of virtue rewarded and evil punished, and over-life-size statues of meditating figures, a gallery of Buddhist art almost one mile in length if set end to end.

The five square-stepped terraces, ballustraded with stone carvings, rising to circular terraces with *stupas* (towers pierced with delicate carvings) lead on up to one last great stone *stupa*. The building itself, and the action of the pilgrim climbing its steps, represents the soul's journey to enlightenment.

The statues of the calm, teaching Buddhas sit as if nothing has ever disturbed their contemplation. In fact the jungle had almost ripped their stone mountain apart, when a huge international rescue operation was mounted in the 1970s, to dismantle and reconstruct the temple.

In the 11th century the religious and administrative capital moved hundreds of miles to eastern Java. The fields were left to farmers, Hinduism became the dominant religion, and gradually the temple buildings fell into ruin.

They were rediscovered by a French team around 1900, and enough of the choking vegetation was cleared to reveal the extraordinary quality of the stonework.

Intermittent excavation and repairs continued through the 20th century, but in 1972 the first major survey of the temple mound revealed that it was getting close to the point of collapse, from trees and creepers ripping apart the stone terraces.

In one of the most spectacular efforts of rescue archaeology ever attempted, the artificial mountain was dismantled. An international team of conservators, architects, and engineers joined hundreds of local workers. Over 800,000 stones were numbered, removed, cleaned, repaired, and replaced. The path to enlightenment is now clear again, for both pilgrims and increasing numbers of tourists.

Opposite: The lower terraces of the temple are decorated with over 1,000 panels of sculpture, illustrating parables of virtue rewarded and evil punished. They are also works of great beauty.

# ANGKOR WAT:
# A WORLD HERITAGE SITE
# ON THE BLACK MARKET

Anyone particularly impressed by the magnificent ruins of Angkor Wat, the vast temple in the Cambodian jungle, can buy themselves a piece on the archaeological black market. The ancient capital of the Khmers has the dubious distinction of becoming one of the most looted monuments in the world.

**Above: Monks gaze at the splendor of Angkor Wat across one of the artificial lakes, which were so complex and expensive to maintain they may eventually have bankrupted the Khmer empire. In the late 20th century, under the Khmer Rouge, the stone towers, symbolic mountains of the gods, became gun emplacements.**

Angkor, one of the world's most impressive stone-built monuments, was sacked by the Thai armies in 1432, clawed back from the jungle by archaeologists in 1898, and looted on a truly industrial scale during the Pol Pot regime and since.

The ruins are so vast—one square mile of the Angkor Wat temple and 124 square miles of the Angkor Thom complex of city, palace, temples, moats, canals, and water tanks, built and rebuilt from the ninth to the twelfth centuries—that they were never exactly lost, just forgotten.

They were mentioned occasionally by Chinese, Portuguese, and Spanish travelers over the centuries, but finally became famous again when a French naturalist, who also happened to be an exquisite painter, wandered in on foot in 1860.

Henri Mouhot was really more interested in butterflies, but started to study the ruins when he realized he was walking not on the jungle floor but on a broad paved road. He was struck by the haunting atmosphere of the ruins, above all the hundreds of huge stone heads on the towers, smiling faintly into the trees.

His drawings are still regularly reproduced, though he was dead of a fever before his journals were published, first in French and then in English. "The howling of wild animals and the cries of a few birds alone disturb the solitude," he wrote, so the antiquarian world flocked.

The local people themselves believed the ruins were the work of giants or gods—which was not so far off, since they were built by Khmer kings who were held also to be divine, and commemorated themselves as gods in the intricate carvings.

By the end of the 19th century, archaeologists, led by the French, had proved they were built by the forgotten Khmer, ancestors of the local people, who rose from being the dominant tribe in one province to become rulers of one of the most powerful trading empires in Southeast Asia.

Their Buddhist and later Hindu temples were heavily influenced by Indian architecture, built as much for symbolism as beauty.

Archaeologists now believe that the enormous cost of building and maintaining the complexes, and the hundreds of miles of waterways and tanks which fed them, bankrupted the empire. There were signs of decay long before the Thais came in the 15th cen-

tury. The Khmers took their more portable treasures and moved to found a new capital at Phnom Penh, about 150 miles away.

The jungle repossessed the ruins, and in 1898 the first major exercise in rescue archaeology was mounted, to save the buildings from being torn to rubble by trees and vines. The French work director said "the fig tree is the ruler of Angkor." Archaeologists worked with hundreds of local laborers to cut down or uproot thousands of trees and saplings, which were tearing apart the stones and toppling towers and statues.

The first rescue was by sheer manpower. Almost a century later the stones were again in trouble, and the Cambodian government invited in Indian conservators, whose work, including chemically stripping stained stones, is now considered to have done more harm than good.

Other archaeological monuments are in acute danger from the volume of tourism. Angkor Wat's problem has been the tourist flight in the wake of the region's renewed political instability, leaving the black-market art thieves to work undisturbed

Under the Khmer Rouge, the tower mountains of the gods became gun emplacements, while many soldiers took up amateur antiquity dealing as a lucrative side line.

At its height there were reports of art thieves taking orders from sheaves of photographs across the border in Thailand, and then going back to hack off carvings to order. At one point they took a short cut and looted an archaeological store instead, taking dozens of carvings which had been deliberately removed for safe keeping.

Angkor Wat is now officially listed as one of the world's most endangered sites, but it is clear that a lasting environmental solution is only possible in the wake of a lasting political and military peace.

Meanwhile, the technology of war has revealed that there is still more out there in the jungle. A map produced by the American space agency, N.A.S.A., of radar images taken by a DC-8 aircraft, has uncovered a large circular mound near Angkor Wat, suggesting an even earlier city, and six more temple sites.

**At one point, art thieves were offering the magnificent carvings for theft-by-order from photographs.**

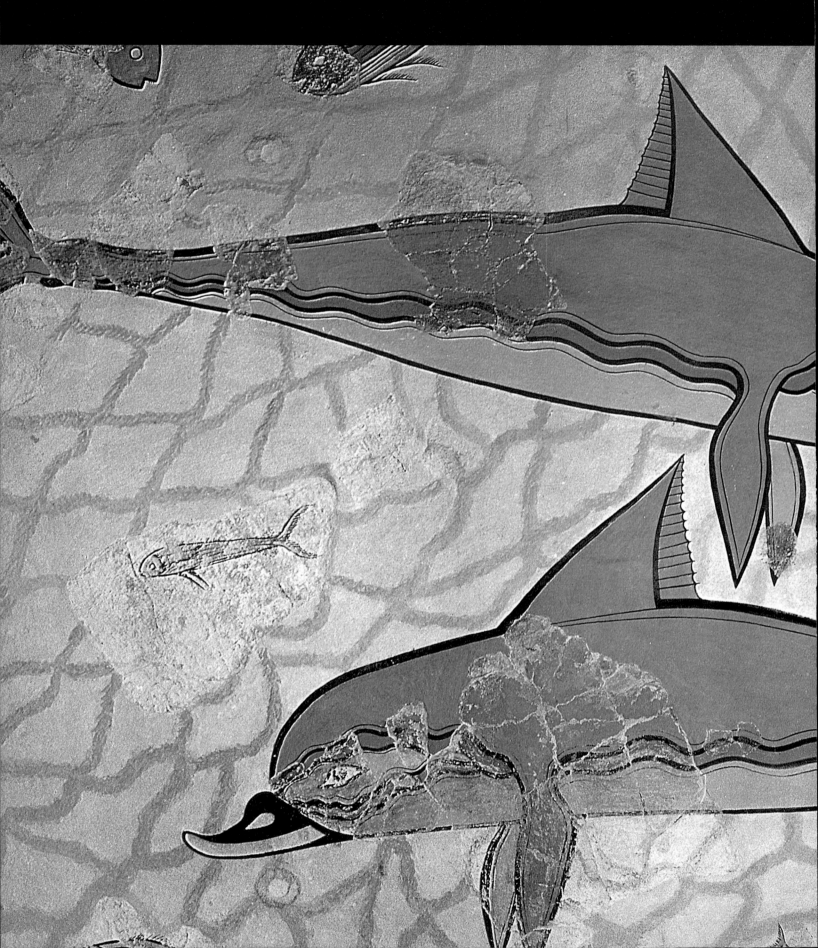

These frescoed dolphins in the sparkling waves,
from the Palace of Knossos, seemed to speak of
a Minoan civilization of carefree prosperity.
Scholars now question this sunny image.

# GREECE

The long shadow of the art and religion, the law and philosophy, the literature and architecture of ancient Greece still lies across the world.

6

# DIGGING FOR HOMER: GREECE

Superficially they look rather alike, Heinrich Schliemann and General Sir Augustus Henry Lane Fox Pitt Rivers: well-buttoned, prosperous mustachioed Victorian gentlemen, full of convention and righteousness.

**HEINRICH SCHLIEMANN**
Heinrich Schliemann (1822–1890) was the son of a poor German pastor. His childhood, spent in a village haunted by legends of lost golden treasure, and a book about Troy showing the great gateway in flames, marked him for life. He made several fortunes and learned a dozen languages to prepare himself for the honor of excavating Homer's city.

Appearances deceive. Schliemann had the purest of motives, the loftiest of patrons, and the operating methods of a Barbary pirate. Pitt Rivers had an inquiring mind, quite unblunted by 20 years in the British Army, a superbly organized approach to problems, and a streak of eccentricity which led him to believe that yaks would flourish on his lands in Wiltshire, England—they didn't.

In the late 19th century, two rival approaches to archaeology were vying for supremacy in the field.

Schliemann's had reigned for a century, and was the only half-legitimated cousin of the grave robbers of old.

If something interested you—Nineveh, say, or the Athenian Parthenon—you bought it, usually from "Johnny Turk." If he wouldn't sell, you tried to take it anyway. You dug what and where you liked, skipping the dull bits as if reading the Bible or *War and Peace*. If you'd signed an agreement, as Schliemann did at Troy, to give half the finds and all the gold to the Turkish government, well that was clearly nonsense; you'd probably been cheated already so it made sense to try and outwit the authorities and get whatever you wanted out of the country as soon as possible.

The approach was seen all over Greece. The Parthenon Marbles were only the most spectacular example; entire temples and tombs were dismantled and taken home. Arthur Evans was better disguised as a modern scholar, but his approach to Knossos was essentially the same: he was ruled by what he knew to be so, not what he observed on the ground.

Pitt Rivers stopped being a career soldier in 1880, when he inherited his uncle Lord Rivers' vast estates, provided he changed his name from Augustus Henry Lane-Fox. His thousands of acres included Iron Age, Romano-British, and Saxon sites, so he turned himself into an archaeologist.

He pioneered the technique of meticulous planning, scrupulous observation, and recording, and inch-at-a-time progress. When he had finished with a site it was scraped to the bare bone; there was nothing left above ground. He found some splendid things, but was among the first to see that a bone needle, a stone lamp, or a broken pot, could tell you more than a golden goblet or a bronze shield.

Mortimer Wheeler, who thought him a hero of archaeology, lamented the fact that 40 years after Pitt Rivers' death in 1900, people were still digging sites like terriers frantically digging out rats.

If Pitt Rivers had excavated Troy, with its layer upon layer of cities, would he ever have got down as far as the gold at all?

If Schliemann had attempted to excavate Pitt Rivers' Cranborne Chase estate . . . ? But he wouldn't have: Homer had nothing to say on the subject of Wiltshire.

Schliemann got the laurel wreaths, and was regarded as the hero in his day. Within a decade scholars were shaking their heads over his excavation of Troy, and declaring that the city was sacked twice, once by the Greeks and once by Schliemann, and Schliemann did the more damage.

Even in his day a lot of the work Pitt Rivers was doing was regarded as worthy, impressive, but desperately dull. Frankly it takes a lot of black coffee to get through all the handsome volumes he published himself on Cranborne Chase. But for all that, his was the lasting influence, felt wherever an archaeologist marks out a grid.

But which has inspired more people to the trade, Pitt Rivers' charts and diagrams, or Schliemann's blazing passionate certainty?

Pitt Rivers believed that the object of archaeology was knowledge, not treasure. The humblest broken pot shard was as valuable to him as a golden goblet, excavated with as much care, and lovingly recorded in the sumptuously produced volumes he published himself.

95

# TROY

Troy, the city of Priam and Paris and the beautiful stolen Helen, the besieging Greeks, and the Trojan Horse, is wrapped in magical stories. It was already a place of legend in Homer's day—legends woven by him into a work of art.

Since 1873, Troy has been bound up with the name of Heinrich Schliemann as closely as with Helen. It is unfortunate that archaeologists no longer trust a word Schliemann wrote, since what he wrote is so vivid.

He wrote of "the great projects I formed when I was a poor little boy," a German childhood in a haunted landscape, where legend said there was a baby buried in a solid gold cradle under a nearby hill, where neighboring villagers were said to have dug up and drunk barrels of Roman beer.

He said that his father, a poor and eventually disgraced pastor, gave him a book about the Trojan War when he was seven, and that he there and then decided to grow up and find Troy. He wrote of desperate poverty, of blighted love, of shipwreck and rescue, of the years he spent mastering languages (he claimed to be able to learn a new language in a fortnight, and to have learned English by learning *Ivanhoe* and *The Vicar of Wakefield* by heart) to prepare himself to learn Greek, read Homer, and find Troy.

But however he did it, he did it: he was poor, he did become rich, married a lovely Greek woman, and finally headed for Asia Minor.

Local legend in northwest Turkey associated two sites with Troy. Schliemann picked the one that he felt more closely resembled Homer's description, and began to dig huge trenches into the hill in 1870, even before his licence to dig came through.

Immediately he hit the tops of massive stone walls, and announced he had found the very walls which had kept out the Greeks for ten years.

This dusty hill is the shining city of Troy, pock-marked and pitted by a century of excavation. It was Schliemann's tragedy that he believed Homer's Troy must lie at the deepest level. He dug straight past the city he craved, and threw aside as rubbish the priceless evidence from the time of his heroes.

The blind poet Homer was writing in the eighth century B.C., about events claimed for the thirteenth century B.C. Schliemann was convinced that Priam's palace was at one of the earliest levels. He dug on furiously, forced, he wrote, "to demolish many interesting ruins in the upper strata." Every generation of archaeologists since has winced. A hillside of archaeological remains was carted away, unexamined, as rubbish.

After two years the workmen uncovered what Schliemann announced was Priam's palace. In fact he had reached a date of about 2200 to 2500 B.C., 1,000 years too early for Priam, and earlier than anyone at that date had believed the Aegean had a city civilization.

In May 1873 he saw the glint of gold in the rubble, and called an unscheduled meal break in order to get all the workmen off the site. It must have been the longest meal break in archaeological history.

"In order to secure the treasure from my workmen and save it for archaeology" he began to cut wonderful gold objects out of the foundations with a large knife, from under a wall threatening to collapse on him.

"My dear wife stood at my side ready to pack the things I cut out in her shawl and to carry them away," he wrote, in his most vivid and almost certainly untruthful images. He cut, she swaddled the jewelry, the goblets, the wonderful diadem, until he had cut 9,000 objects out of the mud. He claimed that they

"My large collection of Trojan antiquities have a value which cannot be calculated, but they shall never be sold. If I do not present them in my lifetime they shall at all events pass in virtue of my last will to the Museum of the Nation I love and esteem most."

After an unhappy first marriage, Schliemann virtually drew up a shopping list for his second: she had to be Greek, interested in classical Greek culture, and, if possible, beautiful. Sophia proved a sound choice and a devoted companion for life. This image of her, shimmering in gold which he believed once gleamed on the brow of Helen of Troy, made an indelible impression on the Victorian imagination.

had been packed into a wooden chest, locked with a copper key, and buried in the foundations of the city wall as the besiegers broke through the gate and the towers of Troy burned.

It couldn't have happened like that, but there was an excellent reason for the secrecy. His permit said that half of any valuables would be given to the Turkish state, and Schliemann was determined to keep the hoard intact.

Schliemann's tragedy was that if relics of Priam and his heroes existed, they were in one of the levels he discarded. Wilhelm Dorpfeld, originally hired by Schliemann to sort out the muddle, identified nine successive Troys—

there are now believed to have been sixteen— and labeled Troy VI, which had evidence of destruction by fire, as Homer's.

In 1996 one of archaeology's great riddles was resolved: what happened to the gold? Schliemann, quite illegally, but vindicated by his own blazing self confidence, smuggled the gold out of Turkey, intending to put it on display in Greece.

Instead he changed his mind again and sent it to Berlin, leaving it "to the German people to be held in perpetuity and preserved undivided." It disappeared during World War II. The bleakest suggestion was the most plausible, that the goblets, earrings, wine flasks and bowls, bracelets, and brooches had been stolen and melted down, worth no more than their weight in gold.

In 1996 the answer emerged, in a glittering exhibition at the Pushkin State Museum of Fine Arts: the Trojan Gold, Helen's Gold, Schliemann's Gold had been kept in Moscow secretly and under heavy guard, ever since July 9, 1945. Germany wants it back, and so does Turkey.

When Schliemann found this golden mask, he sent the message round the world: "I have gazed upon the face of Agamemnon." He was wrong.

# MYCENAE

The Troy that Heinrich Schliemann found was 1,500 years too old. He found his gold, but it wasn't the gold of Helen. He had dug past the Homeric Troy he was looking for, and destroyed irreplaceable evidence for generations of later archaeologists.

When Schliemann tired of Troy he followed Homer further, and went looking for its besiegers at Golden Mycenae, the first civilization of mainland Greece.

Mycenae, near Argos and the Aegean Sea, was only one of five fortified Late Bronze Age citadels of the Argive plain, which began to rise in importance and dominate—and frequently raid—their neighbors from about 1500 B.C. However, Homer said that Mycenae was the capital, and that Agamemnon, its king, led the Greeks in the expedition against Troy.

It was the only Mycenaean site Schliemann was interested in.

This was not a Troy, a forgotten dusty hill. Parts of the massive stone walls, "Cyclopean" because they were said to have been built by the giant Cyclops, the sanctuary, and the gates of Mycenae could be seen, and had been sketched by antiquaries for centuries. Hundreds of Mycenaean rock-cut tombs had been discovered in the surrounding hills.

Their art, heavily influenced by the Minoans whom they conquered, but with scenes of bloodshed and battle replacing the Minoan sunlight and flowers, was well known. Thousands of their undeciphered clay tablets had been found.

In 1876 Schliemann was not looking for any of that; he was looking for the literal truth of his revered Homer's poetry. Again Schliemann found what he was looking for. He had a more recent eyewitness than Homer this time, the historian and traveler Pausanius, who said in the second century A.D. that Agamemnon and his companions were buried inside the fortifications, so that's where Schliemann started.

He found exactly what he had expected to find: deep shaft-cut tombs, so important that the line of the walls had been rebuilt to encompass them; and, deep below, magnificent burials.

There were golden cups and bowls, a beautiful inlaid dagger with a lion hunt, crowns, and jewels—and thin-hammered gold death masks, laid over the skulls.

Again Schliemann's blazing certainty ruled: "I have gazed upon the face of Agamemnon," he announced to the world, after he found a body with the mask of a grave, bearded elderly man. And again, unfortunately, he was wrong —it may have been a royal mask, but as proved by later dating techniques, it was at least 300 years too old.

As with Troy, Schliemann's conviction has proved more persuasive than mere scientific fact. Work continues at the site, and many important discoveries have been made, including the deciphering of the script, Linear B, which proved that Mycenaean is an ancient form of Greek and the Mycenaeans, therefore, are the ancestors of the modern Greeks. That would have pleased Schliemann.

But the king still has no name that archaeologists can stand by, so his gold mask is still displayed with Schliemann's original label: the Mask of Agamemnon.

The walls of Mycenae, with their distinctive huge blocks of stone, and the splendid lion gate, were known to travelers for centuries before Schliemann began excavating there in 1876.

**ARTHUR EVANS**
Arthur Evans (1851–1941)
was knighted for his services to
archaeology, for discovering
the Minoans, the earliest Greek
civilization. The bookish,
short-sighted son of a wealthy
industrialist who was also a
scholar and collector, Evans
worked as a journalist before
returning to his studies and
becoming keeper of Oxford's
Ashmolean Museum at the
age of 33. It was Heinrich
Schliemann who showed him
the strange seals from Crete, and
Evans who succeeded in buying
the patch of land in which
Schliemann was interested. He
started digging in 1900, and
found the Palace of Knossos.

# EVANS AND KNOSSOS

If the wealthy Victorian manufacturer's son had been born with better eyesight, the history of archaeology might have been different.

Arthur Evans had extremely short sight. He spent his boyhood literally poring over books. But at a few inches' range he could see in minute detail, and what he saw was a new civilization: the Minoans, who came before the Mycenaeans, who came before the Greeks.

It was Schliemann who showed the young curator of the Ashmolean Museum, Oxford, some curious seals from the Mediterranean. Evans could see even more clearly the dolphins, fish, and carved octopuses, and he had never seen anything like them before. He bought as many as he could get hold of, and the curio dealers told him they came from Crete.

Knossos was to have been Schliemann's third great triumph. He was convinced that legend was about to lead him to concrete reality once again, that he would follow the sea passage of Theseus to the palace of King Minos and the lair of the Minotaur.

The legend led Schliemann to Crete, and to a hill which was said to be the heart of Minos' kingdom, but it was Arthur Evans who succeeded in buying the site.

Evans was a scholar, not an archaeologist, but in 1900 he hired some local workmen and started digging up Knossos. He found walls immediately, more and more of them, and not just foundations but rooms, stairs, frescoed walls, storage jars taller than a man, and finally an alabaster throne which he was convinced was the throne of King Minos, all in a complex of rooms so labyrinthine it seemed to give some credence to the Daedalus myth.

Everywhere, he found painted, carved, or cast images of bulls. When an earthquake happened, as he lay in bed in the house he built on the site, he wrote that he could hear the roaring of a great bull and feel it shaking the earth.

He dug for 30 years, published his work in four hefty volumes, was made a knight for his services to archaeology, and brought tourists and archaeologists swarming to Crete to the sites themselves.

What so struck the world about the Minoans was that they seemed so nice. Their world, of leaping dolphins, sparkling waves, and blooming meadows, seemed a sunny Mediterranean place, where the people were elegant and happy. They were the most appealing discovery since the smiling Etruscans, and like the Etruscans they seemed to like the more pleasant things in life: wine and oil, butterflies and dancing, beautiful youths and buxom matrons.

But there was no sunlight in the legend of the Minotaur, and later work on other Minoan

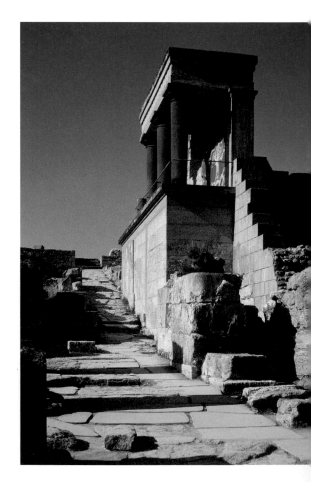

Evans answered any questions about Knossos from his own inner certainty. He had no doubts about his reconstructions on the site, although later generations of archaeologists have many doubts. The site is now the second most visited in Greece, and a conservation nightmare.

Left: Arthur Evans found ruins as soon as he stuck a spade into the ground at Knossos, and was soon faced with an appalling dilemma: structures still standing, up to four stories high, but threatening to collapse as they were uncovered. His solution was radical and contentious.

sites has darkened the picture: evidence suggesting human sacrifice and even ritual cannibalism has been found. One of the most extreme theories interpreted Knossos as a blood-soaked necropolis, a place of dark underground ritual, a palace only for death.

Evans seemed to answer every question about Knossos with an instant inner certainty. He knew how the sunny kingdom ended. He had heard the bull roaring, seen with his own eyes the oil jar toppled in the final earthquake, set ablaze by a fallen torch, which set fire to a palace and a kingdom. This is only one of many of his conclusions which have now been challenged. J. D. S. Pendlebury has pointed out that ancient earthquakes, on the whole, do not cause devastating fires; fire is a modern consequence of earthquakes ripping apart electricity and gas lines. Invasion by the Mycenaeans now seems more likely.

There were masses of inscribed clay tablets at Knossos and other Minoan sites, in two scripts labeled Linear A and Linear B, which may resolve some of the questions. In 1936 Michael Ventris, a schoolboy at Stowe, was gripped when Evans said that he was still struggling with Linear B. Ventris cracked it in 1954, as an early form of Greek, and then died tragically in a car crash in 1956. The linguists are still wrestling with the earlier Linear A

The debate on the real nature of the Minoans continues, but the greatest contro-

versy remains Evans' treatment of the site of Knossos. He was excavating the remains of a five-story building, which had been propped with timber. The timber was gone, and the palace began to collapse as he uncovered it. In order to excavate the great staircase it either had to be destroyed or propped.

There was no suitable timber available locally, and what he could get started to rot in a season, in a climate that varied from torrential rain to scorching heat. So he adopted a radical solution, reconstructing on a grand scale, using metal girders and concrete. The reconstructions of some of the most famous frescoes from fragments have been seriously challenged.

The site is now a huge tourist attraction, and a conservation nightmare. The girders and metal reinforcing rods are corroding, while the original very soft building stone continues to melt like sugar in the rain. The floors and ceilings which Evans supported are collapsing again, and frescoes are fading. Tourists, who had been allowed to walk on original pavements and room floors, have now been barred completely from many parts of the palace. The debate about whether and how to restore it is still unresolved.

It has been murmured that Knossos may eventually have to be closed entirely, which would be a financial catastrophe for Cretan tourism—the site attracts more visitors than any Greek site except the Acropolis.

# ELGIN

Opposite: When in 1800 Lord Elgin changed his mind about taking plaster casts from the Parthenon in Athens, and decided to strip the actual marbles and ship them back to London, it caused immediate controversy which has continued ever since.

Below: When the marbles arrived they astonished and disconcerted: they were not pure, chaste, and "classical" but troublingly fleshy and human.

There was nothing new about picking up wonderful things in Athens and taking them home: the Romans did it, the Byzantines did it, every traveler on the Grand Tour took home at least a coin or a little bronze or a nice marble hand as a paperweight.

It was the scale rather than the principle of Lord Elgin's shopping trip which caused the controversy.

It began in his day, with questions in the British Parliament and outraged letters to *The Times*—it didn't help Elgin's case that one of his ships sank off the Turkish coast, and he had to spend three years paying divers to recover the carvings—and has raged ever since. In politically correct circles one now speaks carefully of the Parthenon Marbles, emphatically not the Elgin Marbles. They are at the heart of a bitter international debate about who owns the past, or at least the past as it has been captured in museums and art collections.

Nobody would have paid much attention if the marbles had come from some dusty hillside in Turkey. Nobody thought it anything except a sublime feat of engineering and human sweat —and one in the eye for the French collectors—when Layard began to send the vast winged bulls and lions back from Assyria.

The Cambridge don, Edward Daniel Clarke, a minerologist, wrote with great amusement about his efforts to take the statue of a goddess, half buried in the fields and still revered as a fertility object, from Eleusis. The peasants protested: what would happen to their crops if "the old lady with the basket" were removed? Clarke simply went to Athens and bribed the Pasha with an English-made telescope. The goddess is in the Fitzwilliam Museum in Cambridge, England—history does not relate what happened to the crops.

But to take the most sublime carvings from the most prominent monument at the very heart of the city which was a symbol for art, culture, and democracy to most of the Western world, was something else, even in 1800.

Lord Elgin wasn't the first to think of removing them. When he arrived in Athens, as British Ambassador to Constantinople, the

French agent was actually negotiating for them. In 1799 the British drove Napoleon's French troops out of Egypt, and gained a stupendous war booty of archaeological treasure, including the Rosetta Stone. Incidentally they also put an end to French negotiations in Athens, and Elgin got the permit to take the real marbles instead of the plaster cast replicas he had already applied to make.

It took up to 400 men almost a year to remove the carvings, and even Elgin admitted that some were so badly damaged in the process that he was forced to leave them behind.

His motives were somewhere between pragmatic and noble. He believed, with many other connoisseurs, that the mere presence of such noble art would elevate the British, and improve their art. He also thought the British Museum might pay him a small fortune for them, which it did, eventually, a very small fortune—£35,000—which, Elgin complained, did not even cover his costs.

The marbles began arriving between 1802 and 1812. The historical artist Benjamin Haydon, who eventually went mad and committed suicide, was among the first to see them in 1808. He had expected images of chaste classical perfection. Instead he saw life, pulsing through the white marble.

"The first thing I fixed my eyes on was the wrist of a figure in one of the female groups, in which were visible, though in a feminine form, the radius and the ulna. I was astonished, for I had never seen them hinted at in any female wrist in the antique . . . when I saw in fact the most heroic style of art combined with all the essential detail of actual life, the thing was done at once and for ever."

At the time when London's British Museum acquired the Parthenon Marbles, Paris—with the "Laocoön," the "Venus de Medici," and the "Apollo Belvedere" all on display at the Galerie des Antiquites—was boasting that it had transferred Rome to Paris.

The British Museum regarded itself as having regained the artistic high ground with the Parthenon Marbles: a medal, showing the head of the Prince Regent floating in glory over the shattered pediment of the Parthenon, was designed to celebrate their acquisition, though perhaps fortunately it was never struck. They went on public display in 1816, and two years later the French sent a "scientific expedition" of 100 men to strip marble from Olympia.

All the arguments which Elgin used are still being rehearsed. The problems of decay, vandalism, and looting of monuments left in the open air is endlessly discussed at international conferences. Carvings are being replaced with replicas in parts of Athens to protect them from the scorching air pollution, and it recently emerged that the city of Rome has replaced many original statues with replicas, in public squares and gardens, for fear of theft.

103

Raphael made his frescoes of the School of Athens for the Vatican in the 16th century, taking careful note of descriptions by classical authors of Aristotle's famous academy. When the foundations of the actual school were uncovered by chance in 1997, under a modern car park and a scruffy olive grove, the layout closely resembled Raphael's imaginings.

# THE SCHOOL OF ATHENS

"Poetry is something more philosophic and of graver import than history." Aristotle.

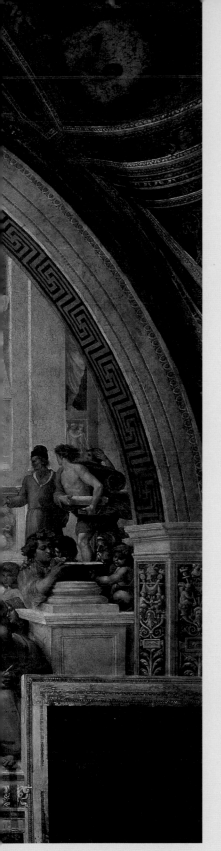

People have been digging up Athens not for centuries but for millennia—treasure-hunters, builders looking for cut stone, antiquaries, and latterly archaeologists from all over the world.

The Acropolis now rises out of a haze of traffic fumes choking a congested modern city vastly larger than the ancient Greek capital. It's hard to believe there could be anything significant left to find under the modern concrete pavements, but part of the enduring fascination of archaeology is the surprises it springs.

The tunneling machines, extending the outdated Athenian underground rail system, are regularly stopped for remarkable finds: in the 1990s these included a marble column inscribed with the names of 21 Athenians who died during the Peloponnesian War in 5 B.C., a life-size bronze head of about the same date, an 11th-century B.C. Mycenaean grave, Roman public baths of the third century A.D., Byzantine frescoed walls, and the grave of a dog complete with the nails from his vanished leather collar.

There was outraged protest when the Greek government decided to cut down a grove of olive and pine trees and build a modern art museum on one of the rare patches of open land in the city center, about one mile from the Acropolis.

As it turned out, there had been a grove on that spot for 2,400 or so years. The workers began by digging up a small car park, and almost immediately hit walls. Work stopped, and the archaeologists were called in. In January 1997 archaeologists announced what it was: Aristotle's Lyceum, the original of Raphael's School of Athens. Greek archaeologists compared it to uncovering the workshop of Leonardo da Vinci.

Aristotle was born in Macedonia, and attended Plato's academy in Athens, the original "grove of Academe." It has been suggested that he was affronted at not being appointed successor to Plato, and he is then said to have become tutor for several years to an athletic boy with military leanings, who became Alexander the Great.

Next, he returned to Athens, set up his own academy, and refined his philosophy, the influence of which was still acknowledged by both 19th- and 20th-century thinkers. It was distinguished by its common sense, and lit by Aristotle's wide range of other interests.

"Now what is characteristic of any nature is that which is best for it, and gives most joy. Such to man is the life according to reason, since it is this that makes him man."

His Lyceum lay just outside the walls—he wasn't a citizen and so couldn't buy property in the city—in 335 B.C., in a grove sacred to Apollo.

The Lyceum was marked on archaeological maps of the city, under the Botanical Gardens, but the real site was further east.

His school, where he taught history, geography, poetry, and politics as well as pure philosophy, is seen as the foundation of the modern university. It rapidly became famous in its own day, and a visit became an essential part of any cultured, educated man's visit to Athens. It was described in detail by visitors and former pupils, and as the site was cleared it was recognized from the layout of buildings in those descriptions.

The first section uncovered was the large exercise yard, where discourses continued while the pupils and teachers walked, and a pit for wrestling. Foundations of lecture halls and libraries have been discovered and more must lie under buildings still standing.

Aristotle thought on his feet. Notoriously, most of his work was in teaching notes, and never committed to books—more of his work survives in notes taken by his scholars than he set down himself. It is almost inconceivable, but some scholars still dare to hope that undiscovered Aristotelian writings may still survive somewhere in the ruins.

# DELPHI: THE END OF THE GODS

The Apollo of Delphi was the god of black jokes.
Herodotus says that Croesus, the legendary wealthy king of Lydia, feared an attack from the envious Persians. He couldn't decide whether to hold fast or launch a pre-emptive strike, so he sent emmissaries to consult the oracle at Delphi. She said that if he crossed the River Halys and attacked with vigor he would destroy a great nation. He did, in 532 B.C., and he did destroy a great nation, his own. His army was annihilated.

Between the eighth century B.C. and the second century A.D., Delphi became the most beautiful, wealthy, and cosmopolitan of Greek sites. It was terraced into the slopes of Mount Parnassus, overlooking the Gulf of Corinth, built around a cleft in the rock from which volcanic gas seeped, sending the oracle into a sacred trance in which she transmitted the words of the god Apollo. Her words were often entirely incomprehensible, and were translated into elegant verse by the temple priests.

People came from all over the Greek world, usually bringing gifts, to ask advice of the oracle, the Pythia. Where her words had a happy outcome the custom was to return and express thanks in concrete terms. On a happier occasion Croesus had given a solid silver bullock.

The site acquired magnificent temples, statues, altars, and treasure-houses, built in all the Greek orders, Doric, Ionic, and Corinthian, and in styles and materials reflecting the donors' origins. The stone includes marble from the mainland, the islands, and Africa. The main temples, of Apollo and Athena, were rebuilt many times, each time more splendidly.

One of the treasuries is said to have held the flax cables from King Xerxes' pontoon of ships across the Hellespont, his bridge for the Persians invading from Asia into Europe. On that occasion the Athenians eventually realized that when the oracle said they should depend on their wooden walls, she meant their ships, not a higher fence—they defeated the Persians in the great sea battle of Salamis, and finally crushed them at the Hellespont.

The tholos, a superbly decorated Doric round temple, of the fourth century B.C., was known to Vitruvius and inspired several Roman circular buildings, and through them was copied into Renaissance times.

There was so much superstitious weight attached to the idea of the oracle that she was formally banned, by the Emperor Theodosius, in A.D. 385. It was a symbolic gesture: she had already spoken her last.

Julian the Apostate had sent to ask if the ancient gods could prevail against Christianity. The last elderly Pythia said that Apollo's sacred olive grove had been felled: "Apollo hath no chapel, no prophesying Bay, no talking spring. The stream is dry that had so much to say."

The site was gradually forgotten. It was rediscovered by 17th-century travelers, whose drawings show a few broken carvings on a green hillside cropped by sheep.

The first major excavation was by a French team in 1892, and work has continued on the site ever since, disentangling the layers of ritual worship, from the earliest Mycenaean offerings almost 3,000 years ago. Some of the most important monuments have been reconstructed, including the only monumental Ionic column and capital found intact, given by the island of Naxos. It stood over 30 feet tall, topped by a splendidly jaunty winged sphinx, and it has allowed the proportions of similar capitals at Ephesus and other sites to be accurately calculated.

The quality of what was found makes art historians and archaeologists wonder what has been lost.

Nero is recorded removing a shipload of 900 statues to melt down for their bronze. Among the handful of survivors was the grave young "Charioteer of Delphi," found in a heap of rubble where he had been tumbled by a fourth-century earthquake. He was almost complete except for his left arm, his hair tied back with a silver inlaid ribbon, his right hand still holding the reins. He is regarded as one of

the most outstanding surviving pieces of ancient sculpture, but he cannot have been the most outstanding statue on the site—he was given to commemorate not a great battle, but the victory of a rather obscure Sicilian prince in a chariot race.

Left: The classical world found its way to this Greek hillside, to ask the advice of the famous Oracle at Delphi, and if they were wise they considered the advice she gave very carefully indeed. Those who prospered returned to share their fortune with the temple.

Above: The elderly Pythia's final task was to announce the end of that world: the last message from the old gods was that the Christian god would triumph.

# ROME

**7**

For a long time,
the study of
Roman literature,
art, and architecture
was synonymous with
scholarship itself, the
only proper concern of
an educated gentleman.
Museums scorned
their own domestic
barbaric cultures in
favor of crumbs from
the table of Rome.

Opposite: The monuments
of Imperial Rome dominated
the city long after the
empire disintegrated.

# THE SCHOLAR CUCKOLD: WILLIAM HAMILTON

**WILLIAM HAMILTON**
William Hamilton (1730–1803) was a successful diplomat, an unusually scrupulous archaeologist for his day, and an obsessive collector, who wanted to mold the taste of the world by publishing his two collections of Greek vases. He hoped to be remembered as an outstanding scholar: he is largely only remembered as the man who lost one of his treasures, Emma Hamilton, to Lord Nelson. Both were by his deathbed in 1803.

Poor Sir William Hamilton is one of the more tragic figures in Roman archaeology. He hoped to be remembered as a great classical scholar, and was remembered instead as a classical figure of fun, the ancient cuckold.

He studied classics, like all proper 18th-century gentlemen, and it gave him a near fatal collecting virus. In the Age of Enlightenment, to study classical art was not just a pleasure but a moral imperative. To own such things was to partake of divinity.

The first decree against looting Roman monuments was passed in the 11th century. In the 12th century, the Bishop of Winchester, Henry of Blois, imported a shipload of Roman sculpture to adorn his magnificent palace at Wolvesey, near Winchester Cathedral.

From Renaissance times they were beyond protecting. Architects, sculptors, painters, jewelers—and gentlemen—burrowed into Roman ruins, in search of not only treasure but inspiration as well.

For a long time archaeology was classical archaeology: anything else was vulgar grubbing in the mud. One of the great Victorian curators at the British Museum, A. W. Franks, had to fight to have prehistoric and post-Roman antiquities displayed at all. The perceived purpose of museums was to display geology, natural history, and Greek and Roman art.

The most spectacular discoveries, like Herculaneum, mined for decades as a private art vault by the King and Queen of Naples, launched international fashions in clothes and furnishings. Every court in Europe, every aristocratic household, demanded its own collection of Roman antiquities, the badge of education and taste.

Hamilton just had an acute form of the disease of his day. He collected until he was nearly bankrupt, not once but several times. Whenever he was about to reach his last penny, he sold a collection—and immediately started collecting again.

He owned fabulous things. He owned the Portland Vase, the most exquisite piece of Roman glass known, dating from the first century B.C.

He owned a collection of Greek vases which would make angels weep, and published them in sumptuous volumes with the object of improving the moral climate of the world.

What he did influence was every expensive gift shop in the world. He directly inspired a Staffordshire potter called Josiah Wedgwood to produce luxury pottery decorated with classical figures drawn directly from Hamilton's vases. It is still being manufactured, and still a bestseller.

The Wedgwood works were named Etruria, because many of the vases were mistakenly identified as Etruscan. They were indeed from Etruscan tombs, but they were there because the Etruscans were just as impressed by them, and imported them in bulk from Greece.

Hamilton collected paintings and drawings, medals and coins, sculpture and weapons. He excavated Roman and Etruscan tombs himself, and, unlike most of the gentleman antiquaries, carefully recorded, like a modern archaeologist, what he found and where.

Hamilton collected compulsively, and only sold a collection to start collecting again. He owned the most beautiful surviving piece of ancient glass, the Portland Vase. The copies made by his friend Josiah Wedgwood were themselves regarded as treasures: Charles Darwin, Wedgwood's son-in-law, sold his for enough money to build a dining room extension at his new house.

He also collected living Roman traditions, festivals, songs, and dances, which could be traced directly back to Roman times.

In 1781 he was tremendously excited when he discovered the festival of Saint Cosmo's Big Toe. This was an annual festival at the shrine in Abruzzuo of Saints Cosmo and Damian, and Hamilton was convinced it was an authentic survival of the Cult of Priapus. The saint's big toe was a euphemism for a phallus, and in the three-day festival wax phalluses were paraded through the town—along with the relics of the saint—and distributed in return for offerings. Hamilton managed to get hold of five specimens, just before the Catholic Church suppressed the festival. He sent them as a present to Sir Joseph Banks, president of the Royal Society, with a message hoping that his big toe would never fail him.

Hamilton hoped to be remembered as a great collector and scholar, but he also col-

lected Emma Hamilton—literally; she was originally the mistress of his nephew who passed her on. Emma was hugely admired for her classical profile, and her "attitudes," poses drawn from his classical works of art. She was much admired by a brilliant young English naval officer who came to visit the Ambassador to Naples. Emma had met her Lord Nelson, and Hamilton had met his Waterloo.

The British Museum held a major exhibition in 1996, to restore Sir William Hamilton's image as a great classicist and archaeologist. The aim was to put him back in the company of scholars like the German Johann Joachim Winckelmann, who published his *Letter on Herculaneum* in 1762, followed by his hugely influential *History of Ancient Art* in 1763, and in the company of other molders of fashionable taste, such as the architects and furniture-designers, James and Robert Adam. Instead, all the reviewers wrote about Emma.

# PETRA: ONE IMMORTAL LINE OF POETRY

"Match me a marvel save in Eastern clime, a rose-red city half as old as time." Dean Burgon, Petra.

Petra is an astonishing place, but it has undoubtedly become one of the most famous archaeological sites in the world because of one line of poetry, by an otherwise forgotten Victorian poet.

Dean John William Burgon won the Newdigate Prize for his poem in 1845—the shining line was cribbed from a poem by an even more obscure friend. At the time he had never visited Petra and he was most disappointed when he did: it wasn't rosy at all, he wrote crossly to his sister.

It was a far more romantic figure who had walked down the Siq, the helf-mile long cleft through a mountain narrowing to an arm's stretch, 40 years earlier. Johann Ludwig Burckhardt, a Swiss scholar and explorer, had traveled through the Ottoman empire in sweeping Arab robes as Sheikh Ibrahim. It was no mere fancy dress: a few years earlier another disguised traveler trying to reach Petra had been unmasked and murdered.

The desert Arabs had never forgotten the city in the rock, and still camped out in the tombs; but in the West, after the Crusaders brushed by in the 12th century, it had become a legendary place.

Burckhardt had found the city lying where an earthquake had tumbled it, but the fantastic tombs and monuments carved into the living rock endured.

Such rock monuments are not unusual, but the combination of the Nabateans' magpie architecture, borrowing from every culture they crossed, and the strawberry ice-cream stripes of the rift of Nubian sandstone they carved, made Petra unique. It was not to all tastes: Henry Layard, discoverer of Nineveh, came in 1840 and groaned: "debased, of a bad period, and corrupt in style."

Burckhardt's journals, published after his early death of dysentery, became world best-sellers and inspired generations of explorers.

The secrets of the mysterious Nabateans, who rose in a few centuries from desert Nomads to build a capital envied by Rome to eventually become a Roman province, are still being unraveled. Geography gave them several vital ingredients for prosperity: water, a defensible site, and a location on an East-West trade crossroads. Gold, silk, jade, amber, and spices flowed past.

The Nabateans seem to have operated their city somewhere between pirate fortress, customs post, and freeway gas station. The rock monuments still cause visitors to stop in their tracks in atonishment, and that was undoubtedly part of their purpose.

With the Middle East peace process, Petra is coming under unprecedented tourist pressure, ringed by increasingly luxurious hotels. The tourists are only interested in the monuments, such as the Treasury, a fantastic stage set 130 feet high, pitted with bullet holes from Arab rifles trying to smash the urn to set a pharaoh's hidden treasure cascading down.

While money pours into tourist facilities, the archaeologists who have been working on the site throughout the century are frequently short of funds, poring through the rubbish dumps, layers of foundations, and pot shards.

Earthquake and changing trade routes, not war or plague, seem to have tumbled the city after a few blazing centuries during which it produced half the annual wealth of Rome.

The classical geographer-historian Strabo, who had never visited Petra, called the Nabateans a sensible people, and said they were so fond of money they imposed swingeing fines on anyone who made a business loss. This view so persuaded archaeologists that they concluded the beautiful pottery, fine as an eggshell and ringing like porcelain, must have been imported from some undiscovered source. In 1980 a bulldozer, gouging out new visitor facilities, chopped the top off a kiln like the top of a boiled egg, and there was the wonderful pottery, still waiting to be fired. Archaeologists, not for the first time, were forced to reassess the Nabateans.

Opposite: The view of the facade of the Treasury is one of the most famous in the world. It is astonishing that any of the delicate carving survives, given that local Bedouin believed the solid stone carved urn held a great treasure of gold, which might pour down if a lucky bullet hit the right spot.

Below: The Nabateans worshipped a god who both lived in the rock and was the rock. They cut their temples and tombs out of the living rock, and these have endured. Their houses, built on the valley floor, were tumbled by an earthquake.

# THE PAINTED PEACE: THE HAPPY ETRUSCANS

D.H. Lawrence loved them: "Whoever it is that has departed, they have left a pleasant feeling behind them, warm to the heart and kindly to the bowels."

The Etruscans are like neighbors who suddenly vanish: such a friendly couple, such a nice house, and yet the baffled people next-door suddenly realize how little they knew about them.

George Dennis, British Consul to Rome in 1848, loved the dead Etruscans far more than the living or dead Romans: "The Romans,

those stern soldiers, owe everything they have of humanity and art to the Etruscans."

The Etruscans were out there, just beside the autostrada and weekend villas in the hills around Rome. From the evidence they left behind they seem so attractive. With their love of the good things in life, their smiling monuments, their companionable married couples laid together in death, almost chattily, it is not surprising that they attract such passionate and unscrupulous admirers.

The Etruscans lived in houses of clay and wood, but laid their dead in stone mansions, so that is where people have looked for them.

There is one Italian who claims to know more about the Etruscans than any historian or archaeologist: he is Luigi Perticarari, a grave-robber, who published an autobiography in the 1980s with an unequivocal title, *I Segreti di un Tombarolo*. The secrets of a tomb-robber cover a career as a specialist looter of Etruscan tombs. He claims to have emptied some 4,000 dating from the eighth to the third centuries B.C. He professes great interest and admiration for the Etruscan culture, as well he might, since it has provided him with a handsome living supplying private collectors and unscrupulous museums.

The smiling Etruscan couple faced death and eternity as equal partners.

His profession is ancient: smashing open Etruscan tombs was almost a spectator sport in the 19th century.

Mrs Hamilton Gray had been much impressed by an exhibition of treasures from Etruscan tombs in Pall Mall, London. So, when wintering in Rome in 1838, she drove out in a carriage to watch tombs being opened. Treasures had been found that season, gold jewelry and tripod lamps still containing perfumed resins—they lit them in a drawing room and were smoked out. At Veii, nine miles from Rome, a site just then discovered, she recorded, "the ground is let out to the different dealers and private antiquaries in Rome." It was often very exciting; some of the tomb-robbers found the perfectly preserved bodies of husband and wife, lying side by side on their stone couches, which crumbled into dust as soon as the light hit them. Often they found lovely things, like the minute golden ducklings, a cloak clasp for a princess, which is now in the Vatican Museum, Rome.

Mrs Gray came on a bad day. She grew frankly bored as the undergrowth was cleared, the rubble and earth dug away from the doorway and steps, and finally the door smashed in. And after all that she was disappointed—though not as much as the treasure-hunter—to find only rough pottery and no sarcophagus. "The tomb had evidently been rifled before," she wrote, without a hint of irony.

Carlo Lerici developed a tool in the 1950s for checking where the robbers had already struck: having located a tomb he would bore a small hole and insert a tube with a periscope head, light, and camera. He almost exceeded Perticarari's record, checking 3,600 tombs. Most were entirely empty, but he also found 20 splendid painted tombs.

More is still being discovered of the Etruscans' villages and towns, of their engineering skills with bridges, drains, culverts, and roads, things thought of as particularly Roman. At Veii where the Romans would have bridged the river, the Etruscans diverted it and built their road on the dry bed.

The Etruscans are best known, however, for their attractive tombs, built like little houses, with tile roofs with terracotta ornaments.

They did go to their graves as if they were going to bed. In the Tomb of the Stuccoes, in the Cerveteri cemetery northwest of Rome, one niche is fashioned as a couch with double pillows, and one has a pair of slippers set ready.

Late in the Etruscan period something seems to have profoundly troubled their world: sinister blue demons come for the dead, swinging hammers and snarling, and in a fourth-century B.C. banqueting scene an elderly man looks frankly terrified, as a grim female demon grips his wrist.

The tranquil sleeping figures still appear though, side by side with the terrors, sometimes in the same tombs.

In most of the painted tombs the walls are full of pleasure—wild-fowling, fishing, drinking, and music. In some tombs there are carved couches for the dead, and painted banqueting guests to keep them company. They show scenes which are most unusual in the ancient world: there are women lying on the couches, too, and they are neither servants nor courtesans, but equals.

The finest paintings were recorded in watercolor in the 19th century, which is just as well. Many have been vandalized since, or as Perticarari's memoirs prove, are still at risk from tomb-robbers like himself. Others have just been breathed on by too many living people, so the colors of the dead world are clouding and fading away.

**Most Etruscan tomb paintings show a happy world, of feasting and hunting, music and dancing. In some later tombs a shadow passes across the sun, and fearful demons are shown coming for the terrified dead.**

# ROME: THE RENAISSANCE
# TREASURE HUNTER'S LARDER

"What a city Rome would be, were it not for its ruins!"
Mortimer Wheeler.

The Roman Forum, in a typically doom-laden 18th-century etching by Piranesi, is a tract of rough countryside, with rocks, shrubs, and sheep, and the ruins of great classical buildings erupting out of it: the slender columns of the Temple of Castor and Pollux, the Arch of Titus, the great hulk of Vespasian's first-century B.C. Colosseum in the background. There is a quality of wonder and nightmare about the image, surrounded on all sides by the sprawl of the modern city.

Rome has been described as the most complex archaeological site in the world. The ancient Roman city was always a next-door neighbor of the modern Romans, and for a millennium the Pantheon and the Colosseum were among its largest buildings.

Roman leaders added new monuments— Julius Caesar rebuilt the cramped Forum and Pompey gave the first theater—and themselves turned archaeologist, to restore the ruins of the past as monuments to themselves. One of the

**Above: The great hulk of the Colosseum remained the largest building in the center of Rome for centuries after the fall of the empire.**

first civic acts of the first emperor, Caesar Augustus, was to restore the temples in the Forum. New mayors in Rome, shaky new Italian governments, still seek to establish their credentials by ambitious restoration projects.

The Forum is littered with inscriptions, ancient and modern, claiming glory. On the Temple of Saturn: "L. Munatius Plancus, consul and imperator, renewed this temple out of the spoils of war." The Altar of Volcanal: "The Emperor Augustus . . . dedicated this to Volcanus from the money which the Roman People sent to him because he was absent at the beginning of the year." On the Basilica Julia: "To the departed spirits of L. Marcius Fortunatus, banker from the Basilica Julia, who lived 40 years, 3 months, 18 days. Set up by Marcia Zoe to a husband of blessed memory, with whom she lived for 24 years."

You could scarcely stick a spade into the ground without turning up some fragment of antiquity. Raphael was inspired to redesign his Vatican frescoes after seeing the frescoed walls of Nero's palace. They were intact to a height of two stories, and uncovered while he was working on the frescoes.

Renaissance architects not only sought to reinvent Roman architecture, seeing it as a spiritual model of rational order as well as a physical guide, but they also actually incorporated stone from the surviving monuments. Much of the stone for the 15th-century Farnese Palace came from the Colosseum and the Theater of Marcellus.

Cassiano dal Pozzo, working from 1623 in the household of the great collector Cardinal Barberini, began a Paper Museum, an attempt to capture in drawings and prints images of everything worth knowing in the world. It was a time of renewed building, and Cassiano sent out teams of artists to record the extraordinary things being uncovered: many now lost: bronze statues, weapons, and tools; foundations of baths, temples, and palaces; and superb frescoes and mosaics.

Piranesi began by drawing pretty souvenir views for the Grand Tourists of the Age of Enlightenment, showing elegant gentlemen in embroidered coats sweeping a slender cane to demonstrate the glories of Trajan's Column.

But he began to hunger for more, to show the bones under the marble and crumbling brick skin. He sketched builders at work, trawled the classical texts on the buildings, and dug himself to see what was hidden.

Finally in 1756, he published his four volumes on the archaeology of Rome, *Le Antichita Romane*. This unprecedented work attempted to show the buildings as he saw them—many have disappeared or collapsed much further since—the buildings reconstructed and in plan. He shows the brick remains of Hadrian's mausoleum, crumbling and sprouting vegetation, and then uses the marks on the stone and brick to demonstrate the wedges, cramps, blocks, and tackles used to construct it. The books were a tremendous success. Catherine the Great bought a set, and the Society of Antiquaries of London elected him an honorary fellow.

The ruins of ancient Rome cast a shadow across the entire world. You'd be hard pressed to find a city—even Anchorage in Alaska hasn't escaped—anywhere in the world without a toga-furled statue, a court-house, a council chamber, a jail, or a library, inspired by the power and civic menace of the buildings Piranesi drew.

The drawings by Piranesi and later artists and architects, as well as attempts to reconstruct the monuments of Rome, have influenced municipal architects and town planners across the world to this day.

# AN EYEWITNESS TO ARCHAEOLOGY: PLINY AND POMPEII

Archaeology is full of bodies, and has inherited far more homes of the dead than of the living. One of the most moving ever found is not a human but a dog, back arched in agony, howling against the tether which prevents it from fleeing the disaster about to overcome Pompeii.

We know what it might have looked like alive. A mosaic shows just such a wiry, leggy dog, tail curled jauntily, not looking quite fierce enough for the warning *Cave Canem*.

Pliny might have known its name. The other unique aspect of Pompeii is that archaeologists, usually picking through shards of pottery and scraps of burned timber for explanations, have inherited an eyewitness account of its last days, in August A.D. 79.

In his famous letter—he apologized to his friend Tacitus for writing about something so trivial—Pliny the Younger described the moment when, after 24 hours of watching Vesuvius erupting, he and his mother decided to flee. The road was already crowded with terrified people, in darkness at noon, "not the dark of a moonless or cloudy night but as if the lamp had been put out in a closed room."

They already feared, correctly, that his uncle, Pliny the Elder, was dead. He had set off across the bay in a boat, in a mixture of intellectual curiosity and heroic determination to rescue a friend stranded in a villa on the shore.

"You could hear the shrieks of women, the wailing of infants, and the shouting of men; some were calling their parents, others their children or their wives, trying to recognize them by their voices." When light returned "we were terrified to see everything changed, buried deep in ashes like snowdrifts."

Buried in the drifts were two Roman cities, Pompeii and Herculaneum, choked along with their people, their dogs, their loaves of bread, their temples, villas, wine shops, and brothels.

For centuries plowmen had been turning up bits of mosaic, tiles, and little bronzes, in fields in the shadow of Vesuvius. The site of the port town, Herculaneum, and the first complete Roman theater, was finally identified in 1710. Pompeii was discovered in 1748. The King and Queen of Naples took a keen interest, but regarded the sites as a private antiques store, sending men tunneling down seeking treasures for their palaces.

Sir William Hamilton, antiquary and British ambassador, was horrified: "Instead of entering there and going on clearing the streets they have been dipping here and there in search of antiquities, and by that means destroyed many curious monuments and clogged up others with the rubbish."

In 1762 the German antiquary Joachim Winckelmann, "the father of classical archaeology," published his *Letter on Herculaneum*, and created a worldwide craze for the Pompeian style, in furnishing, wall colors, and even fashionable dress.

Erratic excavation continued for a century, including treasures such as the Villa of the Papyri, found with its charred library, on which the oil tycoon John Paul Getty modeled his first museum in Malibu.

In 1860 Giuseppe Fiorelli became director, set about consolidating buildings which, as Hamilton observed, were left tottering by undisciplined excavation, and roofed those where the frescoes and floors were already visibly deteriorating. He also invented the method of preserving the bodies of the citizens, the most touching aspect of the city to most visitors, by filling the cavities in the ash with plaster; experiments have recently been

Opposite: The technique for preserving the remains of the humans and animals, struck down in the streets by the disaster which overwhelmed their city, was invented over a century ago. Conservationists are still arguing about how to preserve the decaying corpse of the city itself.

Below: Many a fashionable European drawing room was repainted "Pompeian Red," as 18th-century excavators began to uncover the frescoed walls and mosaic floors of astonishingly well-preserved and colorful Roman houses.

made with transparent resins, so the bones too can be exposed to view.

Archaeologists like Roger Ling have spent decades in the 20th century on less glamorous parts of the site, showing how trade and occupancy patterns had shifted.

Archaeologists have reassesed earlier work, and suggest that far from being a typical provincial Roman town, at the time of its destruction Pompeii was literally a town living on the edge of a volcano, with many of the older families having already fled since an earlier warning eruption, and rootless adventurers suicidally moving in to snap up their property at bargain prices.

This was exactly the kind of population to support more than 30 brothels and dozens of wine shops—although another expert has re-examined the evidence for the brothels and now believes there were only a modest four. Once opulent houses had fallen into poor repair; what had been expensive property was owned by freed slaves; and one luxurious frescoed bathhouse had been reused simply as a storeroom.

Pompeii is in considerably more danger now than when discovered in 1748, and not just because Vesuvius has been grumbling again. The glamour of its violent death and the fascination of being able to walk through its disinterred streets have made it one of the most popular archaeological sites in the world.

Tourist revenue has not been equaled by spending on conservation, and in 1997 the newly appointed director of archaeology, Pietro Giovanni Guzzo, warned that the rate of decay was so dramatic that by the tercentenary of its discovery there may be nothing left. Looting is still a problem, with an estimated 600 items stolen in a decade, but the main problem is sheer pressure of visitors, neglected conservation, and some poorly executed work. Professor Guzzi calculates that it needs a U.S.$300-million rescue project, far more than the Italian government spends annually on its entire national museums and sites program.

It has even been suggested that the ultimate solution may be a replica Pompeii, with tourists banned from the actual site, as at the Lascaux caves.

# BATH: MINERVA IN A SEWER

"The people of Bath never need to light their fires except as a luxury, for the water springs up out of the earth ready boiled for use." Thomas Hardy, *Far From The Madding Crowd*.

In 1727 workers were digging a sewer in Stall Street in Bath, a small city in the west of England, built on hills around a boggy river crossing.

From the bottom of the trench a great golden head gazed back at the laborers. It was the goddess Minerva, the cult image from a long-buried temple, a spectacular witness to the luxury with which Romans stranded at the edge of their empire comforted themselves.

Their empire could be mapped in temples and baths, but a stream gushing over 265,000 gallons of hot water a day was exceptional even by Roman standards. The opulent complex was famous internationally in its day and since. The site is still the foundation of the town's fortunes, and it is still dominated by the sound of the torrent.

The earliest archaeologists were drawn to the ruins. In the eighth century they impressed a Saxon poet: "The wall enfolded within its bright bosom the whole place which contained the hot flood of the baths." For centuries scholars, such as John Leland and William Camden, recorded splendid Roman stones recycled as building blocks.

In the 18th century, as the builders of the Georgian town burrowed into the Roman foundations, spectacular finds tumbled out. The great gilt-bronze head of Minerva, described as "competent if somewhat dull" by Professor Barry Cunliffe who has himself spent half a lifetime at the bottom of Bath trenches, was not the most dramatic.

In 1790 a mass of carved stones collapsed on to a Roman sidewalk as the city built its mag-

nificent new Pump Room. Among them was an astonishing image, the most graphic demonstration of what happened when the pragmatic Romans confronted a strong established cult.

Archaeological evidence proved that, centuries before the Romans, the site had awed visitors, who left offerings. There were Stone Age arrows as well as a Roman scribe's inkpot in the spring. The 1790 image was a massive relief carved head from the temple pediment, a Gorgon—but in place of the classical female head, the fierce staring eyes of a Celtic male god whom the Romans clearly acknowledged as already in occupation.

After the decline of the Roman town, the site remained a famous, and occasionally

Above, left: The bland, imperturbable golden face of the goddess Minerva lay in the earth for 1,500 years, and now gazes down on visitors to the museum built in the ruins of the Roman temple, below the floors of the Georgian pump room.

infamous, healing bath, but the main Roman bath and spring were lost under later buildings.

A 19th-century photograph records a scene to make today's archaeologists weep: a horse struggling up a ramp out of the baths, carrying cartloads of unrecorded Roman material away as rubbish for dumping.

Bath's most scrupulous and passionate archaeologist of the 19th century had left the city by the time the most significant discovery of all was made. James Thomas Irvine came in 1864 as clerk of works for Gilbert Scott's restoration of the abbey, and spent all his free time exploring the Roman remains. Every time a spade was stuck into the ground, Irvine was there, noting every detail. He almost found the Roman spring but that honor went to the City engineer, Major Charles Davis, who found the foundations, the enclosure wall, and eventually the sheet-lead-lined Roman bath while doggedly pursuing a leak.

His excavation methods were ruthlessly practical, and provoked outrage among archaeologists. Major Davis ignored it, and carried on digging and dumping. He sold the lead to help with the costs. Much of the surviving architecture was scrapped to build the present Victorian fantasy of a Roman bath.

Archaeologists are still working through what Major Davis left, including most of the temple precinct which was only uncovered in the 1980s.

Among the the rubbish spared from Major Davis's carthorse, they found a treasure: the actual voices of the Roman citizens, transmitted across two millennia in lead curses rolled up and thrown into the spring. They turned out to be the squabbling, gossiping voices of any small town, invoking terrible curses on the heads of thieves of gloves, cloaks, and women, to name a few: "Docimedis has lost two gloves. He asks that the person who has stolen them should lose his mind and his eyes in the temple where she appoints."

Above, right: The Victorians built this fantasy of Roman life and luxury, complete with rather stumpy figures of toga-draped heroes. It doesn't look remotely like the interior of the real Roman bath, with its barrel-vaulted roof, and they destroyed a great deal of genuine Roman architecture to build it. The steaming green iron-rich water, however, is just as the Romans knew it.

S ome of the most splendid Roman sites are not in Italy but in North Africa, preserved by the relative poverty and underdevelopment of the modern countries, and the hot, dry air from the Sahara.

# LEPCIS MAGNA: THE TRIUMPH OF THE LOCAL BOY MADE GOOD

The Roman baths at Lepcis Magna, in modern Libya, with their domed and barrel-vaulted concrete roofs, at first glance look like a modern intrusion on the site. They were built in the second century A.D., and protected, along with their murals of leopard hunting, by a layer of hot, dry blown sand.

The traditional image of the empire was of legion after legion of superbly trained fighting men, marching out from Rome to conquer the known world. Archaeologists increasingly reveal what a motley coat the empire wore, with locally recruited administrators, governors, farmers, tax collectors, and soldiers.

The Roman empire at its height stretched right across the entire North-African coast, from the straits of Gibraltar to Alexandria. North Africa even supplied an emperor, Septimius Severus, who reigned from A.D. 193 to 211. He was born in Lepcis Magna, and he repaid the favor by making it one of the most splendid Roman provincial cities, and now one of the most impressively preserved.

The fertile land on the edge of the desert was vital to Rome for food supplies, including grain and olives—the oil was burned for lighting, as well as cooking. Production was clearly on an industrial scale, and the remains of several complexes of large olive-presses have been excavated. Julius Caesar punished a minor rebellion with a fine of three million Roman pounds' weight in olive oil.

The trade served the empire but also made the local landowners rich. By the time of Septimius's birth Lepcis Magna already had the largest theater in Roman Africa, given to the city by one wealthy businessman, Annobal Rufus. The market was already a century old, and had been made more dignified and impressive by adding flanking buildings and pillared porticoes to it.

Excavations further along the coast show the same pattern, of older buildings being made more splendid, and increasing use of marble in new buildings.

At Sabratha, west of Lepcis, a marble pillar records the bounty of Flavius Tullius, who "brought in an aqueduct at his own expense and also built 12 fountains and adorned them with marble veneer and statues and moreover promised and paid to the town 200,000 sesterces for the upkeep of the same aqueduct." There was a measure of enlightened self-interest about Flavius, since he almost certainly made his money growing olives, for which he would have needed an assured water supply. The plaque goes on to record that his grandson Gaius Flavis Pudens was "the first in this town to put on a most splendid spectacle of a gladiatorial show lasting five days." The grateful council voted to put up a statue to him at public expense; Gaius accepted the honor but paid for the statue himself.

When Septimius came to power Lepcis Magna was given a new marble overcoat, and broad streets and squares proliferated.

Rome kept a close eye on the colony. The remains of several large forts have been excavated, and many inscriptions record the visits of emperors: Hadrian in A.D. 128, and Septimius himself in a vast marble triumphal arch at Lambaesis, headquarters of the Third Legion.

Septimius revisited his own native city in A.D. 207, and a new forum and basilica were among the splendid public buildings erected to greet him. There was a triumphal arch, of course, with reliefs showing him sweeping into the city, driving a carriage with his two sons at his side. The marble for this definitive monument to the local boy made good came all the way from Asia Minor.

As the cities of North Africa grew in wealth, what was once built in mudbrick was replaced with stone, and what was stone was rebuilt in marble, until their opulence rivaled Rome itself.

Left: The forest of columns marks the vast extent of the theater at Lepcis Magna, the largest theater in Roman Africa, and the gift of a single wealthy businessman. The city produced an emperor, Septimius, and his return to revisit his home was the excuse for another burst of lavish public building.

There were cold feet at the furthest end of the Roman empire.

The soldiers in the garrisons strung out along the 74 miles of Hadrian's Wall were not—as used to be thought romantically—sun-tanned Roman legionaries who had marched in neat ranks all the way from southern Italy. Nevertheless, most of them were a long way from home, and they were cold.

Hadrian's Wall, begun just 70 years after the first permanent Roman invasion of Britain in A.D. 43, was the northwestern frontier of a vast empire which stretched for 1,500 miles to the Sahara desert, and all the way east into present Iraq.

on guard duty, and did not own any armor. The soldiers on Hadrian's Wall may have had quite a lot of free time, and wives and families just down the road.

Excavations have uncovered not just the milecastles (1.6 miles apart), and the pairs of turrets between them, with their living quarters, bathhouses, exercise grounds, stables, and kitchens, but the villages that inevitably sprang up around them, and the cemeteries nearby.

Another romantic myth about the Roman empire was that it ended suddenly, like the light going out, plunging Britain straight into the Dark Ages. It is clear from the wall, as from all Roman sites, that the truth was much more gradual and confused, with the wall gradually losing strategic importance in the Roman fight to keep control of Britain.

# HADRIAN'S WALL: COLD FEET ON THE BORDER OF EMPIRE

After his death in A.D. 138, the official Roman biographer of the Emperor Hadrian cited his 80-mile wall, far away in foggy Britain, as one of the great achievements of his reign.

The frontier was briefly pushed even further north, when Antoninus Pius, immediately after Hadrian's death in 138, built a turf wall 100 miles north.

The line soon fell back to Hadrian's Wall, which remains the best-known of all the frontier monuments in the empire. In all the arguments about how far and how deep Roman influence spread in their conquered territories, it is the most impressive testimony in Britain to the organization and authority of the Roman rulers and engineers. Every aspect of construction, down to the size of the blocks to be used in the turf ditch, was regulated. The public-service-minded Romans are a gift to archaeologists: since everything had to be recorded, often in duplicate, triplicate, or even quadruplicate, the chances of records surviving are quite good.

Equally romantic is the view that the Roman army was made up of finely honed fighting men, straining at the leash to march off and smite barbarians. Tacitus says that in Syria there were soldiers who had never been

The wall, marching across open countryside, could never be lost. The Venerable Bede, in his history of 731, said it was built in the third century to keep out the Picts and Scots, and that it was eight feet wide and 12 feet high —which may have been based on his own measurements of the eastern end near his monastery at Jarrow. It had to wait for the antiquary Reverend John Hodgson, in 1840, to re-establish the correct date, and attribute the entire wall to the emperor Hadrian.

The survival of so much of the wall is remarkable. It was a tempting store of ready-cut building stone for centuries, and distinctive stones have been traced in manor houses, churches, and farm buildings all along its line. It was also regulary mined by treasure- and antique-hunters, before John Clayton, an amateur archaeologist who lived for 98 years from 1790, inherited one of the best preserved forts at Chesters. He set out to study the entire length of the wall and to buy up as much of it as possible. Most of it was gradually acquired by the state in the 20th century, but miles

Despite centuries of serving as a convenient source of cut stone for houses, barns, and churches, Hadrian's Wall remains the most impressive frontier monument of the Roman Empire.

remain in private hands, although a management program was agreed in the late 1990s for its entire length.

One of the most touching aspects of the site is that the soldiers have voices. Hundreds of inscriptions on stone, from altars and memorials to graffiti have been found, but in the 1970s archaeologist Robin Birley found 1,500 letters, written in ink on wafer slivers of birch and alderwood, preserved by the chance of pockets of clay keeping them from air, at the Vindolanda site.

The soldiers included men from modern-day Hungary, Bulgaria, Germany, and France, but also many recruited locally to maintain the permanent garrisons. Many may have had wives and families in the villages which grew up around the forts. The letters include an invitation to a birthday dinner party on September 11 from the commander's wife, and a less grand but more useful letter which immortalizes the fact that the soldier's anxious family has sent him a gift of two pairs of underpants, sandals, and warm socks to keep out the chill.

This monastery in the Sinai was
founded in the age of Justinian
to shelter monks studying the
Old Testament as the literal

The yearning to find the concrete evidence of the literal truths in the Bible, including the marks of the Great Flood, the mountain where Noah's Ark came to rest, and the tumbled walls of Jericho, inspired a great deal of 19th century archaeology all over the Middle East. Even for agnostics, such archaeology had one great attraction: it was usually exceptionally well-funded.

# BIBLICAL ARCHAEOLOGY

8

# CHRISTIANITY AND THE ARCHAEOLOGY OF FAITH

I n the late 19th century a most unsuitably dressed group of field archaeologists was at work on a green hill in County Meath, Ireland.

The site was Tara, legendary home of the High Kings of Ireland. The site had as much Celtic romance as any Victorian heart could desire: carved crosses, tombs of saints, tombs of kings, fairy rowan trees, and an ancient stone which authenticated High Kings by crying out in recognition when the true claimant stood on it.

The site lies on one end of the Boyne Valley complex, which is a kind of archaeological theme park. It has hundreds of Bronze Age barrows, as well as the huge burial mound of Newgrange. There is the legendary site where Saint Patrick lit the paschal fire of Easter and overcame the forces of pagan Ireland, a superb Cistercian abbey, a Norman castle on every hilltop, and from more modern times the site of the seminal Battle of the Boyne where the forces of King William of Orange scattered the Jacobites.

The diggers were interested in none of these. They were from a secretive and well-connected society, the British Israelites: they were digging for the Ark of the Covenant. Not surprisingly they didn't find it, but they did enormous damage to the genuine monuments which to this day, archeologists are still trying to disentangle.

The search for the literal truth of the Bible, Old and New Testaments, was a driving force in 19th-century archaeology.

If the archaeologists could find Babylon and Nineveh, Nimrud and Ur, why not the wall on which the moving finger wrote terrible words in fire at Belshazzar's feast, why not the Tower of Babel, why not the Ark of the Covenant,

why not Noah's Ark? Why not the legendary Holy Grail itself?

There were considerable practical attractions in Biblical Archaeology, even for the most sceptical scholar. You might have difficulty getting funding to dig up yet another Bronze Age barrow in Wiltshire or Mississippi. Announce that you were looking for Solomon's Temple, or the birthplace of Abraham, and there was a good chance that the Palestine Exploration Fund, set up in 1865, would send you to find God and glory in the sunny warm Middle East—although you did risk, like the unfortunate Captain Charles Warren, being attacked with rocks by Muslims who obstinately believed that most of the Holy Land now belonged to Islam.

There were great disappointments, but unswerving faith usually compensated for them.

In the early 20th century a German team set out to excavate Jericho, confidently expecting to find the walls which fell down when Joshua, on the advice of the angel of the Lord, marched in silence around the walls for six days and then blew his great war trumpets.

They found the city, and the walls, and the walls were indeed cracked. They went home happy—it was decades too early for the science which would prove that they had just exploded biblical chronology. The walls dated back 10,000 years, in a world which was only supposed to have been created 6,004 years ago.

The American archaeologist W. F. Albright (1891–1971), son of a Wesleyan missionary in Chile, is credited with giving a scientific

Opposite: This beautiful Nuremberg Bible shows the sort of craftsmen the artist was familiar with, fashioning a splendid Ark for the Covenant. In the 19th century there were many groups of believers who turned to archaeology, believing they would find the Ark of the Covenant if only they looked hard enough in some very unlikely places.

respectability to Biblical Archaeology, looking not for literal truth but for illumination of the text. As director of the American School of Oriental Research, he spent decades on sites across Palestine and the Middle East. He lived to see and write of the find which the 19th-century Bible students must have dreamed of: the Dead Sea Scrolls, biblical texts 1,000 years older than any existing Hebrew copy.

The fundamentalists flourish side by side with the scientists. They also took great heart from the Dead Sea Scrolls. If they had survived, why not the Ark, why not the Holy Grail? The search for the Grail still generates shelves of new books every year, and in the late 1990s at least two major expeditions to find the Ark were being planned—and even one to find Atlantis.

# THE WALLS FALL DOWN: JERICHO

Above: Jean Fouquet, in this 15th-century French manuscript, painted Jericho as a comfortable French medieval town, besieged by Joshua and his trumpet blowers, all in their Sunday best. The real Jericho astonished everyone when it was revealed just how very old it really was.

The walls didn't fall down —the theory did. A German group in the early 20th century, driven as so much 19th-century archaeology had been by a belief in the literal truth of the Bible, set out for the Jordan Valley to dig up Jericho. They were looking for the walls which fell down when Joshua blew his horn. Instead they found a city the dates of which exploded the traditional chronology of the Bible. Man had been living behind the shelter of the walls of Jericho for thousands of years before biblical scholars had declared that God made the world.

The desert north of the Dead Sea is not the golden sand-dune desert of Hollywood. It looks more like an abandoned building site, a desolation of rubble and grit.

Water is still behind some of the most bitter disputes in the Middle East, and water defines its archaeology.

Man had to keep moving unless the soil was fertile enough to support crops which could feed him and his animals through the cycle of a year. The key to fertility was water, and at Jericho it poured out of the earth. Archaeologists saw in the earliest foundations of Jericho by the spring, one of the first sites where nomads finally stopped moving and settled down to become farmers.

From the air the *tell*, the great mound which marks the site of ancient Jericho, looks like the surface of the moon, after 150 years of archaeologists burrowing into it.

Kathleen Kenyon, of the British School of Archaeology, who dug there for most of the 1950s, pushed back the date when the nomads first settled there to 9000 B.C.

By 6000 B.C. farmers were herding flocks and cultivating and storing barley, and there may have been as many as 3,000 people living in Jericho.

Jericho did indeed have walls, however. As the oasis grew into a village and the village into a town, stone walls rose and rose, made more massive by an exterior ditch, surviving in places to a height of 23 feet, with an 11-foot tower, reached by a staircase securely inside the walls, overlooking all.

The P.P.N.A. people—Pre Pottery Neolithic phase A, named because they used vessels made of stone, not pottery—lived in small round mudbrick houses, often built and rebuilt on the same site.

Their huge walls argue a highly organized society, and also one that feared somebody else would come after their water. Some archaeologists have interpreted them as defense for the town from flood and erosion, not invasion.

In any case, the evidence seems to point to a city repeatedly abandoned and resettled, possibly due to earthquake or climate change, rather than violent invasion.

The second settlement, centuries later, seems to have been of a closely related people, still using stone vessels, and living in rectangular huts: they left very striking evidence of their interiors, in the clear marks of braided circular rush mats impressed firmly into the baked clay floors.

Their stone implements include some made of obsidian, from distant Turkey: surplus food supplies are their most plausible merchandise.

They also left some of the most startling evidence of ancestor worship, in a collection of decorated human skulls. The earliest burials were deep under the floors of the houses, but Kenyon was astonished to find a cache of skulls, carefully stored in a niche dug out of a wall. These skulls had been removed from the bodies, given shells for eyes, covered in plaster, and molded and painted to resemble living flesh. They are still disquieting objects, even gazing out of a museum display case.

Jericho did indeed have walls, level upon level of them, the earliest proving organized communal activity millennia earlier than expected.

# THE QUEEN OF SHEBA AND GREAT ZIMBABWE

Great Zimbabwe, unique among archaeological sites, gave its name to its country, when Rhodesia became Zimbabwe. It is a site where legend and unpleasant myth have stubbornly outlived scientific evidence.

In 1871 Karl Mauch knew exactly what he had found: there was a timber doorpost to prove it. It was, he decided, cedar—he deduced this, touchingly, by comparing it with the smell and color when burned of the cedarwood pencil in his pocket. It could therefore only be a cedar of Lebanon. Solomon's palace used cedars of Lebanon, and the Queen of Sheba had visited Solomon, and this, this baffling collection of massive walls and towers stitched into huge rocks, this was the remains of Sheba's palace, built in admiration of what she'd seen at Solomon's place. It was the glittering biblical city of Ophir.

Karl Mauch is one of the most heart-breaking figures of 19th-century archaeology. Many of the swashbuckling adventurer-explorers had useful personal fortunes from trade, like Schliemann, or inheritance, such as Evans. Mauch, a geologist and a German carpenter's son, had his own broad shoulders, his passion, and his rather patchy reading.

He had to work his passage to go exploring, and since the ship took him to Africa, he set off to explore the African interior. Eventually he heard of some promising ruins, near enough for him to walk carrying all his baggage. He found huge walls and massive towers, fitted together without mortar out of millions of pieces of granite, threaded in among the rocky outcrops rising from the plain where the Shona people lived.

He sent a letter back to Europe announcing he had found Ophir, although even the dauntless Mauch must have been slightly disappointed that there were no diamonds, no peacocks, and no elephants, only the towering stone walls.

It would be nice to report that he came back to Europe to find himself famous and courted. In fact he came back to find himself as poor and as sneered at as ever, and he died by falling out of a window in a cement-works.

The site he found sparked a particularly unpleasant debate where the paths of archaeology, anthropology, and racism crossed, which lasted a century.

Archaeology has been bedeviled by the conviction that anything out of the ordinary must have been built by people from somewhere else. From Stonehenge to the burial mounds of the North American Plains Indians, the scholarly community has had the greatest difficulty in believing that anything splendid could have been built by the primitive ancestors of the farmers and hunters. In Europe, and sometimes even in the New World, the Romans, Greeks, or Phoenicians tended to be given the credit for building anything bigger than a cowshed.

At Great Zimbabwe this slowness in perception acquired the unpleasant extra

Left: The curved walls and elegant conical towers of Great Zimbabwe were thought too beautiful and sophisticated to be of native construction.

**KARL MAUCH**
Karl Mauch (1837–1875), a German engineer turned explorer, never had enough money to support his dauntless courage. He walked inland carrying all his gear on his broad shoulders, until he found the puzzling ruins of Great Zimbabwe. He was convinced he had found the palace of the Queen of Sheba. He died without the public recognition he craved, but at least he died without discovering how mistaken he was.

dimension of refusal to accept that the native black Africans could have built anything as elegant as any medieval building of their supposed white European superiors.

The splendid walls and towers of Great Zimbabwe were duly credited to the pharaohs, the lost tribes of Israel, the Phoenicians, Arab traders, Romans, or Portuguese traders. When Cecil Rhodes visited the site in the 1890s, the local people were told to prepare for the visit of the Great Master to the temple which once belonged to white men.

The first excavator, J. T. Bent, initially suspected the truth, that the beautiful ruins were built by the ancestors of the local Shona, and then argued himself out of his initial good sense, concluding that they were not "in any way connected with any known African race."

The next official archaeologist, Richard Hall, apart from creating the usual devastation of discarding 13 feet of "rubbish," came to the same conclusion: Zimbabwe was built by "more civilized" northerners.

The British Association for the Advancement of Science sent an archaeologist to take a longer, cooler look; after several years Gertrude Caton-Thompson said that every scrap of evidence suggested local builders and a medieval date. That was in 1931, but it did nothing to resolve the controversy. A beautiful Rhodesian travel poster of 1938 shows a black African slave kneeling among the ruins, offering a huge nugget of gold to the ghostly white figure of the Queen of Sheba. As late as the 1970s some authors were still insisting on a Phoenician origin.

It is now, at last, accepted that the ruins are the evidence for a wealthy and sophisticated culture, trading as an equal power with most of those previously credited with the buildings. It reached its height, literally in terms of the buildings, around the 13th and 14th centuries, began to decline in the 15th century, and was abandoned in the 16th century, though its influence can still be traced in local building styles. The site is a World Heritage Site, and is the most spectacular memorial to the fact that the native people of South Africa were not savages living in mud huts when the civilized Europeans arrived.

133

# JERUSALEM: ARCHAEOLOGY UNDER A SHOWER OF STONES

Jerusalem has never been a city at ease, and its troubled history, past and present, has presented peculiar problems for archaeology.

In A.D. 70, when a Roman army under Titus besieged it, the historian Josephus recorded the starvation of the population: "Gaping with hunger, like mad dogs, lawless gangs went staggering and reeling through the streets, battering upon the doors like drunkards, and so bewildered that they broke into the house two or three times an hour." He tells of a woman—like a good reporter he identifies her carefully, "Mary, daughter of Eleazar, of the village of Bethezuba, the name means House of Hyssop," who roasted and ate her own baby, and then offered the remains to the food raiders, taunting them to join her ghastly meal.

David captured and built on the city of the Jebusites, which perhaps dated back to 1800 B.C.; Solomon built his great temple and palace over that; Nehemiah rebuilt on the ruins after the Babylonian exile, over a century after the Babylonians sacked the city in 587 B.C.; and after that things become extremely complicated.

In one corner below the Temple Mound, which was excavated in 1967, the 16th-century A.D. city walls of Suleiman the Magnificent lie on a 12th-century crusader tower, which is on a sidewalk surviving from an Ommayad palace of the seventh century, built on a Byzantine sixth-century building. That in turn was built on ruins of a Roman Tenth Legion camp, which was built after the siege on ruins dating from Herod the Great's city. Added to the tumult of ancient wars is the roar of present politics, which has meant that for centuries much of the old city has been out of bounds to archaeologists.

It is not surprising that one of the earliest and most ancient structures found is a preparation for war, the stone tunnel built by Hezekiah to bring the vital water source from the spring of Gihon within the walls, before a threatened Assyrian siege in 701 B.C.

Throughout the 19th century biblical archaeologists craved, much as the Crusaders had, to get their hands on the holy sites of Jerusalem, where they expected to find the solid evidence of so much of the Old and New Testaments. Their efforts were largely confined to plots within the convents and monasteries of Christian orders.

In 1867 Lieutenant Charles Warren, of the British Royal Engineers, was funded by the Palestine Exploration Fund to dig under the city walls and Temple Mound. He came under a hail of rocks from outraged Muslims in the mosque above, and was forced to tunnel instead, sinking over 50 tunnels and shafts, in dreadful conditions. Work frequently stopped while they waited for pit props and tunnel frames to arrive from England. He had been warned to expect about 60 feet of rubbish under the modern city: it was about 130 feet and more in places, he complained, and in any breach the rubble and loose shale poured in like a flood of water, filling their tunnel to the roof. Nevertheless he was triumphant over the massive stone walls and arches they uncovered: "We now have a most complete idea of the appearance of this wall built by King David."

A century later Kathleen Kenyon was able to excavate enough of the walls to prove that

Opposite: This exquisite image of Jerusalem, from the 15th-century *French Book of Hours* of René of Anjou, demonstrates the romance which surrounded the image of the Holy City, as alluring to archaeologists as it had been to Crusaders and pilgrims.

poor Lieutenant Warren was wrong: the walls, like virtually all the most impressive visible surviving stonework, were Herod's, not David's. However, she was able to establish that the traditional sites of the Crucifixion at Golgotha, and of Christ's burial and resurrection, lay outside the city walls of his day. The sites themselves are entirely out of bounds to archaeologists, within the Byzantine Church of the Holy Sepulcher, where even the paint surface and color of the restored Great Dome took years of negotiation between the three Christian denominations which share control of the church.

In 1996 the Israeli government proposed to open one of the old archaeologist's tunnels as a tourist route. Just as they had when Lieutenant Warren started digging, the Muslim faithful were affronted, and saw it as an attempt literally to undermine their religion. Extremists from both sides rallied against the plans, and in the rioting and disorder that followed, dozens were killed.

Against the background of bitter political unrest, there are still remarkable discoveries.

The tractors clearing land to widen the road to a new Jewish settlement, on Palestinian claimed land at Har Homa, were parked each night on a patch of rough land beside the road. As clearance work began on the edge of the tractor park, the foundations of an octgonal Byzantine church were found. Well-preserved remains of a fifth-century mosaic floor were found, but in the center of the floor a limestone rock protruded oddly.

The site is just beyond a fast modern road which has been built on the same route that it has followed since biblical times: the road from Jerusalem to Bethlehem.

Israeli archaeologists, and the Greek Orthodox church which owns the site, are convinced they have found the ruins of the Church of the Kathisma, the "church of the seat," which became a major pilgrimage site as early as the third century A.D. The piece of limestone was believed to be the rock where the Virgin Mary, heavy with child, rested briefly on her journey with Joseph to Bethlehem , where she would give birth to Jesus, Christianity, and centuries of religious warfare.

# CELTIC ASCETICISM ON THE RIM OF IRELAND

On the extreme southwest coast of Ireland, on a hillside overlooking the sea, there is a small building representing an extreme of Christian architecture. The solitary ascetic Celtic strain, utterly resistant to centralized authority or regulation, was a thorn in the flesh of Rome for centuries.

The Irish saints and monks had more in common with the desert hermit Copts of Egypt and the Sinai than with most of the Christian countries in between.

The early Irish poem "The Hermitage," translated by Frank O'Connor, is attributed to the sixth-century Irish Saint Manchan, but was probably written two centuries later.

> "Grant me sweet Christ the grace to find— Son of the living God! —A small hut in a lonesome spot To make it my abode."

The little building, the shape and size of an upturned boat, has been a conundrum to archaeologists. Gallarus Oratory had traditionally been given a seventh- or eighth-century date, but its elegance, and a window now interpreted as Romanesque, have suggested to some a much later date, perhaps 12th century.

Gallarus Oratory is the only surviving perfect example of its type in Ireland, a building of the utmost simplicity and refinement. It was entirely built in dressed stone, laid without mortar, and is still watertight, though there is evidence of later rebuilding. It is related in style to one of the most beautiful and important of the many early ruined churches in the area, Kilmakedar.

Little is known of Saint Gallarus, and the building is now interpreted as an oratory chapel on a major pilgrimage route, which included, in typical Celtic style, climbing the highest nearby mountain, and visiting the shrines on the Blasket Islands, which are still, even with modern boats, storm-bound for days at a time.

The Dingle peninsula is littered with early Christian remains. Some are datable through Latin inscriptions in Ogham (a linear script for inscriptions on stone) but the buildings are often as difficult to date as Gallarus.

Dry-stone construction is a living tradition. Near the oratory there are dozens of *clochans*,

an Irish word literally meaning little stone huts, but translated as the "beehives" they exactly resemble. They may date originally to the earliest monastic foundations, but they have been continually repaired by the owners. Most have never been touched by archaeologists, beyond a recent survey of all the monuments.

Many are still in use as toolsheds or henhouses, though some owners have recently fenced them in and charge admission. One smallholding has, in one thistly field beside the farmhouse, several beehive huts, a passage grave, and a three-chamber stone house made of linked clochans, with a soutterain, an underground passage for storage or protection. The *bean-an-ti*, the lady of the house, pointed to the apparently best preserved clochan, and said cheerfully: "My husband and his people rebuilt it a bit, to use it as a dairy."

It is no coincidence that this proliferation of ancient stone building is sited as far west as you can get before falling into the Atlantic. Fasting, contemplation, and exile from both home and human company were a strong element in Celtic Christianity. The writings of the early Irish saints are full of complaints of being followed into exile by acolytes, forcing them to remove to somewhere even more remote: Scotland, Orkney, the Shetlands, the northeastern coast of England, or France.

There was a phrase for it, White Martyrdom —as opposed to the Red Martyrdom of death— which meant a sacred vow never to set eyes on your homeland again. One saint who moved to a small Scottish island discovered that on a clear day he could still see the tops of the Mountains of Mourne, and was forced to move again.

In the case of the Kerry saints, according to strong local legend and extremely unreliable later devotional texts, this compulsion drove Saint Brendan the Navigator to the logical next step. He and a crew of monks launched a sheepskin boat, within site of Gallarus Oratory, and sailed west to discover North America. Archaeologists can't find evidence for it, but author and sailor Tim Severin recreated the boat and the voyage in the 1980s, and successfully crossed the Atlantic, though he didn't follow the saint's example in saying Mass and lighting a fire on a whale's back.

Opposite: This elegant little dry stone building, mirroring the shape of the boats in the bay below it, has kept out rain and wind for 800 or 1200 years—the archaeologists are still debating its age. Dating dry-stone construction is notoriously difficult.

# COPTIC CHRISTIANS: A LIVING LINK TO ANCIENT EGYPT

T he Coptic Christians regarded themselves as a people apart, a sorely persecuted chosen people.

From the fifth century on they were split from the Roman church, after a bitter theological dispute over the nature of Christ, which helped to preserve their way of life and language. But it was precisely the fact that their language was not unique, but preserved the fossilized remains of the language of the ancient Egyptians, which was their most significant service to archaeology.

They are also one of the most mislabeled people in history, not helped by a flood of forgeries of sculptures and manuscripts which appeared in the 1960s.

There are Coptic works of art in most major museums and libraries in the world, and most are wrongly labeled. The Copts themselves are wrongly labeled: they only acquired the name from the Muslims in medieval times, meaning "Egyptian" and used to describe Egyptian Christians.

Coptic, in 19th-century museums, became an equally useful tag for anything brought back from Egypt, or thereabouts, which plainly wasn't ancient Egyptian, Roman, or Greek. The Copts only date themselves, and their Calendar of Martyrdom, from A.D. 284 and the persecution of Christians by the Emperor Diocletian.

Josephus, the Jewish historian, notes with evident surprise that "the tribe of the Christians, so called after him, has still to this day not disappeared." He was writing 60 years after the death of Christ.

One of the places where the new religion spread rapidly was Egypt, where its central message of redemption, resurrection, and immortality seemed to fill a void left by the old certainties of the Egyptian gods.

They added their own distinctively ascetic note, of solitary hermits in the desert, and hermits grouping individual cells into monasteries, a life of prayer and meditation.

Although the stylized, stocky Coptic figures, the intense gaze of the painted saints and scholars, and the brilliant colors in painting, manuscript illumination, and textiles are quite distinctive, they preserved many elements of ancient Egyptian art. The decoration on a funeral monument, showing Saint Kolluthos laying a protective hand on the shoulder of a young woman as an assurance of welcome into the Communion of Saints, is drawn directly from identical gestures found on many pharaonic monuments.

The same effect is seen in their language. It didn't look anything remotely like Egyptian hieroglyphics, but it was a descendant of ancient Egyptian, written in Greek script. It even preserved some of the spoken sounds of the language of the pharaohs.

One of the scholars who knew the ancient language, though by then Coptic survived only in written form, was Jean François Champollion. He presented his first paper on the Coptic language at the age of sixteen. It was to lead him eventually to one of the legendary triumphs of linguistics, deciphering the famous Rosetta Stone.

The Coptic traditions are still alive in religion, still followed by several million people, and in tattoos. Tattooing seems to have been a

**JEAN FRANCOIS CHAMPOLLION**

Jean François Champollion (1790–1832). The brilliant young French linguist could read Greek, Arabic and Coptic by the age of 13. He devoted 15 years to unlocking Egyptian Hieroglyphics, and published his famous "Letter to Monsieur Dacier" in 1822. The unacknowledged work of several peers helped him to the crucial realization that the symbols represented both sounds and ideas. By 1828 he was giving lecture tours of Egypt, combining showmanship and scholarship. Four years later he was dead.

This plate from a 19th-century travel book shows Saint Catherine's monastery at the foot of towering mountains. The Copts, in jealously guarding one of the most ancient Christian traditions, were also performing a great service to archaeology by preserving elements of far older cultures.

Coptic custom from very early days: close examination of Coptic painting has revealed tattoos on ancient figures of saints and hermits. The permanence of the tattoo was, and is, seen as a living reminder of the faith.

The traditional tool was a metal comb, of seven needles mounted in wood, and the pattern picked out in lamp-black. The designs go straight back to Coptic manuscript illumination and textiles: the Resurrection and angels, mermaids and splendid saints on horseback—who may be distant descendants of pagan horse gods from northern Europe, brought into Egypt by Roman soldiers recruited along the Danube, another pagan relic fossilized in one of the oldest Christian traditions.

139

# THE ARK: THE SEARCH CONTINUES

Karl Mauch would have approved of Jack Grimm. Mauch, who died in 1875, had found Great Zimbabwe in 1871. Then, he had made the inspired and utterly mistaken leap of faith that he had found the Queen of Sheba's legendary city, Ophir, simply because he had found a wooden doorpost and decided it must be a cedar of Lebanon.

Jack Grimm, an old-fashioned adventurer and oil prospector, could have come from a Jack London novel, and actually came from Oklahoma. He died in 1998, aged seventy-five. Everywhere he went, he carried a piece of wood in his briefcase, and went to his grave convinced it was a piece of Noah's Ark, which he had personally salvaged on one of the three expeditions he had made to Mount Ararat, when he hadn't been busy hunting the Loch Ness Monster or the Abominable Snowman.

Biblical Archaeology, the search for the physical evidence of the literal truth of the Bible, began in the 19th century, and continued staunchly in the teeth of the gale of Darwinism. It continues to this day.

A remarkable and unique legal action was fought out through the Australian courts in 1997. It concerned the literal truth of the *Book of Genesis*, and was taken under consumer protection legislation.

The Old Testament is most precise about the Ark. God told Noah to build it out of gopherwood, and to make it 300 cubits long, 50 cubits wide, 30 cubits high—a Titanic of 4,000 years ago, almost 500 feet long.

Above: This detailed 16th-century tile panel demonstrates the technical problem Noah faced, as argued in court 300 years later: how, precisely, was he to fit all this teeming wildlife into his elegant little ship?

When the rain stopped the dove brought back a leaf, and the Ark came to rest on solid land: Mount Ararat, now on the border of Armenia and Iraq.

If gopherwood could survive the Great Flood, surviving a mere four millennia should be easy. Innumerable teams of believers have gone looking for it, and the conspiracy theorists say the C.I.A. found it, in a series of photographs taken from spy planes or satellites, showing a dark lump sticking out of the shoulder of the snowy mountain. Stone, say the sceptics. Yes, but the stone is petrified gopherwood, say the faithful believers.

In the 1990s Dr. Allen Roberts, an archaeological researcher and holder of doctorate in Christian Education from a Florida Bible college, was on an endless lecture tour, trying to raise money for a full excavation, not at the traditional site but at a site 13 miles from the mountain, where he was convinced the Ark lay. In his lectures he explained that petrified timber—gopherwood—rivets, and the remains of animals had been recovered.

Professor Ian Plimer, professor of geology at Sydney University, tried rational argument, which historically has never been much use against absolute faith.

He estimated that if Noah had just 24 hours to get two of every living creature on earth into the ark, he would have had to load them up at the rate of 460 creatures a second. He calculated the exact tonnage of dung, and the millions of gallons of urine Noah would have had to contend with over the 40 days and 40 nights of rain. He said that the large dark object at the site was not a petrified ship but a natural fold of rock, and that it was not 4,000 but 110 million years old.

Finally he sued, claiming that Dr. Roberts was misleading his backers and breaching the Fair Trading Act. As a former Australian Humanist of the Year, fighting Christian fundamentalism, he took his oath in court on the Bible. The judge saw it as a matter which should never have come before the courts, and found against Professor Plimer.

The arguments and the legal action seem likely to drag on for years. Meanwhile, the fundamentalists and conspiracy theorists saw the legal action as more incontrovertible evidence of the malign forces against which they have to battle, to demonstrate that some truths are self-evident.

The nightmare image by Gustav Doré, of the Ark settled on its rock high above an earth littered with the drowned corpses of the unjust, is still accepted as the literal truth by many.

In 1911, National Geographic magazine devoted
an entire issue to the discovery of Macchu
Picchu, The Lost City in the Clouds. Later more
sceptical scholarship has not effaced its glamor.

## 9

While North American archaeologists hunted for phantom Viking settlements and the mythical Mound Builders, their peers in South America found and uncovered vast monuments which had been built long ago by lost peoples, stretched out on the mountain tops or buried in the dense jungle—more, in fact, than there was time to excavate.

# THE AMERICAS

# YEARNING FOR VIKINGS: THE KENSINGTON STONE AND AMERICAN ARCHAEOLOGY

Above: The Kensington Stone was solemnly examined at the Smithsonian Institute, before being proclaimed the most important find in North American archaeology.

When the American lawyer John Lloyd Stephens, and his traveling partner the English artist Frederick Catherwood, stumbled on the magnificent Mayan ruins at Copan, they were amazed that American archaeologists had shown so little interest in them. There was an explanation: they were too busy searching for the Holy Grail.

In the United States, archaeologists wasted a lot of time in a painful state of envy: they had no Greek temples, no Roman aqueducts, no medieval cathedrals, none of the things which classical scholarship taught them constituted civilization and culture.

It was, surely, reasonable to expect that they might have some splendid Viking remains if they just kept looking: a wonderful carved feasting hall, a longship coffin for a noble prince lapped in gold. So they looked, high and low.

In 1898 they found it: the Kensington Stone, covered in runes, on some land near the village of Kensington, in Minnesota County. It was nothing if not dramatic, a cry of anguish from the survivors of a disastrous expedition: "After we came home found 10 red with blood and ded. Have 10 men by the sea to look after our ships 14 days from this island."

There were just a few worrying details. It appeared to contain a few words identical to manuscripts owned by Olof Ohman, the farmer who found it. Some of the words, such as "ded" were written in runes, but appeared to be English. The vocabulary and grammar on the stone were modern.

But it was what people desperately wanted to find, so they believed. In 1949 Dr. M. W. Stirling, of the Smithsonian Institution, called it "probably the most important archaeological object yet found in North America."

The Kensington Stone is now quite discredited, but is still the center of a memorial park, and still passionately believed in by many.

Meanwhile, in South America archaeologists had more huge monuments of ancient culture than they could cope with.

There was a pattern of things being noticed, but not investigated for centuries. A Spanish traveler in Peru saw wonderful stone ruins near

The runes were genuine, but the grammar and vocabulary were modern—and one word was in English. The Kensington Stone is a fake, but still an example of the genuine ancient Viking tradition of jokey inscriptions. The Vikings who took shelter in a tomb at Scara Brae, in the wind-battered Orkney Islands, north of Scotland, left an inscription saying they had slain a dragon.

Chavin in the early 17th century, and said they were a shrine as famous among the local people as Rome or Jerusalem. It had to wait until the 1920s, for Peruvian archaeologist Julio C. Tello to uncover the Chavin culture, a people whose artistic influence spread far beyond their Peruvian highland base.

The Incas told the Spanish there had been nothing but savages before them, but some of the Spanish travelers noticed stone monuments which were clearly not Inca. One was Tiwanaku in the Bolivian Andes, now believed to be the ceremonial capital of a lost empire which lasted from about the third to the eleventh centuries.

Work continues on the great carved columns of the Toltec; on Chan Chan in Peru, the largest mudbrick city in the world; on the Olmecs with their fierce were-jaguars and huge glaring football-shaped stone heads, dating from the twelfth to the fifth centuries B.C., half buried in swamps along the Gulf Coast.

In North America it took a long time to value what they did have. Even Thomas Jefferson, credited with the first scientific excavation of an Indian burial mound, scoffed at the idea of "Indian Monuments."

In the 1960s, the decade of student revolt and questioning conventional wisdom, a group of younger archaeologists, led by Lewis Binford, launched the "New Archaeology." This valued cultural, economic, and social history as much as monuments, and condemned traditional archaeology for seeking to demonstrate and date, rather than question and explain.

On some North American historical sites in the 1930s the anthropologists and building historians literally came to blows. Now a corporate merger, north and south, east and west, has been signed between the New and Old Archaeologies. Many of the tenets of the new, the questioning, the formulation and testing of hypotheses, the embracing of other disciplines, have become standard.

So it must have been a momentary aberation which caused one distinguished British archaeologist to snort, at the mere mention of the New Archaeology: "Hah! The Americans had to invent that because they didn't have anything to dig up of their own."

# L'ANSE AUX MEADOWS AND THE MISSING VINEYARD

**W**as Vinland, the land of vines, just another mythical blessed place, haunted by the lost souls of archaeologists? The question tormented American archaeologists for decades.

The sagas said the Vikings got to North America. They were hunted up and down the Eastern seaboard during most of the 19th century, and frequently found, through deliberate trickery or wilful self deception.

It was clear that there had been trading links between the Vikings and the Inuits, right across into the Canadian arctic: Viking carvings and metalwork turned up in Inuit sites, and in the 1940s a large Inuit boat was excavated, the gunwhale of which incorporated a chunk of a much older Viking ship.

There is less to see at L'Anse aux Meadows, at the northeast tip of Newfoundland, than at almost any other World Heritage Site. There is no longship, no banqueting hall. Instead there is a flat, bleak headland jutting into the sea,

*Some of the long, low sod huts, sheltered against the ceaseless Newfoundland wind, have been reconstructed to show the Viking's bleak toehold on the New World.*

with some green bumps in the thin soil, the marks of cooking fires cold for 1,000 years, and some reconstructed long, low houses built of turf sods.

The finds include some loom weights, a few arrowheads, lots of iron nails, masses of scrap iron. It is, nevertheless, a hugely important site, the only proof that the Vikings did, as they claimed, get to America.

The problem was the wine. The Viking sagas were quite clear about it.

Eric the Red was exiled from the Viking settlement which clung for 500 years to the inhospitable shores of Iceland, so he sailed east in 982 and found Greenland—he named it to sound warmer and more appealing and thereby attract settlers to come and keep him company. Bjarni Herjolfsson sailed from Iceland to Greenland in 986 to visit his father at that settlement, missed his turn, and found an unknown land, with green meadows and forest, further east. Eric's son, Leif Ericsson, set off to find Bjarni's land in 1001, and did. He established a small colony, traded furs and

occasional blows with the natives, the Skraelings: roughly translated, pitiful wretches. He
called it Vinland, Wineland, an even better
advertizing slogan than his father's Greenland,
because there were grapes growing there.

Even the most bitter tough-skinned grape
couldn't survive the Newfoundland climate. It
has been suggested that the word means something else, or that the Vikings really meant
blueberries—which frankly, for a people
whose sagas reveal them as intensely interested
in food and drink, seems unlikely.

In the 1950s a Norwegian traveler, Dr.
Helge Ingstad, began a systematic search for
Vinland. He read the sagas and studied old
maps, scanned the coastline from the air, and
then landed by boat at any remote fishing village which seemed hopeful. In 1960 a local
fisherman, George Decker, took him to see
some bumps and mounds he had seen on the
edge of Epaves Bay, near the village of L'Anse
aux Meadows.

His wife, the archaeologist Anne Stine
Ingstad, began digging in 1961 and at the end
of the first season found scrap iron and distinctive rivets, which could not possibly have been

made by the indigenous peoples.

A decade of work by Dr. Ingstad and the
Canadian Parks Service followed. The site was
said in the sagas to have been occupied for over
50 years. The foundations of eight buildings
were found, including living houses with sleeping platforms and hearths, stores, workshops,
and a blacksmith's with a furnace set carefully
apart from the rest of the settlement to guard
against setting fire to the other buildings.

But no wine. The sagas were passed on
orally and not written down until the 13th century, so there is always the possibility of error:
Helge Ingstad has suggested that the word
means not "wine" but "meadow." It has also
been suggested that the settlement was not a
true village, but a periodically occupied camp
where boats were repaired.

A later site director, Birgitta Wallace, has
suggested that L'Anse aux Meadows was only
the gateway to Vinland, a much larger terri-
tory, and that the grapes grew much further
south. The theory is not universally accepted,
but it does at least keep alive the Grail quest:
the hope that the site of a major settlement
may still be found.

# JEFFERSON, THE "FATHER" OF AMERICAN ARCHAEOLOGY, DIGS UP HIS OWN BACK YARD

Among the odder laurel crowns heaped on the American president, philosopher, and author Thomas Jefferson is the title "the father of American archaeology."

Years before he became president, he had become briefly disenchanted with the demands and conflicts of politics, and had retired for several years to live and work on his estate in Virginia.

He was extremely interested in scientific research of all kinds, and aware of the papers published on the infant science of archaeology, in England, Germany, and Scandinavia, where scholars as well as treasure hunters were beginning to dig into earth banks and mounds.

William Stukeley had already published his beautiful and accurate drawings of Stonehenge, and the discovery of the entrance to the huge burial mound of Newgrange had sent travelers by boat and horseback all the way to the Boyne Valley in Ireland.

In North America the hunt for the Moundbuilders had begun.

Thousands of mounds were being destroyed as settlers and farming spread west. Some contained dozens of burials, some none. Some contained pottery and weapons, obsidian arrows made of stone traded from hundreds of miles away, clay and stone effigies, cedar-wood masks with shell inlays, combs, and hair decorations worked from turtleshell, mica, copper, and silver. Some contained only disappointing bits of burned clay and bone, which were generally thrown away.

The conviction was general that the most imposing mounds, man-made hills such as Monk Mound, 100 feet high and covering 16 acres, could not have been built by the even more savage ancestors of the local Native American peoples.

Jefferson, curious about everything, had several mounds on his own lands, so in 1784 he got some workmen and carefully cut a trench across the full height of one of the largest.

He was not looking for treasure, but for sense. He was not a man for monuments, he confessed: "I think there is no remains as respectable as would be a common ditch for the draining of lands."

The principle of stratigraphy, that deeper means older and that careful study of the layers can give insight into chronology, was cautiously beginning to emerge in both geology and archaeology, even 70 years before Darwin's explosive *On the Origin of Species*.

Jefferson carefully removed the soil and recorded the what and where of everything he found. There were many burials, at different levels in the mound.

"These were lying in the utmost confusion, some vertical, some oblique, some horizontal, and directed to every point of the compass, entangled, and held together in clusters by the earth," he recorded. "So as, on the whole, to give the idea of bones emptied promiscuously from a bag or basket, and covered over with earth without any attention to their order."

The bones at the lowest level, he noted, were far worse preserved than those higher up. From this he deduced that the mound had not been built all at one time, but used and reused for successive burials of bones collected

Thomas Jefferson (1743–1826) briefly wearied of politics and retired to his extensive estate in Virginia in the 1780s. Out of curiosity he set his workmen digging a deep trench into the heart of a mound on his land, and conducted the first scientific excavation in North America. He published his conclusions, returned to politics, and became Third President of the United States. He kept the extra title of Father of American Archaeology.

together over a long period. There were the remains of up to 1,000 skeletons in his comparatively small mound, he believed.

He also, far more controversially, stated that he could find nothing to suggest that the mound was not raised by the ancestors of the present-day Native Americans living in the area: he pointed out that the mound was opposite some hills where there had once been a Native American town.

The hunt for the lost tribe of Moundbuilders continued to occupy a vast amount of time and energy in North America throughout the 19th century.

Jefferson moved on to other preoccupations, but he is still credited with the first scientific archaeological excavation in North America, and one of the earliest anywhere. If not precisely the father of American archaeology, he was certainly its benevolent godfather.

# GREAT SERPENT MOUND, A PUZZLING MONUMENT

Like the Nasca Lines, stretching for miles across the desert in Peru, Great Serpent Mound is one of those puzzling archaeological monuments which could never have been fully appreciated by the people who made it.

Above: Viewed from the air, as its builders could never have seen it, Great Serpent Mound is revealed as a vast snake, its undulations traced across the ground in tons of mounded soil.

From the air the Nasca lines form into straight tracks or drawings of monkeys or spiders, from the ground they are mere scrapes in the earth.

Great Serpent Mound, in Ohio, is a series of undulating hills at ground level. From the air it is clearly seen as a huge snake, over 1,200 feet long, 20 feet wide, and 5 feet high, with a burial mound in its mouth. These structures are notoriously hard to date, particularly when they may have a long and varied period of use,

but Great Serpent Mound is believed to date from between 500 and 100 B.C.

Such monuments tend to attract clouds of wild theories, from coded messages of apocalypse to landing strips for alien spacemen. One possible explanation is that they were indeed made to be viewed from the air, that they were laid out to please the eyes of the gods.

In North America, as with Thomas Jefferson's mounds, the 19th-century conviction was that these monuments were also built by aliens, by Vikings or even the Toltecs from Mexico, the lost people of Atlantis, or the Lost Tribe of Israel.

The alternative theory was that if the serpent, and the mounds, were native, then they must represent one great lost nation: the Moundbuilders were identified as the Adena People, of the midwest and southeastern United States.

Caleb Altwater, a postmaster, opened many mounds which have long since been flattened, near his home at Circleville, Ohio. He published a paper on them in the first edition of the journal of the American Antiquaria Society in 1820: he attributed the earliest mounds to the Moundbuilders, and believed they were Hindus, from India, passing through on their way to Mexico.

Ephraim Squire, a newspaper publisher in Ohio, opened hundreds of mounds, or recorded sites being destroyed by settlers, with a local physician, Edwin Davis, between 1845 and 1847. Their book, *Ancient Monuments of the Mississippi Valley*, was the first publication of the new Smithsonian Institution in 1848. It did give careful measurements and plans, and they did spot that the mounds were built for different purposes, but they still felt that their construction was beyond any Indian, by nature "averse to labor."

The search for the Moundbuilders ignored the fact that mounds were of many different types and served different purposes. Some were vast projects, requiring high organization of large numbers of people, such as the serpent, which it makes sense to see as a center of major religious ceremonies. Some were modest heaps of soil over single burials, perfectly within the capabilities of a surviving family group. Whereas others were huge burial mounds raised over wooden burial chambers, such as Grave Creek Mound on the Ohio river in West Virginia, which is almost 70 feet high and would have required moving thousands of tons of earth.

Some were raised by hunter-gatherers, as seasonal ritual meeting places for a scattered people. Others, of the sedentary farming Mississippian culture, are interpreted as the foundation mounds for large wooden buildings. These may have been either temples or the homes of chieftains, such as the 20 pyramidal mounds around a large plaza at Moundville in Alabama, believed to have been a fortified town with up to 1,000 people living there by around A.D. 1150.

In 1881 John Wesley Powell, who had spent much of his own youth digging into mounds, before establishing the Bureau of American Ethnology to study North American Indians, recruited Cyrus Thomas to settle the Moundbuilder question. Thomas spend years on the task. He read all the reports, and spent seven years doing fieldwork himself. Thousands of mounds later he came back with the answer, although it took decades before it was universally accepted: there were no Moundbuilders. The mounds were built for many purposes, practical and ritual, over a very long period in time, and by many different people. They were not built by aliens, but by the direct ancestors of the modern Native Americans, who in many cases were still living in their shadow.

Below: The stylized bird's claw, made out of a sliver of mica as thin as a shadow, is typical of the the elegant works of art made by the Hopewell Indians. The images of humans and animals would have been too fragile to use as jewelry or even handle, and are believed to have been made as ritual offerings.

# JAMESTOWN, THE COLONY THAT FAILED

J amestown has been considerably more successful as a visitor attraction than it was as the first permanent English settlement in America.

The Virginia colony has a precise starting date: it was born on May 14, 1607, and many of that first small group of colonists didn't make it past the first winter—the records show deaths due to "a wound given by the Savages," "the swelling," and "the bloudie fluxe." The site was good for defence but, with river on three sides and swamp on the fourth, miserable for health.

In 1610 Lord Delaware, life governor of Virginia, returned to the James River with three ships of supplies and 150 more settlers, just in time to save the survivors. Tobacco, the first cash crop, gave the settlers a precarious stability and prosperity, and the little colony had the dubious distinction of having the first black slaves in America. Delaware himself died and was buried at sea in 1618, on his way back to deal with a swelling revolt against the deputy governor he had left behind.

There were difficult relations with the Powhatan Indians from the start. They helped the settlers through the first bitter winter of 1607, but relations rapidly soured. In 1609 their leader pleaded for fairer dealings, and Captain John Smith, of Pocahontas fame, copied down his words: he warned of the settlers attempting to take by force what had been offered in friendship. "I therefore exhort you to peaceable councils; and above all, I insist that the guns and swords, the cause of all our jealousy and uneasiness, be removed and sent away."

His exhortations were useless. In the spring of 1622 the Indians attacked and killed 350 settlers. Repeated raids continued, there was a serious fire in 1676, and in 1699 the colony

was abandoned. The survivors, and the seat of government, moved to Williamsburg.

Jamestown had already taken in the survivors of an even less fortunate settlement, Martin's Hundred, which was further down the James River toward Chesapeake Bay. Only a handful of settlers remained when it too was attacked in the spring of 1622, and razed to the ground. Martin's Hundred appears on the earliest maps of Virginia, but it was never settled again.

The archaeologist Ivor Noel Hume resurrected it from scraps of rubbish and the shadows of timber in the soil, over five seasons from 1976.

He had originally been asked by Colonial Williamsburg to identify a spot of no historical interest whatsover, in the grounds of Carter's Grove, an 18th-century mansion, so that they could build a temporary exhibition for the 1976 Bicentennial.

His work proved how much it is possible to

The Jamestown settlers' timber, mud, and thatch houses have been reconstructed, where nothing remains of the originals except the shadows in the soil of long since rotted timbers.

This sentimental 19th-century print shows John Smith leading a group of extraordinarily well-dressed settlers in giving thanks for their safe arrival on a very foreign shore. The contemporary records show that the little colony was in serious trouble from the start.

recover from a site which has disappeared apparently without trace. There were cooking-pots and broken skillets, a bill hook and two crushed helmets, and luxury items like fragments of Delft tiles. And there were bodies, dozens of them, some in a proper cemetery, some evidently buried in haste under attack, and one, nicknamed "Granny," in a rubbish heap where she had apparently crawled, injured, to die.

At Jamestown, 40 years earlier, the excavators had tried and failed to find the distinctive triangular palisade described in contemporary accounts. As Noel Hume remarked, the techniques which worked perfectly well for stone or brick foundations at Williamsburg were useless where the diggers were looking for nothing more substantial than dark stains in the soil,

left by long-rotted fence posts. Techniques had improved, and at Martin's Hundred Noel Hume was able to recover the lines of huts, outbuildings, and fences. On one hut site he found evidence of an underground structure, baffling until he found contemporary documentary evidence revealing that the poorest settlers built underground shelters with the roof resting directly on the soil.

In one hut, where he also found a cannon ball, Noel Hume found a scrap of gold, a tiny piece of gold wire thread, and through it identified the owner of the house and the most important person in the colony. A 1621 law restricted gold-laced clothing to "council and heads of hundreds" and a census of 1625 identified the administrator of Martin's Hundred, William Harwood, as the only man in the settlement who owned a cannon. Cannon ball and gold thread: Harwood must therefore have been the owner.

Jamestown itself was excavated by the Virginia Archaeology Service in the 1930s and 1950s, which uncovered traces of the quays, houses, fields, traces of the fire—which broke out not in a timber hut but in one of the few brick buildings.

Beside the archaeological site there is now a flourishing re-creation of the colony, including full-size replicas on the river of the settlers' ships, *Susan Constant*, *Godspeed*, and *Discovery*, and of the Powhatan Indian village.

On the banks of the James river, rubbish dumps, scorch marks, and the faint shadows in the soil of rotted timbers helped archaeologists recover the short, unhappy history of the earliest English settlements in Virginia.

# MESA VERDE, THE CATTLE RANCHER'S TREASURY

It wouldn't be fair to dismiss Richard Wetherill out of hand as a treasure-hunter: he did contact the Smithsonian Institution and Harvard University's Peabody Museum. They don't seem to have taken the request for scientific advice and help from a Colorado ranger entirely seriously.

Above: When a cattle rancher found a lost city of houses clinging like swallows' nests to the walls of a canyon, none of the great national museums took his reports seriously. Archaeologists only woke up to the importance of his discovery when the cattle rancher was found shipping out artifacts by the wagon load.

But in 1888 Wetherill had indeed found a deserted city, 600 years old, built into a canyon wall, with room upon room of pots, implements, arrows, and turquoise jewelry. He had even found the mummies of some of the inhabitants, and he gave them a name, from the Navajo for ancient people: the Anansazi.

Neither of the great museums offered any help, though he was eventually to sell Indian artifacts to American museums by the freight-train load.

Wetherill and his family continued to clear and sell the contents of room after room of the Mesa Verde and Chaco Canyon cities, until the authorities finally realized the scale of what he

had found and then banned him from any further efforts.

The first outsiders to take note of the buildings, like honeycombs on the floor and walls of Chaco Canyon, New Mexico, were two artists and a map maker. They were traveling with a U.S. Army division which was tracking down hostile Navajo in 1849. The Kern brothers and Lieutenant James Hervey Simpson were far more interested in the extraordinary complexes of stone and adobe building. When their journals were published they attracted a steady trickle of the curious, including the photographer William Henry Jackson, whose images of buildings clinging to the wall of an 800-foot cliff, in 1876, spread the word even further.

Over the 20th century, thousands of settlement sites were identified, over 25,000 square miles, centered on Four Corners, where Utah, Arizona, New Mexico, and Colorado meet. This is the most extensive complex of archaeological remains in the United States.

Wetherill found the Mesa Verde buildings, according to legend, while tracking lost cattle in a snowstorm. He went back with his brother-in-law, wife, and employees, and when they raised $3,000 dollars from the first sale of their finds he realized they'd stumbled on a far more profitable occupation than ranching.

He made a handsome living out of treasure-hunting, but he was also extremely impressed by the culture that he had stumbled upon. The earliest settlers wove baskets, and lived in underground houses.

In 1895 Wetherill turned his attention to the Chaco Canyon. Here the culture had advanced to making pottery, with distinctive and elegant black-and-white geometric decoration, and living in pueblos of hundreds of square single rooms. These were grouped around circular semi-underground buildings, which resembled their earlier homes but were now used for religious rituals. In one of the largest pueblos, Pueblo Bonito, he found rooms and burial pits heaped with goods, including hoards of thousands of turquoise beads, which archaeologists believe were traded as far away as the Pacific.

Populations of up to 5,000 had been estimated for the largest pueblos. The settlers grew many crops, and saved every drop of rain that fell, but archaeologists have since questioned whether the sites could ever have supported such large permanent populations, and suggested they may have been gathering places for ritual ceremonies.

It was clearly a hard life, lived on the edge of subsistence: among the Mesa Verde mummies, traces of osteoarthritis were found in every single adult over thirty-five.

The Anansazi settlements have a further archaeological significance: they helped to establish the science of dendrochronology, dating by counting tree rings.

Stone and adobe buildings are notoriously difficult to date, but the builders had also used whole pine trunks, an estimated 250,000 trees in the Chaco Canyon settlements, brought from up to 40 miles away.

The theory of dating by counting the rings which trees add every year, and whose size is determined by climate, was devised by an Arizona astronomer, Andrew E. Douglas. The extremely dry desert air not only preserved basket work, textiles, and human flesh, it also preserved the trees perfectly, so that he was eventually able to work out a chronology covering some 2,000 years.

The system provided accurate dates for the buildings, and enabled a sequence to be established, from the first basket-weavers around the year A.D. 200, through the introduction of pottery around 600. It also suggested that prolonged drought—made worse because they had probably felled every tree in the region—may have led to all the pueblos being abandoned by the year 1300.

Chaco Canyon is now a National Monument, and dendrochronology a standard scientific tool.

The earliest houses were sheltered in pits. In later settlements the underground rooms, accessed by ladders, evolved into ritual centers.

# THE BLOODY BALL GAME: THE MAYANS AT COPAN

I f the Mayans were right, the Millenarianism of the end of the 20th century, the rise of anxiety, superstition, alternative religions, and survivalist cults, was entirely justified, but just a little premature.

The end of the world really is nigh, according to their calendar, one of the most sophisticated of the ancient world.

They had interlocking long and short calendars, on which the long lives of gods and kings and the short essential lives of farmers and seasons can be tracked, and they give dates with great precision. The world will end, their calendar predicts, in A.D. 2012.

The earliest true Mayan settlement discovered by archaeologists so far is at Cuello, in modern Belize. It dates from about 1200 B.C., but lineage and ancient pedigree were very important to the Mayans, so they demonstrated that their world had started far earlier. Their clock starts on a specific date: August 12, 3114 B.C. The end is equally precisely stated: the world finishes in A.D. 2012.

Archaeologists took a surprisingly long time to become interested in the Mayan empire, whose gods prized astronomy, mathematics, and fountains of human blood.

Major discoveries are still being made, including cave paintings, and undisturbed royal tombs in what had been believed to be solid stone pyramids. The seventh-century tomb of Pacal the Great was found in 1952 at Palenque, in Mexico, with a magnificent carved slab over the coffin. Tombs were found at Copan by American and Honduran archae-

ologists in 1989 and 1992, with jade objects including masks, ritual knives, and containers.

The Mayans stretched across thousands of miles of Central America, from southern Mexico through Guatemala, Honduras, Belize, and El Salvador, from about 1200 B.C. to A.D. 1500, rising to greatest power and wealth from about A.D. 250–600.

It took over a century to crack the glyphs, the inscriptions covering all their sites. Russian scholars made the running in the 1950s. The answer, as with Egyptian hieroglyphics, turned out to be a mixture of pictograms and phonetic symbols, while the numbers were made up of dots and dashes.

There had been Mayan books as well, beautifully painted on cloth and wood, and kept as treasures. Spanish missionaries destroyed as many as they could get hold of but a handful was sent back to Europe as curiosities, and attracted scholars from the early 19th century.

Once the language was cracked, the Mayans proved extraordinarily helpful to archaeolo-

The earliest ball court so far discovered is pre-Mayan, over 3,500 years old. They are found at all major sites. The game, played with heavy, solid latex balls, which have also been recovered, was very important— the losers lost their lives.

Carved images of gods, priests and kings dressed as ball players are found at many sites. This player, raising his arm to the figure of a diving god, is one of hundreds from Santa Lucia Cotzumalhuapa, in modern Guatamala, whose puzzling monuments combine Mayan, Aztec and many other influences.

Cauac Sky literally left his mark on Copan: he built the most monumental inscription in South America, a stairway of 72 broad high steps, all covered in glyphs. It was tumbled by earthquake centuries ago, and archaeologists have been working for a decade to reconstruct the giant jigsaw puzzle.

The American lawyer and English artist, John Stephens and Frederick Catherwood, literally hacked their way through the jungle to Copan, now in Western Honduras and a World Heritage Site. In 1839 it was hard to see anything through the vegetation, and the wall, 100 feet high, was almost too vast to notice—a real case of not being able to see the wood for the trees. Beyond it they found the flight of broken steps, ascending a 100-foot pyramid, colossal statues of men and animals, and inscriptions everywhere.

Stephens and Catherwood traveled on, drawing and recording, and saw many other sites, all with the same inscribed stones. Stephens brilliantly concluded, at a time when the Phoenicians, Lost Tribes of Israel, or Vikings were being credited, that the stonecarvers were native, and ancestors of the Mayan Indians at that.

In the center of Copan, the ruins of which cover a river valley floor, is a huge open space, surrounded by pyramids and *stelae*, carved stone pillars up to 13 feet tall.

At one end of the central enclosure is a ball court, clearly of ritual more than recreational importance. Ball courts have been found at all major Mayan sites. Games using solid rubber balls and stone hoops were evidently played, and archaeologists have found evidence suggesting that winning was a matter of life or death, with the losing team sacrificed on the spot to the Gods.

All the city sites seem to have been gradually abandoned from the ninth century on: as usual the solution seems to be several small answers rather than one dramatic disaster. The climate may have changed slightly, as the cities grew too big to be sustained by the surrounding farmland. The Mayans themselves didn't disappear: millions of people still living in their ancient territories today claim direct descent from them.

gists. With their sophisticated calendar, they recorded not only the year but the month and the day of the week, of births, of conquests, of coronations, and major rituals.

At Copan the inscriptions record that 18 Rabbit, a descendant of a famous and powerful king, Smoke Jaguar, was toppled by Cauac Sky, ruler of a smaller neighboring state, on May 3, 739. An axe symbol suggests what happened next to 18 Rabbit.

# THE AZTECS UNDER MEXICO

In 1978 electricity workers were digging a pit for a new substation for the underground railroad, near the cathedral in the heart of one of the most crowded and polluted cities in the world, Mexico City. They uncovered a giant carved disk, the moon goddess Coyolxauhqui, remarkably well preserved after 400 years buried away from the night sky. Construction work immediately stopped as archaeologists came in to assess the find.

It has proved remarkably difficult to destroy anything completely in human history. Even where every stone has disappeared above ground, lost buildings show up in parch marks in crops, or shadows in slanting evening sun. In Mexico archaeologists realized almost immediately that they had found the Great Temple of the Aztecs' island capital, Tenochtitlan, a pagan affront to the Spanish, on top of which the Conquistadors destroyed and built their own city.

The discovery of the Great Temple didn't come as a complete surprise to Professor Matos Moctezuma and the archaeologists who had been making remarkable discoveries for over a decade, as Mexico's new subway was built.

There are now many keyholes in the traffic-choked modern city through which the Aztec ruins, only a few yards down, can be seen. The huge stone platform of the temple of Ehecatl-Quetzalcoatl has been opened to the sky again, in a sunken square beside a station.

The archaeologists were not working blind: there were many records of what had existed. The Spanish had no regrets about slaughtering pagans, flattening magnificent temples, or melting down superb works of art for their gold, but they were fascinated and repelled by the remarkable civilization they were trying to wipe out. They recorded their own observations and also many of the Aztecs' own pictogram writings and beliefs. Given the importance of agriculture, most of the Aztec gods were tied to fertility, the seasons, and climate, and an extremely complex calendar system. They also absorbed many of the beliefs, and built on the monuments, of the people they supplanted, the Toltecs, and their great god, the feathered serpent Quetzalcoatl.

Hernan Cortez took Tenochtitlan in August 1521 after a siege which lasted months. The Spanish recorded towers and temples, walls and houses, all in stone, built by a civilization with no iron, no beasts of burden, and no wheeled vehicles, rising up out of the lake: "Never was there seen, nor heard, nor even dreamt, anything like that which we then observed."

It was the last to be captured of the great native Meso-American cities, which began about 1200 B.C., their wealth based on maize grown in the rich soil of the Central Valley. Aztec accounts say that Tenochtitlan, founded in the early 14th century, grew within 200 years to 200,000 inhabitants, considerably larger than London or Rome at that date, wealthy on the tributes paid in gold, goods, or food by every other town.

Apart from tributes, the city was supported by fields on artificial strips of land in the lake, the *chinampas*, where a huge variety of fruit and vegetables were raised, and sold at a market in the city which the Spanish admitted was unrivaled by anything at home. They were also astonished by the splendor of the palace of Montezuma, its gardens, fountains, aviaries, and menageries.

As excavation proceeded at the Great Temple it became clear that the Spanish had only managed to destroy the top of six levels of a repeatedly rebuilt pyramid, with its feet in the waterlogged foundations of the city itself. The Aztecs simply built higher and more magnificently each time they renewed the temple, a rite demanded by the gods every 52 years.

It must all have dripped with human blood, for their religion demanded rivers of blood. The original carved goddess was depicted hacked to pieces by her brother, who had previously joined her and their 399 other brothers to slaughter their mother—a statue of her shows her with a garland of human heads and hands, strung like beads, around her neck.

One of the kings alone is said to have slaughtered 20,000 human victims, and among the find was a beautiful carved stone jaguar, with a hollow in its back to receive the beating hearts ripped out of living human breasts.

Finds included smaller temples and painted shrines, life-size statues, stone altars used for human sacrifice, and thousands of offerings to Huitzilopochtli, god of sun and war, and Tlaloc, god of rain and water. These were either buried or placed in stone boxes, and all carefully oriented. There were animal remains, including a jaguar skeleton with a green stone ball in its mouth, birds, turtle and crocodile remains, snake skins, and many offerings of fish and shells brought from the distant coast.

The pressure for more space, through the construction of new taller buildings, is unrelenting in Mexico City. The presumption is that more spectacular finds are likely, of the old Aztec city the Spanish could thankfully only bury, not destroy.

Opposite: The Spanish tried to destroy the great capital of the defeated Aztecs, but much of it survives just under the skin of the modern city. This carving, from the Great Temple, is a representation in stone of real skull racks, built to hold severed human heads, found at every major Aztec site.

Below: The small Aztec temple —baptized with a Christian name, Santa Cecilia Acatitlan— was a local complex north of the capital. The reconstructed pyramid gives some idea of the original appearance of the vastly larger Templo Mayor at Tenochtitlan.

# SIPAN: THE UNLOOKED
# FOR ROYAL TOMBS

In February 1987 looters at Sipan, a village on the north coast of Peru, stumbled on something which neither they nor any archaeologist knew existed: an untouched royal tomb, full of gold. Until that night the main contribution of the Moche culture to archaeology was thought to be its wonderful pottery.

The Moche flourished between the desert and the coast of Peru from the first to the eighth centuries, diverting what water there was in canals and ditches to their crops.

They left vast mudbrick pyramids and platforms, now drastically eroded, and thousands of looted graves, from which a seemingly endless stream of marvellous pots poured on to the art black market.

The Moche had no writing, but more is known about their everyday life than any other South American culture because they modeled everything: portrait heads and gods, animals, workers, and the crops they grew, the sick and maimed so vividly portrayed that modern medicine can diagnose their ills, human sacrifice, women cooking, and straining women giving birth helped by midwives.

One type had a particular black-market value: their erotic pots, showing every possible and improbable sexual position. One archaeological writer has commented, straight faced, that these must relate to some religious ritual, "given that few of the acts depicted would have resulted in impregnation."

Small amounts of gold, beautifully worked, had been found over the decades of looting. The tomb of the Lord of Sipan was something else, instantly prompting comparison with Tutankhamen.

The grave robbers battled over their loot, the police heard and local archaeologist Walter Alva—who has since found two more royal tombs—was sent in to work under round-the-clock armed guard.

The archaeologists found, as they expected, that the tomb, dating from about A.D. 300, was in chaos, nothing left in its original place by the robbers. As they worked they noticed that a large section of brick had been disturbed at some stage. They dug in and found the tomb's guard, a man whose feet had been cut off so he couldn't abandon his post. Beyond him were six coffins, five less important containing three women, two men and a dog. The uncoffined bodies of a child and two llamas were also found at the site.

Alva initially assumed that the women had been killed to accompany their lord, but later research proved they had died long before, and were largely decomposed within their shrouds when they were put into the tomb.

The sixth wooden coffin contained the Lord of Sipan, literally covered, from head to toe, in gold and turquoise.

The finest jewel was a tiny gold ear ornament, only the size of a button, its component pieces no bigger than pin-heads, as delicate as a piece of Swiss clockwork. It is of a human figure, carrying a club, and wearing a gold-and-turquoise headdress, collar, jewelry, and carrying a war club, like its owner—except where the Lord is wearing a necklace of large gold peanuts, the little figure is wearing one of microscopic owl heads.

Another tiny gold piece shows a spider with a human head on its back, crouched on its web; it is made of seven different pieces, with three gold beads loose inside the base to rattle with every movement.

Not everything that glittered was gold: the Moche had mastered gold-plating copper, with a layer of gold so thin that it doesn't show in cross-section under a microscope, so that it still appears to be solid gold.

After several years of experiment, with the benefit of modern laboratories, scientists managed to duplicate the results using only materials available in ancient Peru. The Moche seem to have invented a system of electroplating, using chemical reactions to bond the gold, a process which was thought to have been invented in Renaissance Europe 1,000 years later.

Opposite: The tomb robbers at Sipan were hoping for a cache of beautiful Moche pottery, coveted by collectors. Instead, they found a prince, covered in gold from head to foot.

# MACHU PICCHU, THE MISINTERPRETED CITY IN THE CLOUDS

The term "prehistoric," meaning before the invention of writing, seems particularly feeble when applied to the Incas. They built stone roads along 2,500 miles of mountain ridges until their empire, the largest in South America, stretched from Ecuador to Chile. They had a supremely efficient government, a large feared army, wonderful metalwork, superb textiles, unrivaled stonework laid without mortar so precisely that it is still impossible to slide a knife blade between the blocks—and no form of writing except knotted cords as mnemonics.

The Inca rule expanded for three centuries from about A.D. 1200, until it spread over six million people, from dozens of ethnic groups, united by the official language, Quechua. (Strictly speaking, the "Inca" was the emperor; they called their empire Tahuantinsuyu, the Land of Four Quarters.) They readily incorporated local leaders, customs, and gods, but all their subjects paid taxes in goods or labor on government projects.

Its peak, however, lasted barely a century, when Cuzco became the administrative capital and the home of the greatest Inca shrine, the treasure-stuffed Temple of the Sun. In 1532 the Spanish arrived. The Incas fought skirmishing battles for 40 years, longer than any other South American people held out, but Spanish-introduced diseases wreaked more havoc than Spanish soldiers, and finally Cuzco fell to siege.

The last emperor, Atahualpa, was taken prisoner, and the shock of seeing chains on a ruler believed descended directly from the sun god seems to have been terminal. It took the Spaniards weeks to melt down about 24 tons of gold and silver treasure sent to ransom him—the odd object that even the Spanish soldiers thought too beautiful to melt shows the quality of what was lost. They described solid gold fountains, and real trees with golden birds in the branches in the Inca's garden—and melted them down. Atahualpa was killed anyway.

The last of the Inca's people withdrew to a new settlement in the jungle. The romantic belief for much of this century was that this was Machu Picchu, high above it, a fortified city in the Andes which was never taken—the Spanish could scarcely have breathed at such altitudes, yet alone fought.

Machu Picchu has partly become such a symbol of fortitude and romance—the most popular tourist site in Peru, despite the difficulty of getting there, and the political instability of the region—because the man who found it again had a head so filled with romance.

As so often, in 1911 Hiram Bingham found a city which had never been lost, except by Western authors. The ruins were deserted. But local people, descendants of the Inca, were still growing crops on 400-year-old terraces, their retaining walls of the distinctive Inca masonry.

The ruins of Machu Picchu, strung along a mountain ridge, could be seen from several miles away.

Hiram Bingham taught Latin American history at Yale, but he was an authentic Indiana Jones prototype. He spent all his holidays traveling, hacking through jungles, fording raging rivers, and climbing vertical mountain faces. He hunted down the Olmecs, the Toltecs, the Mayans, and the Aztecs, but he found his true goal when he heard about the city in the clouds.

Bingham says, in proper fairy tale style, that he heard of the last stronghold of the last Inca from an innkeeper. Others suggest that he heard about it, more prosaically, in Cuzco from other archaeologists who were already interested in reports about Machu Picchu, and in the fabled jungle settlement, Villacamba. Bingham came close to the real ruins of Villacamba, but then decided it must be the ruined city on the mountaintop.

His version of the story is that he set off up the slopes with the innkeeper, and when the climb got too difficult and the rest of the group stopped, a ten-year-old farmer's son led him to the top of the mountain.

Bingham returned season after season, explored and photographed every inch of the site, went on to become a U.S. Senator, and continued to write and lecture about it until his death in 1956.

Archaeologists now believe that Villacamba was the last major Inca settlement, and that Machu Picchu may have been part of an exceptionally grand royal farming estate, and a center for major religious festivals, not a city at all.

The heart of the complex is a long open space, with a staircase leading to a stone outcrop, and a pillar carved from the bedrock, known as "the hitching place of the sun." The sun still rises over it, but the settlement seems to have been abandoned not long after the Spanish arrived, perhaps because there were no longer enough people to maintain the temples and terraces, nor an emperor to require it.

"Would anyone believe what I have found?" Bingham wrote of what was immediately dubbed "the city in the clouds." The resounding answer from contemporary archaeologists is: on the whole, no.

Above: The steps led to the circular platform of an observatory, built to track the vital movements of their greatest god, the sun. In a cave below it a tomb, probably of a priest, was found.

Left: The brilliant green terraces between the superb Inca masonry give a clue as to what really went on here. The lost city Hiram Bingham found was never lost, and probably not a city. It was most likely a farm, and local people will still climb the slopes of the mountains to cultivate terraces leveled by the Incas.

# EL PLOMO, CHILE:
# THE SADDEST SACRIFICES

At the furthest reach of the 2,500 miles of mountain ranges which made up the Inca empire, on top of the highest peak of all at El Plomo in Chile, a pitiful victim was found in 1954.

Like most of the other major South American cultures, the Incas practiced human sacrifice. A typically elegant piece of Moche pottery, from about A.D. 400, shows a dragon-headed god with a knife in one hand and a severed human head in the other, and a beautiful Aztec stone jaguar was made to hold warm hearts ripped out of living breasts.

With the largest empire in South America to keep a grip on, the Incas perhaps had more need to placate the gods than most.

Offerings of produce or precious objects seem to have sufficed for everyday occasions; human sacrifice was for when it was necessary to draw the attention of the gods more urgently. Adult sacrifices have also been found in the high mountains. Archaeologists have speculated that the offerings of children—and most of those found were exceptionally well dressed, and well nourished, and so presumably from wealthy families—may have represented the greatest sacrifice, for the times of greatest or most urgent need.

Many of them have been found near the mountain roads which stitched together the huge length of the Inca empire—a boy found on Mount Aconcagua in 1985 was near the route of an ancient Inca path which is now the main highway from Argentina to Chile.

Until an even better preserved girl was found in 1995, nicknamed "Juanita," the El Plomo boy was the best preserved of dozens of naturally mummified children found on mountain summits, in caves and also under rock overhangs.

Juanita was found at 19,000 feet on Mount Ampato, the El Plomo boy at over 15,000 feet. Both the archaeologists, who carried the mummies down from the heights on their shoulders, and the people who sacrificed the children, were working at the limit of human strength. Johan Reinhard, a North American anthropologist who has led many of the expeditions, and found both Juanita and the following year "Saritya," has identified several resting sites, with evidence of extensive camps, on the paths to the places of sacrifice.

A few thousand feet below Juanita, two more children, a boy and a girl, were found, but they were less deeply frozen and therefore less well preserved.

A 16th-century Spanish account says that boys and girls were often buried in pairs, "with all the items that a married Indian would possess." The bodies were found with dozens of pieces of pottery, wooden utensils, and tools, and a pair of sandals.

Juanita's body, still deeply frozen, has been entirely preserved along with a fine alpaca-wool cloak, and a man's cape which one archaeologist has suggested was to give to the husband she would take in the afterlife.

Her body was exposed completely by chance: hot ash from a nearby volcano partly melted her covering of snow and ice.

The Babes in the Wood myth, the childhood terror of being taken into some terrible place and abandoned, is found across many cultures and countries. It came true for the El Plomo boy 500 years ago. He went to the top of the mountain in his best clothes, and handsome leather shoes.

Unlike Juanita he was not frozen but desiccated. The bitter dry cold which killed him, as he wrapped his arms around his knees and huddled

Right: The boy from El Plomo, huddled against the cold with his head cradled on his arms, is the most touching of the child sacrifices found in the high Andes. He went to his death dressed in his finest clothes. This was one of the first newspaper photographs of the find.

Naturally mummified adult human sacrifices are still being found. Archaeologists speculate that in times of special need, the Incas sent the gods the most valuable offering they could make— their children.

away from it, also preserved his skin and finger-nails, his woollen tunic and leather shoes, his braided hair with feather-and-shell decora-tions, and his pitiful collection of little toys—a doll with a feather headdress, a splendid feather purse, a gold alpaca, and a silver llama.

He was about eight, and it was even possible to blood-type him—he was group "O."

Like Tollund Man, the El Plomo boy is the most haunting of the mummies because of the extraordinary tranquility of his face. The chil-dren were killed, or at least knocked uncon-scious, by heavy blows to the back of the skull, but there is no mark of violence on his face. He looks as if he simply closed his eyes and fell asleep, and one hopes he did.

Shipwrecked cargo boats, sunk with their goods
scattered around them, are giving a unique
insight into trading patterns in the ancient world.

# MODERN TIMES

10

For centuries, underwater archaeology was confined to the accidental discoveries of fishermen and sponge divers. Technology has made it a new science, one of many that are stretching the frontiers of archaeology.

# THE ANCIENT HISTORY OF MODERN TIMES

The gentlemen archaeologists of the Age of Enlightenment would have needed reviving with burned feathers at the idea of searching around in trash dumps, water treatment works, or in the greasy recesses of huge pieces of factory machinery.

The idea of historical archaeology, archaeology of periods for which modern written records existed, was once controversial.

The barriers between anthropology, social and cultural history, and archaeology are becoming more and more permeable. The proper concerns of archaeology now include industry, engineering, science, concentration camps, gardens, theaters, and trash cans.

Archaeologists spend a lot of time in trash dumps. A good pile of trash can tell them a lot more about the inhabitants of a site than the most splendid building. But are they drawing the right conclusions?

In 1973 Professor William Rathje, of the University of Arizona, set his students to carry out an archaeological experiment on the hapless citizens of Tucson. The Garbage Project

Maritime archaeologists sometimes work on dry land. One of the most famous ancient boats, the Sutton Hoo ship, was found in Suffolk, England, in 1939 with all its treasure heaped as grave goods around the prince whose coffin it became. The ship, dating from about A.D. 650, was recorded down to the last rivet, although every scrap of timber had rotted into the Suffolk soil.

has since spread to other cities and other states. Thousands of tons of rubbish have been delivered to the university, stored in giant refrigerators, sorted, and then analyzed, to reveal what people buy, what they eat, and what they throw away.

One of their more unexpected findings occurred during a beef shortage in the 1970s. When meat is scarce one would expect every scrap to be used, and nothing except gristle and bone to be thrown out. In reality the archaeologists found clear evidence of panic buying: more meat was wasted and thrown away during the shortage than when it was in plentiful supply.

The experiment has been going on for long enough to allow the archaeologists to advise local authorities on how to build dumps, what kind of rubbish to expect, and how fast it will rot away.

The study has often found that while rubbish doesn't lie, people do. Asked how many cans of beer they bought a week, most people said none, and only a small fraction more than

eight. Their bins told another story: over half bought more than eight and only 15 percent had none.

Maritime archaeology often remains controversial, because the lines between pure archaeology and treasure-hunting are blurred on many wreck sites.

Maritime archaeology doesn't even require water, however. One of the most ancient ships was recovered from one of the driest places on earth: a Nile boat was found in a pit beside the Great Pyramid in Egypt. Every inch is known of the Sutton Hoo ship, a sumptuously rich Anglo Saxon burial far from the sea in eastern England, but not an inch of timber survived: the boat was recovered entirely from the impressions it left in the soil.

The first archaeologists to strap on an aqualung and go underwater were breaking new ground. In due course, somebody will undoubtedly climb into a spacesuit to investigate the monuments of the Space Age, the debris on the moon, and the abandoned *Mir* spacecraft.

In 1939 excavators dug into one of the low mounds dotting the fields at Sutton Hoo, Suffolk, in England, and found the outline of a beached ship holding the richest burial ever found in Britain. Treasure, including a solid gold buckle weighing over one pound, was heaped around a coffin-shaped space in the hull. The body, coffin, and the 7th-century ship itself had entirely disappeared. The ship could be traced down to the last rivet from its ghostly image in the soil.

# ARCHAEOLOGY GETS ITS FEET WET

A 19th-century Swiss doctor, Alphonse Morlot, was proud to proclaim himself the first underwater archaeologist and left a wonderfully funny drawing of himself at work as proof.

**JACQUES COUSTEAU**
Jacques Cousteau (1910–1997), diver and oceanographer, is best known for the remarkable series of underwater nature films he made. As one of the inventors in 1942 of the aqualung, however, he gave archaeologists gills, allowing them to work freely underwater for the first time.

In 1853, a long drought shriveled Lake Zurich and other Swiss lakes, exposing rows of wooden stakes. They were soon identified as remains of Bronze Age dwellings, and when swords, jewels, and bronze pots started to turn up in the mud, antiquaries flocked.

Most contented themselves with pottering around on the shore, or dropping grapples from boats. Not Dr. Morlot. His drawing shows a sort of underwater Ned Kelly, in homemade bucket-helmet with glass window, linked by an air-line to an assistant in a boat, trudging along the lake bed in weighted shoes, with a forked stick, a spade, and a net bag to carry up anything interesting he finds.

It was another century before underwater archaeology was established as a science, but men had been diving for treasure for centuries.

The first to recover sunken archaeological artifacts were certainly fishermen, cursing over ripped nets. If they were lucky, they snagged something like a Greek bronze which would pay for the damage; if unlucky, lumps of unidentifiable timber from lost ships. Fishermen had been grumbling about the great Roman ships drowned in Lake Nemi, near Rome, since medieval times—Mussolini eventually resurrected them by the simple expedient of draining the entire lake.

For centuries the scholars kept their feet dry, though a flamboyant figure, Père André Poidebard, French Jesuit priest and archaeologist, did fly a plane in the 1920s to spot sunken sites. They sent men down holding their breath, in primitive diving bells, or the early clumsy, heavy diving helmets and suits. The ship carrying the Parthenon Marbles, whose removal from Athens by Lord Elgin was already regarded as scandalous by many, sank off the Peloponnesus in 1802, and it was local divers who were sent down to retrieve them.

The aqualung was invented in 1942 by Jacques Cousteau and Emile Gagnan, but it was another decade before George Bass, of the University of Pennsylvania Museum, became the first archaeologist to train as a diver and go down for a look himself. He worked with diver and anthropologist Peter Throckmorton to establish many of the rules of the new discipline. They built the *Asherah*, the first two-seater archaeological submarine, and in a decade of diving with a team from the Bodrun Museum made a series of sensational discoveries in a graveyard of ancient ships off Turkey.

The first underwater archaeology conference had already been held, in Cannes in 1955, reflecting the obvious lure of the Mediterranean for archaeologists, which combined thousands of wrecks and submerged structures, with comparatively shallow, clear, and warm waters.

One of George Bass's more spectacular discoveries, the Ulu Burun shipwreck, was first spotted by a Turkish sponge-diver in 1982, in almost 150 feet of water off the southwest coast of Turkey, after which it was named. He told a friend he had seen "metal biscuits with ears" on the seabed—a vivid description, immediately recognized, of the distinctive copper ingots.

The ship was a Bronze Age trader, found with all her cargo, a complete picture of who was selling what around the shores of the Mediterranean in about 1316 B.C.

After a decade of diving, the finds include pottery from the Levant, about ten tons of copper in hide-shaped ingots—the "biscuits" —from Cyprus, and tin from Afghanistan. There were also goods for the luxury market: tortoise shells, an elephant's tusk, some gold including a lovely scarab with the name of Nefertiti, mother of Tutankhamen, ebony from Africa, amber from northern Europe, ostrich eggs, lumps of blue glass which the Mycenaeans prized for jewelry, vast quantities of resin and orpiment, an arsenic compound used for cosmetics and pigments.

Personal possessions included a hinged wooden writing tablet, with wax-covered leaves.

Food on board, analyzed from the traces in terracotta amphorae, included olives, honey, figs, pomegranates, and herbs such as cumin, saffron, and coriander—some for trade, some undoubtedly for lunch.

The humblest part of the cargo was also the last to be loaded before her disastrous final voyage, and permitted the most accurate dating: some bundles of firewood, which gave a date of about 1316 B.C.

Dr. Bass believes that the ship's home port was in northern Syria, and has reconstructed what he thinks was its seasonal anticlockwise trading route around the Mediterranean, by the Levant, Cyprus, Anatolia, Crete, and back to North Africa, buying and selling all the way.

It was, he said modestly, "one of the greatest archaeological sites ever found—although I should probably not say so myself."

George Bass has proved that it is possible to excavate as meticulously underwater as on land—raising questions about the enormous cost of raising sunken ships to the surface in order to study them.

# BRINGING UP THE BOATS:
# THE MARY ROSE AND THE VASA

Two of the most famous ships ever recovered were comparatively modern. They were resurrected, with immense effort and expense, from the cold, deep water where each sank within sight of its berth.

The *Mary Rose*, sunk off the coast of southern England, and the *Vasa*, which sank in Stockholm harbor on her maiden voyage, are more famous than any of George Bass's far more ancient ships because their recovery became media spectacles.

The ships had much in common. The *Mary Rose* was Henry VIII's favorite warship until she sank, with several hundred lives, just off Portsmouth during a battle with the French in 1545. The larger *Vasa*, a sumptuously carved Swedish warship, sank in 100 feet of water, again within sight of land, while packed with crew and guests who were on board for her maiden voyage in 1664.

Both ships sank very fast: the *Mary Rose* possibly because she had been repeatedly modified to carry larger modern guns; the *Vasa*, it has been suggested, because the design was flawed and she was top-heavy with sail.

The *Vasa* was "discovered" by engineer Anders Franzen in 1956, after he spent years studying contemporary records to identify the exact site. Diver Alexander McKee found the *Mary Rose* in 1967 by tracking thousands of pieces scattered on the seabed.

In each case the ship had been discovered at least once before. A team in a diving bell brought up some bronze cannons from the *Vasa* in 1664, while, after complaints from local fishermen, the diving brothers John and

Charles Deane went down and found the *Mary Rose* in 1836. They brought up some cannon, which went to the Tower of London, and other curios, including bottles and pieces of timber which they sold.

It took another century before the technology existed to attempt to raise such ships.

Divers from the Swedish navy spent months tunneling through deep mud under the *Vasa* to attach cables, before she was gradually brought back to the surface in 1961. Divers then spent years recovering hundreds of pieces of timber, which broke off and scattered artifacts, from the seabed.

The lesson was learned for the *Mary Rose*: all that work was done before the attempt to raise the ship. Prince Charles was one of the divers who went down to do the preparatory work, before most of the ship was brought up in 1982, watched by millions live on television.

The contents of both ships have brought everyday life on a 17th-century warship to vivid life.

The contents of the *Mary Rose* included musical instruments, a sack of shoes awaiting repair, and the barber-surgeon's complete collection of remedies, including syringes, surgical tools, jars of partly used ointments—and his velvet hat, which alone required years of conservation work.

The conservation problems were immense. The same technique was used for both hulls: keeping them saturated, then gradually replacing most of the water with a solution of polyethelene glycol, then gradually allowing the timber to dry out.

The cost of the conservation was so vast that it led many archaeologists to question the wisdom of such heroic effort. Freeze-drying water-sodden timber has already been used as a successful alternative for smaller boats, but George Bass has also proved that it is possible to carry out a complete archaeological survey underwater. In several parts of the world entrepreneurs are planning underwater archaeological parks, where sites will be conserved underwater, and visited by tourists either diving, or peering into the water through glass, like the first underwater archaeologist, Dr. Morlot, and his bucket.

Above: The *Mary Rose* was resurrected after lying submerged for 400 years. Millions watched on television as she rose slowly from the water in a steel cradle.

Opposite: The sumptuously carved *Vasa* may have been a dangerously top-heavy design and doomed from the start. Like the *Mary Rose*, raising the ship from the water was only the start of years of complex and expensive conservation work.

In the 1990s divers plumbing the murky waters of the modern harbor of Alexandria, found that tons of Alexander the Great's transformation of a little Egyptian fishing village into his royal capital have survived, and only 20 feet below the surface.

Divers had gone down before, and had found the odd piece of carving among the rocks and rubble, tumbled by an earthquake and a tidal wave in A.D. 335.

They were working in vile conditions, among oil slicks and islands of floating rubbish, in the path of the sewerage outfall for the modern Alexandria of five million people.

Even though the water was so shallow, the earlier divers could see little trace of the gardens, palaces, and splendid public buildings, the broad avenues meeting at right angles, decribed by contemporary travelers, after Alexander the Great swept irresistibly into Egypt in 332 B.C., had himself crowned Pharaoh at Memphis, and founded his new city in 331 B.C.

He is said to have designed the city by throwing his military cape down on the ground, to give an outline of the shape he wanted to create.

In less than a decade, before his thirty-third birthday, Alexander was dead. The general he left behind in Egypt as governor eventually became the first pharaoh, Ptolemy, founder of the dynasty of Ptolemies who ruled Egypt until the Romans came in the first century B.C. Under his reign Alexandria began to expand as a center of civilization and learning that made it one of the wonders of the world.

In the late 1990s the team headed by Franck Goddio, president of the European Institute of Marine Archaeology in Paris, brought a battery of modern archaeological technology into play: satellite mapping, infrared cameras, radar, and magnetometers to penetrate the gloom and measure the difference in materials.

# PALACES UNDER THE SEA: CLEOPATRA'S ALEXANDRIA

This dream-like image, by the 18th century German architect Fischer von Erlach, is a reconstruction of one of the wonders of the ancient world, the Pharos, the lighthouse which gave its name to all others. Alexander's capital city lived on in the imagination after the most splendid buildings were tumbled by an earthquake.

They found that a remarkable amount of the royal quarter, the most splendid part of Alexander's city, does survive; foundations of large buildings, steps, pedestals and statue bases, massive blocks from the quays, inscriptions in Greek and Egyptian hieroglyphics, sidewalks and columns, are crusted with deposits and sea creatures or buried in sand.

The excitable journalists taken down by submarine to inspect the site were only interested in one person: Cleopatra, the last of the Ptolemy pharaohs, who either amused herself with debauchery as Egypt collapsed around her, or played an end game of diplomacy to try and save her empire, depending on which historian is writing.

The news that Cleopatra's palace had been found went round the world. The press wanted to see the bed chambers where she dallied with Caesar and Mark Anthony, the pools she lounged by under a silken canopy, if possible even the basket that carried in it the asp which killed her.

The team stressed that after 3,500 dives they were certain they had found the royal quarter, and could make more accurate maps of it, but were still a long way from identifying individual buildings.

Somewhere, however, there could be the remains of true wonders. Traces of the lighthouse, the archetype of all others, built on the island of Pharos which Alexander joined to the town with a causeway, do still survive. Some archaeologists believe it is possible they may find remains of the Great—possibly the greatest—Library.

They have not ruled out the possibility of finding the tombs of Marc Antony and Cleopatra, and of another tomb which has been sought for centuries in the most likely and unlikely areas, the resting place of Alexander the Great himself.

His murdered father, Philip of Macedonia, has already been found. After extensive excavation and study of the finds, archaeologists believe that his is the reconstructed head, found in a wonderful golden casket marked with the royal Macedonian star, at Vergina in Northern Greece.

Alexander's body has never been found, although contemporary accounts say it was preserved in honey, in a golden coffin, and displayed at Alexandria until the fourth century A.D. It has been hunted around the ancient world since then, but it may never have left his city, and may be waiting for the archaeologists.

Left: In 1803, as this watercolor by Luigi Mayer shows, Cleopatra's Needle still stood among the ruins of Alexandria, before it was shipped off as a present to London. Divers have recently discovered that a remarkable amount survives below the water in the harbor.

# COOKING POTS AND THE INDUSTRIAL REVOLUTION

A century ago the archaeology of iron-working wouldn't have been seen as a suitable interest for a gentleman, and industrial archaeologists still sometimes regard themselves as the pariahs of their profession.

They frequently lament that while the merest battered fragment of Roman mosaic will attract excavation and conservation funds, the wonders of the world of industrial history are thrown aside without a murmur of protest. When in the 1990s London Transport proposed to put a concrete lining into Brunel's tunnel under the Thames, the first in the world, a pioneer of tunneling technology still in use, and a shrine to engineers from all over the world, one industrial archaeologist groaned

"What would they say if I wanted to pebble dash the Parthenon?"

Archaeologists are still at work on two very different metalworking sites: the greatest iron-works of ancient Europe, and a vast works in Germany which was still producing iron right up until 1986.

For 500 years, until about A.D. 300, the Stara and Nowa Stupia ironworks, in modern Poland, were a scene of intensive metalworking which would not be seen again until the Industrial Revolution.

It is estimated that on one of the hundreds of furnace sites over 112 tons of iron was smelted from over 1,800 tons of ore, using almost 2,000 tons of charcoal.

Over the 190 square mile site, over 440 smelting sites have been discovered, each with its little huddle of metalworkers' huts.

The site was known from the 19th century because the remains of the ironworks were the greatest nuisance to local farmers. They broke up and sold as many of the slag heaps as possible, since they still held pure iron ore. Tons of iron remain on the site, along with the remains of furnaces, molds, discarded castings, and charcoal-burners' works.

The techniques of ironworking changed very little until the Industrial Revolution, and then changed so rapidly that works became obsolete almost as soon as they were built. In the 20th century change became even more rapid and vast plants were built and demolished without anyone considering them as historical sites, worthy of detailed recording if not conservation.

The Volklingen Iron Works, in the Saarland in Germany, were still in production until 1986, and are now a UNESCO-registered World Heritage Site, like the Taj Mahal and the Pyramids.

They won the status because change has been so fast, combined with the cyclical booms and slumps in the industry, that the Volklingen is believed to be the most complete surviving works in the world, with a whole range of blast furnaces dating from 1885 to 1967. The earliest were steam powered, and the works were early pioneers in developing and using gas-powered machinery.

Although the works was founded in 1873, it closed in 1879, and was then bought and reopened in 1881 by Carl Röchling. His family remained in control of the plant for over a century, until a series of mergers in the 1970s. They kept the plants working through the decades of dispute and battle between the French and Germans over the Saarland, and through both world wars. Under the League of Nations administration after the Treaty of Versailles which ended World War I, the Volklingen was the only Saarland mill to remain in German ownership. In 1944 as the Allies advanced, Carl Röchling's grandson, Karl Theodor, refused to obey Hitler's scorched-earth policy and blow up the plant— only two months later he was shot, possibly by a Russian prisoner-of-war, while inspecting the works. His father was sentenced to ten years in prison for his war work.

When the works finally closed the German government bought everything on the site at scrap value, and all the company's records, and the industrial archaeologists came in, past bemused local people who had worked in the plant all their lives.

**The great Volklingen Ironworks became an archaeological site as soon as it closed in 1986. The industry has been changing so rapidly during the 20th century, that it is believed to be the most complete works surviving anywhere in the world.**

# ANY OLD IRON?
# THE ARCHAEOLOGY OF
# YESTERDAY'S REDUNDANCIES

In 1708 a cooking-pot manufacturer bought the lease on a derelict furnace in Shropshire, and launched the Industrial Revolution.

The entire archaeological history of the industrial revolution survives in Shropshire, from Abraham Darby's revolutionary furnace of 1709, to this Victorian works, and the modern factory, which is still in production.

Abraham Darby's furnace, at Coalbrookdale, Shropshire, is the heart of the most spectacular industrial-archaeology site in Britain, and a World Heritage Site.

Archaeologists are still picking their way through the slag heaps of at least 400 years, probably more, of metalworking. The history of Britain's rise to lead the world in cast-iron technology, and its decline to a point where the valley now lives on tourism, apart from one metalworks and one power station, is all to be traced in the valley. Its products are scattered among the Georgian and Victorian buildings: iron bootscrapers and railings, iron lintels and window frames, iron chimneypots and door steps. The furnaces and foundries, warehouses and bridges, railroads and canals, now mostly hold living museums, and tea shops.

Darby moved to Coalbrookdale because it was already an established center for the manufacture and distribution of iron. The furnace he leased was built in 1638, and blew up in 1700, when the wonderfully named tenant, Shadrach Fox, gave up and went to work for Peter the Great.

A year after he moved into Coalbrookdale, in 1709, Darby succeeded in smelting iron using coke instead of charcoal. Making iron from charcoal required a huge volume of wood, which was then made into charcoal in comparatively small quantities by craftsmen charcoal-burners. Coke could be produced on an industrial scale from what then seemed an unlimited supply of coal, and it transformed the production of iron. With cast iron the era of the artisan working by rule of thumb was

over, and the age of the engineer had arrived.

Darby couldn't have realized that he'd started a revolution, but it transformed his cooking-pot industry; within a decade he had expanded to a new larger furnace further down the valley, and his pots, including the 400-gallon Missionary, the pot seen in countless cartoons of cannibals simmering a missionary stew, sold as far away as Honolulu.

His son expanded the works beyond the valley and cast the first iron railroad wheels in 1729. The valley produced the first iron tracks in 1769, and parts for Richard Trevithick's first steam locomotive in 1802.

In 1779 Abraham Darby III cast the world's first iron bridge. It was opened to traffic on New Year's Day 1781, and gave the valley its new name: Ironbridge Gorge.

The original furnace closed in 1818, in the depression after one of its busiest periods in the Napoleonic Wars. It was gradually buried under later industrial building. Throughout the 20th century, before industrial archaeology had been conceived as a discipline, some historical-minded scientists remembered where it was and said that it should be preserved as a national treasure.

In 1969, to celebrate the 250th birthday of Darby's sensational breakthrough, the then owners, Allied Ironfounders Limited, peeled away the later buildings to expose the furnace. The engineers cheered, but the prospect of industrial archaeological tourism would at the time have seemed a joke. By the 1990s, it had become one of the most popular tourist sites in Britain.

This is not just an iron bridge, it is *the* Iron Bridge, the first in the world, cast in 1779. It gave the gorge its new name.

# AND DID THOSE FEET?
# A RETIRED CHIROPODIST
# LOOKS DOWN

Miss Phyllis Jackson listened to the lecture on problems of identification in an Anglo Saxon cemetery in Lechlade, Oxfordshire, with some impatience.

In the early years there was a fine tradition of the amateur archaeologist: General Pitt Rivers, who literally established the ground rules for meticulous excavation, was a career soldier; Austen Henry Layard, whose *Nineveh and its Remains* became a world bestseller in 1849, was an attorney by training.

As the scholarly art of archaeology became a serious science, the amateurs were squeezed out. They are now cautiously returning to the field. Climatologists, social historians, linguists, botanists, and art historians may often be found working alongside conventional archaeologists. We can look into the battered face of Philip of Macedon, father of Alexander the Great, through techniques of reconstructing living faces from skulls, originally developed by the British team of Richard Neave and John Prag to serve forensic pathology.

Miss Jackson, with her unrivaled understanding of the workings of the foot, is merely an extreme example of the diverse disciplines that are now being brought to bear on archaeological problems.

At the Anglo Saxon cemetery at Lechlade, a distinguished archaeologist was explaining that some of the bodies were buried with rich grave goods, and some with none. There were no identifiers except the grave goods, and he explained that it was impossible to deduce anything from the skeletons themselves.

Miss Jackson, then in her late seventies, was not impressed. Had it never occurred to them to look at the feet? Miss Jackson is a retired chiropodist, and her respect for archaeology, and contempt for the attitude of archaeologists to feet, are unbounded. She has found foot bones stored jumbled up with hand bones, because many archaeologists can't tell the difference. Egyptian mummies have been unwrapped, she says with disgust, by experts who haven't even bothered to unwrap the feet.

Miss Jackson was able to sort out the Lechlade cemetery in a trice, and for her work won a Pitt Rivers award for amateur archaeology.

It all turns on the heels and the cuboid bones. Miss Jackson has spent a lifetime working in small and frequently inbred communities on the border of England and Wales, and she knew that foot peculiarities bred remarkably true over generations. She has frequently spotted family resemblances among feet not acknowledged in the offical bloodlines.

Miss Jackson also knew that a group of Polish refugee patients had found it impossible to wear British shoes, because their feet were an entirely different shape—they were saved by a batch of cheap East European shoes which started to turn up in local shops, but which her English patients couldn't wear.

Miss Jackson is an extreme example of the new skills and knowledge gradually being admitted into what has been the hermetically sealed profession of archaeology.

Miss Jackson demonstrated, and the archaeologists have generally accepted, her view that the Saxon foot shape was entirely different from the native British foot. The Lechlade

Opposite: The feet (above right) are those of of a local British citizen buried at Lechlade, a Saxon cemetery about 13 miles east of Cirencester. The genetic ancestry between the feet (below right) of the mid-4th-century citizen of Cirencester (Roman Corinium) is very clearly demonstrated.
The foot of a male Saxon buried in the Lechlade Saxon cemetery (bottom left) is quite different in shape. The structural difference between this and the other two feet is very distinct. To Miss Jackson's great annoyance, excavated feet are usually lacking their toe-bones, giving this rather truncated appearance when reassembled.

grave goods demonstrated that the Saxons, a few generations after they invaded, were considerably wealthier than the natives—but interestingly she found that a few of the graves with goods, though less lavish, were native.

Miss Jackson is convinced she can solve many riddles of movements of ancient peoples and how they interacted with the native populations, if she can only get hold of their feet. She identified a piece of metal from one grave, which had baffled archaeologists, as part of a crutch, having instantly spotted the signs of club foot in the bones. She has found the foot of a child, aged no more than five or six, who had worked so hard in that short life that the foot was literally worn out.

She has now prepared a layman's guide to foot shape, which she is distributing as widely as possible in the archaeological community; she recommends a cat litter tray full of sand as the ideal working medium for sorting foot bones. And she is convinced she could resolve the Out of Africa/Simultaneous Evolution argument—if only she could get the bones.

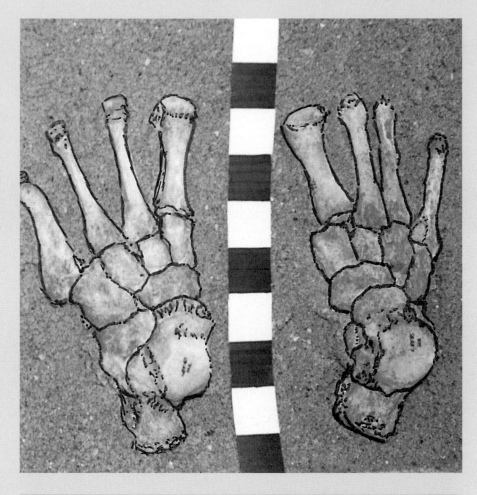

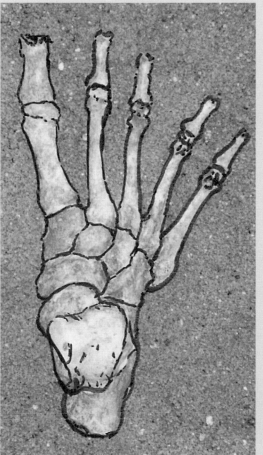

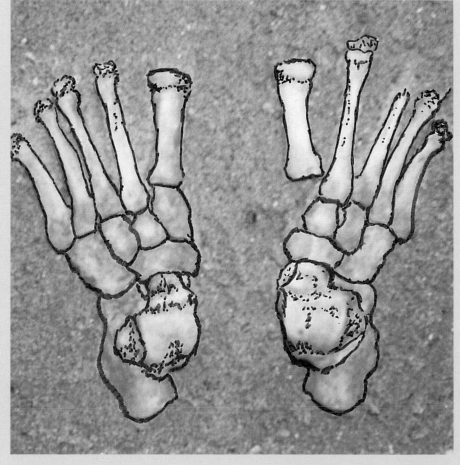

Durrington Walls s post circle

Above: Durrington Walls, in Wiltshire, reconstructed here by Peter Dunn, is another wood henge which has disappeared without trace above ground, like the far larger complex recently identified at Stanton Drew.

# MORE SCIENCE, LESS DIGGING, AND STILL THE WATER RISES: CONCLUSION

It's not hard to imagine what would have happened 150 years ago if somebody had announced the discovery of a vast unexcavated Bronze Age henge, a once-in-a-century find of world significance: there would have been a stampede.

In 1997 Geoffrey Wainwright, chief archaeologist of English Heritage, the official British state body for archaeology and conservation, announced that they had discovered a huge henge in the west of England.

The site is at Stanton Drew, near Bristol, 70 miles west of Stonehenge. It is 5,000 years old, at least as old as Stonehenge and six times larger, four times the size of any previously discovered henge.

It was a vast, columned temple, almost 100 yards in diameter, formed of 400 huge wooden posts from the largest trees the farmers could find. It may have had a thatch roof, and was surrounded in turn by a ditch, with an entrance over 100 feet wide on the northeastern side. Like Stonehenge, the alignment of the posts, ditches, and entrances may have had astrological significance, as well as providing what was clearly a major ritual gathering site.

Not a sod of earth was turned in order to reveal the monument. The posts rotted millennia ago, the ditch filled in. Only some much later standing stones—half a dozen in the back garden of a pub—remain above ground. One fell over in the 17th century, exposing the human bones below.

The work was done entirely through aboveground surveying, using a magnetometer to measure soil resistence.

Dr. Wainwright, who comes in a noble line of irascible archaeologists suffering fools not at all, was asked why he didn't dig it all up, and snapped: "Why should I? Silly question."

The days of heroic archaeology, often carried out by gentlemen amateurs—and a rare scatter of lady amateurs—are over.

The presumption now is against digging at all, if scientific methods can produce as good or better information. If a site is dug, it is likely to be buried again for its own protection, rather than being exposed as a tourist attraction: the

conservation problems at sites such as Pompeii and Knossos are there as a horrible warning. Recording, analysis, and publication are seen as more important than the primal excitement—which even the most cerebral archaeologists acknowledge—of burrowing into the earth, in search of wonderful things.

Science will become even more cunning. More and more disciplines—even Miss Jackson's feet—will be welcomed into archaeology instead of being regarded with myopic suspicion. But digging will certainly continue. The twin forces of development and affronted nature will force it.

The era of rescue archaeology has arrived. The increasing sprawl of cities, the country roads growing into highways and highways into freeways, drive the archaeologists into salvaging as much information as possible. They are often working literally in the shadow of bulldozers, forced to dig at a speed which Belzoni might have admired. The question of who owns the information uncovered, the developers or the excavators, and what the responsibility is to share such knowledge, is becoming increasingly contentious.

But in the end the future may belong to the marine archaeologists. The most grim projections for global warming and rising sea levels put half the world's Heritage Sites under the water.

If archaeology teaches anything it is that things come to an end: the sea-level rises or water disappears, the trees are all felled, the rains fail, the river changes course, and in the space of one lifetime great cities are abandoned to the creeping desert or the waves.

As Aubrey wrote:

"How these curiosities would be quite forgott,

did not such idle fellowes as I am putt them downe."

# GLOSSARY

## Archaeology

Literally, the study of ancient people. Jacob Spon, a 17th-century German physician, traveler and scholar, is credited with inventing the term in 1674.

## Anthropology

The study of humankind. Overlaps—sometimes contentiously—with archaeology, and paleontology (the study of fossil plants and animals) in tracing the very earliest human remains.

## Artifact

An object made, used, or adapted—as in rocks used as tools—by humans. The history of archaeology is bedeviled by centuries of enthusiasts removing the objects without noting the context in which they were found.

## Barrow

An earth mound, particularly of the Bronze Age, usually covering a burial.

## B.P.

Before Present, alternative to the traditional B.C. and A.D. (Before Christ and Anno Domini). Has the advantage that it makes sense across all cultures and religions. To standardize the dates, 1950 was taken as the archaeological "present."

## Carbon 14 Dating

One of a range of techniques measuring the rate of decay of radioactive isotopes, to date organic material up to 50,000 years old. Thermoluminescence can be used to date pottery, reheating it and measuring light emitted to determine when a clay object was originally fired.

## Crop marks, or parch marks

Buried features such as walls, invisible at ground level, seen from from the air as stripes of different color in crops. Still regularly used, the phenomenom was precisely described by William Camden in 1586, of a vanished Roman port in Kent: "It is at this day a corn field, where when the corn is grown up one may observe the draughts of streets crossing one another (for where they have gone the corn is thinner) and such crossing they commonly call S. Augustine's cross."

## Cuneiform

One of the earliest forms of writing, appearing as wedge-shaped letters pressed into wet clay, originally using a thorn.

## Dendochronology

Dating timber by counting tree rings, added every year. As well as age it can provide evidence of climate, which affects the thickness of the rings. Technique first used in archaeology in the 1920s, to date the timber in American Pueblo Indian villages.

## Excavation

Generally denotes physical uncovering of the site, either by removing the entire surface in carefully recorded layers, or by sinking trial trenches to reveal the levels of deposits. Total excavation leaves nothing behind. Mortimer Wheeler said: "I have been an archaeologist—a destroyer of the past."

## Field Archaeology

Literally, archaeology which involves working on the ground—though new scientific techniques mean they may not actually have to dig and get their hands muddy. The opposite extreme is Desktop Archaeology, often used now in considering planning applications, and an increasingly computerised discipline. This type of site study uses all existing documentation, maps, censuses, tax rolls, church records, surveys, and any earlier excavation reports. Historic archaeology is that of any period for which written records are available.

## Glyph

A symbol in writing. Hieroglyphic writing, as in ancient Egypt, uses pictures to represent either ideas or sounds.

## Grave goods

Objects buried with a human body, a custom invaluable to archaeologists.

## Inhumation

Burying a human body. Cremation, burning the body, is more common in many cultures.

## Megalithic

Literally, using large stones, in monuments such as Stonehenge.

## Prehistoric

Often used to mean "very old" but properly, before the invention of writing.

## Potsherd, or sherd

Fragments of broken pottery, dull but essential tools in devising a dating sequence.

## Rescue Archaeology

Excavation to salvage as much information as possible from a site about to be destroyed by development. Increasingly paid for by the developer as a condition of planning permission.

## Relative dating

The age of objects in relation to one another, without necessarily determining the date they were made. Absolute dating is determining age in years.

## Stratigraphy

Study of layers of deposits, generally assuming that deeper means older. Scholars had worked out that there were too many layers to accommodate the traditional Biblical date for the creation of the world, 4004 B.C., long before Darwin published the *Origin of Species* in 1859.

## Three Ages System

Division of history into Stone, Bronze, and Iron Age, useful in Europe but problematic in other parts of the world where Stone Age cultures survive. Originally devised by Christian Thomsen, in 1819 to tidy up the displays at his museum in Copenhagen.

# BOOK LIST

Archaeology: Theories, Methods and Practice, by Colin Renfrew and Paul Bahn, *Thames and Hudson*, second edition 1996

The Oxford Companion to Archaeology, editor in chief Brian M Fagan *Oxford University Press*, 1996

The Story of Archaeology, editor Paul Bahn, *Phoenix Illustrated*, 1996

A Short History of Archaeology, Daniel Glyn, *Thames and Hudson*, 1981.

Eyewitness to Discovery, edited by Brian M Fagan, *Oxford University Press*, 1996

Wonders of the Ancient World, National Geographic Atlas of Archaeology, *National Geographic Society*, 1994

The Atlas of Ancient Archaeology, Jacquetta Hawkes, *Heinemann* 1974.

Finding the Lost Cities, Rebecca Stefoff, *British Museum Press*, 1997

A History of American Archaeology, G R Willey and J A Sabloff, *Thames and Hudson*, 1974.

Martin's Hundred, by Ivor Noel Hume, *Curtis Brown*, 1982

Australian Rock Art, Robert Layton, *Cambridge University Press*, 1992.

Flinders Petrie, A Life in Archaeology, by Margaret S. Drower, *Gollancz*, 1985

Still Digging, by Mortimer Wheeler, *Michael Joseph*, 1955.

Mortimer Wheeler, Adventurer in Archaeology, by Jacquetta Hawkes, *Weidenfeld*, 1982.

Vases and Volcanoes, by Ian Jenkins and Kim Sloan, *British Museum Press*, 1996

Ancient Faces: Mummy Portraits from Roman Egypt, Susan Walkeer and Morris Bierbrier, *British Museum Press*, 1997.

Death and Burial in the Roman World, J M C Toynbee, *Thames and Hudson*, 1971

The Palace of Minos at Knossos, Arthur Evans, *Macmillan*, 1930

The Illustrated Archaeology of Ireland, edited Michel Ryan, *Country House Dublin*, 1991.

Knowth and the passage tombs of Ireland, George Eogan, *Thames and Hudson*, 1986

The Dingle Peninsula, Steve MacDonogh, *Brandon*, 1993.

Olduvai Gorge, my search for Early Man, Mary Leakey, *Collins*, 1979.

Prehistoric Avebury, by Aubrey Burl, *Yale University Press*, 1979

Roman Bath, by Barry Cunliffe, *English Heritage*, 1995

The Oldest Road: the Ridgeway, Fay Godwin and J R L Anderson, *Whittet Books*, 1987

Hadrian's Wall, a guide, *English Heritage*, 1996

Petra, by Iain Browning, *Chatto & Windus*, 1989

Stonehenge, by David Souden, *English Heritage*, 1997.

The World of the Bible, Roberta Harris, *Thames & Hudson*, 1995.

The Archaeology of the Bible Lands, Magnus Magnusson, *Bodley Head*, 1977

The Bog People, P. V. Glob, first published 1969, *Faber and Faber*, 1977

A History of Seafaring based on Underwater Archaeology, George Bass, *Thames and Hudson*, 1972

Murder in Mesopotamia, Agatha Christie, first published 1936, *Fontana paperback*, 1962.

Aubrey's Brief Lives, edited by Oliver Lawson Dick, first published Secker and Warburg 1949, *first Penguin English Library*, 1972.

Early Irish Myths and Sagas, translated by Jeffrey Gantz, *Penguin Books*, 1981.

# INDEX

Numbers in *italics* refer to captions.

Abbeville 14
Abominable Snowman 140
Aborigines 18
Above-ground surveying 183
Abraham 48, 128
Abruzzuo of Saint Cosmo 111
Abu Simbel *66*, 68
Abyssinia (see Ethiopia)
Aconcagua, Mount 164
Acropolis 10, 105
Adena people 151
Aegean 96
Afghanistan 171
Africa 14, 20, 106
Age of Enlightenment 110, 117, 168
Age of Giants 14
Agememnon, King *98*, 99
Air Ministry 29
Alaska 40, 117
Albright W. F.128
Alenque 156
*Aleppo Codex* 52
Aleut people 40
Alexander the Great 6, 73, 77, 105, 174, 180
Alexandria 9, 58, 70, 123, 174
Allied Ironfounders Ltd 179
Altamira 17
Altwater, Caleb 151
Alva, Walter 161
American School of Oriental Research 129
Americas 16, 143
Ampato, Mount 164
Amun 70
Anansazi 154
Anatolia 50
Anchorage, 117
*Ancient Monuments of the Mississippi Valley* 151
Andes 145, 163
*Antichita Romane, Le* 117
Angkor Wat temple 9, 90, *90*

*Animal, Vegetable, Mineral?* 7
Ankor Thom complex 90
Anno Domini 6
Antony, Marc 175
Anyang 78
Apollo 105, 106
"Apollo Belvedere" 103
Apollo, Temple of 106
Aqualung *169*, 170
Arab manuscripts 60, 85
Ararat, Mount 140
Argentina 164
Argive plain 98
Aristotle 7, 104, *104*
Arizona, University of 167
Ark of the Covenant 128, *128*
Armenia 141
Amada, Temple of 66
Arnhem Land 18
Art thieves *91*
Artemidorus 73
Asherah submarine 170
Ashmolean Museum 30, *48*, 100, 100
Assyrians *44*, 46, *47*, 48, 77, 102, 134
Aswan Dam 66
Atahualpa 163
Athena, Temple of 106
Athens 9, *101*, 104, 170
Athens, School of 7, 104, *104*, 105
Atlantis 129, 151
Attai Mountains 39
Aubrey Holes 29
Aubrey, John, 6, 11, 26, *26*, 29, 183
Australia 16, 18, 140
*Australopithecus 21*
Austria 39
Avebury 6, 8, 11, 26
Avebury, Lord 7
Ayloff, Mr 27
Aztecs 158, 163

Babel, Tower of 128
Babylon 11, 128

Babylonian texts 45, 50, 134
Babylonians 46, 48, 77
Baghdad 4
Ball court *156*, 157
Banks, Sir Joseph 111
Barberini, Cardinal 117
Barrows 27, 36
Basilica Julia 117
Bass, George 170, *171*, 172
Bath 8, 120
Beatles, The 7, 21
Behistun 45
Beijing 77
Belize 156
Belshazzar's feast 128
Bent J. T. 133
Berlin 97
Bethezuba 134
Bethlehem 135
Belzoni, Giovanni *60*, 61, 67–68, 183
Bezeklik *85*
Bible, The 11, 128, 130, 140–141
Biblical archaeology 127, 140
Binford, Lewis 7, 145
Bingham, Hiram 163,*163*
Birley, Robin 125
Blasket Islands 137
Bodrun Museum 170
Bog people 7, 38, *39*
Bogazkoy 50
Boise, Charles *21*
Bolivia 145
Bolzano Museum 39
Book of Genesis 140
Book of Isaiah 52
Borobudar 9, 88
Borsippa temple 45
Botta, Paul Emile 46
Bouchard, Lt 58
Boyne Valley 30, *31*, 128, 148
Boyne, Battle of the 128
Brahmans 88
Brendan, Saint 137
Bretons 32, *33*
British Assoc. for Advancement of Science 133

British Israelites 128
British Museum 7, 38, 45–48, 58, 60, 72, 103, 110– 110
British School for Archaeology 131
Brittany 32
Bronze Age 6, 11, 26, 32, 39, 54, 77, 78, 128, 170, 183
Bru na Boinne 30
Brunel's Thames tunnel 176
Buckland, Wm 14, *15*
Buddhist temples 88, 89, 91
Buddhist texts *85*
Bureau of American Ethnology 151
Burgon, Dean John Wm 112
Burial mounds 86, 145
Burckhardt, Johann, L. 7, 112
Bush Barrow 29
Bushmen of the Drakensberg 17
Byzantines 102, 105, 134–135

Caesar, Augustus 6, 117
Caesar, Julius 6, 116, 123, 175
Cairo 70
Calendar of Martyrdom 138
Cambridge 102
Cambodia 90–91
Cambry, Jacques de 32
Camden, Wm 6, 120, 184
Canada 146
Canadian Parks Service 147
Cannes 170
Carbon dating 29, 39
Carnac 8, 32, *33*
Carnarvon, Lord 62
Carter's Grove 152
Carter, Howard 7, 62, 71
Castor, Temple of 116
Catalan atlas *85*
Catherwood, Frederick 144, 157
Catherine the Great 117
Catherine, Saint *139*
Caton-Thompson, Gertrude 133
Cauac Sky 157
Cave paintings 14, 16, 17, 156
Cedar of Lebanon 140

Celts 32, 136
Central America 156
Cerveteri cemetery 115
Chaco Canyon 154, *154*, 155
Champ-Dolent 33
Champollion, Jean François 7, 58, 61, *138*
Chan Chan 145
Charcoal burners 178
"Charioteer of Delphi" 107
Charles, Prince 173
Chavin culture 145
Chesil Beach 36
Chi, Pinyin Li, 78
Chien, Zhang 85
Child, Vere Gordon 35
Chile 162, 164
China 6,11,14,16,67,75, 78
*Chinampas* 159
Chinese Academy 78
Christ, Jesus 6, 135, 138
Christianity 53, 107, 128, 136–138
Christie, Agatha 48
Church of the Holy Sepulcher 135
Church of the Kathisma 135
C.I.A. 53, 141
Circleville 151
*Cirencester* 180
Cistercian abbey 128
Clarke, Edward D. 102
Clay cylinders *44*
Clayton, John 124
Cleopatra 175
Cleopatra's Needle 175
*Clochans* 137
Coalbrookdale 178
Coffins 39, 161, 175
Cold War 11
Colosseum 116, *116*
Confucian philosophers 85
Conquistadors 158
Cook, Thomas 70
Copan 9, 144, 156
Copts, The 137–138, *139*
Corze, Alexander 7
Corinth, Gulf of 106
Corinthian order 106
Cortez, Hernan 159
Cousteau, Jacques *170*
Coyolxauhqui 158
Cranborne Chase estate 7, 94
Creation, The *15*
Crete 6, 100,*100*
Croesus 106
Crucifixion, The 135
Crusaders 112, 134, *134*
Cuello 156

Cult of Priapus 111
Cuneiform 44–45, 47–48, 50, *51*, 68
Cunliffe, Prof . Barry 120
Cunningham, Wm 29
Curse of the pharaoh's tomb 63
Cuzco 163
Cyclops 99
Cyprus 171

Daedalus 100
*Daily Telegraph, The* 47
Danish Royal Society 6
Darby III, Abraham 179
Darby, Abraham 6, 178
Darius, King 45
Dark Ages 6, 124
Dart, Raymond 21
Darwin, Charles 11, *11*, 14, 20, *111*
Darwinism 140
Davis, Edwin 151
Davis, Maj. Charles 121
Dead Sea Scrolls 8, 52, *53*, 129
Deane, John and Charles 172–173
"Dear Boy" *21*
Decker, George 147
Deir El Medina 8. 65
*De la Création* 14
Delaware, Lord 152
Delft tiles 153
Delphi 9, 106
Deluge Tablets 45
Dendrochronology 155
Denmark, King of 47
Denmis, George 114
Denon, Vivant 61
*Description of Egypt* 61
Dingle peninsula 137
Diocletian, Emperor 138
DNA match 69
Don, River 22
Dorchester 37
Dordogne 17
Dore, Gustav 141
Doric order 106
Dorn, Ronald, 18
Dorpfeld, Wilhelm 97
Douglas, Andrew E. 155
Druids *24*, 27, 29, *29*, 32
Dunhuang 85
Dunn, Peter *182*
Durrington Walls *182*

Early Man Shelter 18
Earthquakes 101, 113
East India Co. 45

Ebla 45
Ecuador 162
Egypt 6, 45, 51, 56, *61*, 103, 138, 169, 174
Egypt Exploration Fund 71
Egyption hieroglyphics 51, 138, 156, 175
Egyptology 60, 63, 69
Ehecatl-Quetzalcoatl, temple of 159
El Plomo 9, 164, *164*
El Salvador 156
Elamite texts 45
Elamites 46
Eleusis 102
Elgin Marbles (see Parthenon Marbles)
Elgin, Lord *102*, 170
Ericsson, Leif 146, *147*
English Heritage 183
Epaves Bay 147
Ephesus 107
Er-Rubayat 73
Eric the Red 146
Erlach, Fischer von *175*
Essene cult 53
Ethiopia 21, *42*
Etruria 110
Etruscans 9, 100, 110, 114, *114*, 115
Euphrates river 48
European Inst. of Marine Archaeology 174
Evans, Arthur 94, 100, *100, 101*, 133
*Far From the Madding Crowd* 120
Farnese Palace 117
"Fatima" 73
Fayum, 9, 71
Finland 69
Fiorelli, Giuseppe 119
First Emperor's Army (see Terracotta soldiers)
Fitzwilliam Museum 102
Foot bones *180*
Fortunatus, L. Marcius 117
Fouquet, Jean *130*
Four Corners 155
Fox, Shadrach 178
France 16, 32
Franks 32
Franks, A. W. 110
Franzen, Anders 172
*French Book of Hours* 134
Frere, John 11

Fu Hao tomb 78
Gagnan, Emile 170
Galerie des Antiquites 103

Gallarus Oratory 9, 137
Gallarus, Saint 137
Garbage Project 167
Gauls 32
Geoffrey of Monmouth 28–29
German Army 33
German East Africa 20
Germany 38, 97, 176
Getty, John Paul 119
Gibraltar 123
Gilbert 121
Gleninsheen Gorget 11
Glob, Prof Peter 27, 38
Global warming 55, 67, 183
Globe Theatre *166*
Goddio, Franck 174
Gold Hill tomb 87
Golden Mycenae 98
Golgotha 135
Gorgon 120
Graf, Theodor 73
*Grand Menhir Brise, Le* 32
Grand Tour 102, 117
Grave Creek Mound 151
Gray, Mrs Hamilton 115
Gray, Tom 20–21
Great Dome 135
Great Pyramid 169
Great Serpant Mound 9, 150
Great Temple of the Aztecs 9, 158, *159*
Great Wall of China 8, 76, 77
Great Zimbabwe 9, 132–133, *133*, 140
Great Flood 14, 18, 47, 127, 140
Greece 73, 93, 97–98, *101*, 110, 175
Greek classical painting 73
Greek Orthodox Church 135
Greek languages 8, 101, 175
Greeks *100*, 133
Greenland 40, 146
Grimm, Jack 140
Guatemala 156
Guzzo, Prof Pietro Giovanni 119
Hadar 21
Hadrian's mausoleum 117
Hadrian, Emperor 123, *124*
Hadrian's Wall 9, 124, *125*
Hall, Richard 133
Halys, River 106
Hamilton, Emma *110*, 111
Hamilton, Marquesse of 26
Hamilton, Sir Wm *110*, 111, 118
Han Dynasty 83, 85
Han tombs *82*
Hanging Gardens of Babylon 46
Hangzhoe 84
Haniwa figures 86

Harappan 54, 55
Hardy, Thomas 36, 120
Har Homa 135
Harvard University 154
Harwood, Wm 153
Hatshepsut 8, 70
Hattusha 50
Hattushili 51
Hattushili III 51
Hawara mummies 7, 8, 72, *73*
Hawkes, Jacquetta 29, *29*
Haydon, Benjamin 103
Heibei province 83
Helen of Troy 96, *97*
Hellespont 106
Henry of Blois 110
Henry VIII, King 172
Herculaneum 6, 110, 118
Herjolfsson, Bjarni 146
*Hermitage, The* 137
Hermione 73
Herod the Great 134
Herodotus 106
Hezekiah 134
Higuchi, Takayasu 86
Himalayas 77
Himoko, Princess 87
Hindu priests 85
Hindu temples 88, 91
Hittites 50–51, *51*, 68, 77
Hoare, Colt 29
Hodgson, Rev. John 124
Holy Land *126*, 128
Holy Grail 128, 144
Homer 11, 18, 94, 96 98
Hominid fossils 21
Honduras 156
Hongshan culture 82
Hopewell Indians *151*
Hrozny, Bedrich 51
Huangdi, First Chinese Emperor
    Qui Shi 81
Huitzilopochtli 159
Human sacrifice 29, 48, 101,
    159, 161, 164, *164*
Hume, Ivor Noel 152
Hypostyle Hall 68

*I Sereti di un Tombarolo* 114
Ibrahim, Sheikh 112
Ice Age 22
Ice Baby 8, 40, *41*
Ice Maiden 8, 38–39
Ice Man 38–39
Iceland 146
Imperial Tombs 8
Incas 6, 44, 145, 162, 164
India 54, 85, *85*
Indian Archaeological Survey 54

Indonesia 67, 88
Industrial archaeologists 176
Industrial Revolution 6, 11, 176,
    178
Infant mortality 40
Ingstad, Anne Stine 147
Ingstad, Dr Helge 147
Inuits *40*, 146
Ionic order 106
Iran 45
Iraq 48, 124, 140
Ireland 31,38, 128, 136, 148
Iron Age 6, 11, 22, 36, 38, 94
Iron Age forts 36, 53
Iron Bridge *179*
Ironbridge Gorge 6, 9, 179
Ironworks 176
Irvine, James Thomas 121
Islamic religion 6, 85, 128
Israel 52
Italy 39

Jackson, Phyllis 180,*180*, 183
Jackson, Wm Henry 154
Jacobites 128
Jacq, Dr Christian 68–69
Jade 82, 156
Jade Gate 85
James River 152
Jamestown 9, 152, *152*
Japan 77, 86
Jarrow 124
Java 14, 88
Jebusites 134
Jefferson, Thomas 145, 148, *149*,
    150
Jericho 9, 127–128, 130, 130,
    *131*
Jerusalem 9, 134, *134*
Jingdi, Fifth Han Emperor 81
Johanson, Donald 20–21
Jones, Inigo 26, 29, 29
Jordan 52, 130
Josephus 134, 138
Joshua 128, 130
*Journeys in Lower and Upper Egypt*
    61
"Juanita" 164
Judaism 53
Julian the Apostate 107

Kai-shek, Chiang 78
Karnak temple 51, 68, 70
Kattwinkel 20
Kensington Stone *144, 145*
Kent's Cavern 14–15
Kenyon, Darne Kathleen 7, 131,
    134
Kepler *14*

Kern brothers 154
Kerry saints 137
Khayan Omar 55
Khirbet Qumram 53
Khmer empire 90
Khmer Rouge 90
Khorsabad 46–47
Kiev 8, 22
Kilmakedar 137
Kimeu, Kamoya 21
Knossos, Palace of 9, 92, 94, *100*,
    *101*, 183
Koboyashi, Tatsuo 86
Kofun 86
Koganezuka Kofun 87
Kolluthos, Saint 138
Korea 69, 77
Kublai 85
Kuwait 60
Kuyunjik 47

L' Anse Aux Meadows 6, 9, 146,
    *146*
Laetoli 21
Lambaesis 123
"Laocoön" 103
Lascaux caves 8,*12*, 16,*17*, 119
Latin 137
Lawrence of Arabia 36
Lawrence, D. H. 114
Layard, Austen Henry 45–46,
    102, 113, 180
Le Mans cathedral 33
League of Nations 177
Leakey, Louis 20, *21*
Leakey, Mary 20, *20,21*
Leakey, Richard 20, *21*
Lechlade 180
*Letter to Monsieur Dacier* 138
*Letter on Herculaneum* 111, 119
Leland, John 120
Lepcis Magna 9, 122, 123
Lerici, Carlo 115
Liaoning province 82
Libya 123
Lindow Man 37–38, *39*
Linear A and B scripts 99, 101
Ling, Roger 119
Lintong 81
Llwyd, Edward 30
Loch Ness Monster 140
London *102, 103, 115, 166*
London Transport 176
London, Tower of 173
Lost City in the Clouds *142*
Lost Tribes of Israel 133, 151,
    157
Lothal 54
*Lucy in fhe Sky With Diamonds* 7,

21
"Lucy" 20
Luxor, temple 70

Lyceum 105
Lydia 106
Macedonians 72
MacEnery, Father James 14
Machu Picchu 9, *142*, 162
Maes Howe 34
Maiden Castle 36, *36*
Mallowan, Max 48
Malta 30
Mammoth bones 8, 22, *23*
Manchan, Saint 137
Mangcheng 83
*Manual of Discipline, The* 52
Mao, Chairman 77
Marcellus, Theatre of 117
Marine archaeology 169, 183
Marshall, Sir John 55
Martin's Hundred 152
Martyrdom 137
*Mary Rose* 9, 172, 1 73
Masada 53
Mask of Agememnon 99
Mauch, Karl 132, *133*, 140
Mayans 6, 144, 156, *157*, 163
Mayer, Luigi *175*
McKee, Alexander 172
Mediterranean 50, 100, 170
Megalithic art 31
Memphis 174
Merlin the Magician 28
Merv 55, 85
Mesa Verde 9, 154
Mesolithic Age 6
Mesopotamia 45, 47–48, 55, 77
Metalworking 178
Mexico 151, 156, 158
Mezherich 22
Microfilm 53
Middle Ages 6
Middle East 6, 43, 48, 54, 128
Middle East peace process 113
Minerva 120, *120*
Minoan civilization 6, 92, 99, *100*
Minos, King 100
Minotaur 100
*Mir* spacecraft 169
Mirrors 86
Missionary pot 179
Mistletoe 39
Moche culture 161, *161*, 164
Moctezuma, Prof Matos 158
Modern Ages 6, 167
Mohenjo-Daro 8, 54, *55*
*Mona Lisa* 28
Mongol Yuan empire 85

Monk Mound 148
Monte Pellegrino 16
Montezuma 159
*Monument Celtiques* 32
Morlot, Dr Alphonse 170, 173
Moscow 97
Moses 69
Mouhot, Henri 90
Moundbuilders 143, 148, 151
Moundville 151
Mourne, Mountains of 137
Muhammad 6
Mummified bodies 40, 58, *60*, 63, 65, 69, 72, 154, 164, 180
Mummy portraits 7, 8, 73, *73*
*Murder in Mesopotamia* 48
Mussolini, Benito 170
Mycenae 6, 9, 98, 99, 100–101, 105, 107, 171

Nabateans 113, *113*
Nabonidus, King 6, 11, 48
*National Geographic magazine* 142
Najombolmi 18
Naples, King and Queen of 110, 118
Napoleon 32, 58, 60, 103
Napoleonic wars 179
NASA 91
Nasca Lines 150
Navajo Indians 154
Neave, Richard 73, 180
Nebuchadnezzar, King *45*, 46
Nefertari, Queen 68
Nefertiti 171
Nehemiah 134
Nelson, Lord 60, 110, 111
Nemi, Lake 170
Neolithic Age 6, 26, 30, 36
Nero 107, 117
New Age travelers 24, *31*
"New Archaeology" 145
New Testament 134
Newdigate Prize 112
Newfoundland 6, 146, *146*
Newgrange 6, 8, 30, *31*, 128, 148
Nile Valley 6, 66
Nile, River 58, 66, 70
Nileboat 169
Nimrud 46, 128
Nineveh 8, *43*, 45–47, 94, *47*, 128
*Nineveh and its Remains* 46, 47, 94, 180
Nintoku, Emperor 86
Noah's Ark 127–128, 140, *140*, 141
Norman castle 128

North Africa 122
North America 6, 145
North American lndians 133, 145, 149, 151
Nowa Stupia Ironworks 176, *176*
Nubia 66, 68
Nuremberg Bible *128*
Nutcracker Man 20–21, *21*

O'Connor, Frank 137
O'Kelly Prof. M. J. 31
Objects of archaeology *95*
Ogham script 137
Ohman, Olof 144
Old Persian texts 45
Old Testament *52*, 69, 126, 134, 140
Olduvai Gorge 8, 20, 21
Olmecs 145, 163
Olympia 103
Ommayad 134
*On the Origin of Species* 11, *11*, 14, 148, 185
Ophir 133, 140
Oppert, Jules 47
Oracle of Delphi *107*
Orkney Islands 30, 34, 145
Osaka 86
Otsukayama Kofun 86
Ottoman Empire 46, 112
"Out of Africa" theory 18, 181
Oxford University *15*, 30, *48*, 100
Ozymandias 68, *69*

Pacal the Great 156
Pagan horse gods 139
Pakistan 54
Paleolithic Age 6, 17–18
Palestine 129
Palestine Exploration Fund 128, 134
Pantheon 116
Paper Museum 117
Papyri, Villa of the 119
Paris 103
Paris Universal Exposition 17
Parnassus, Mount 106
Parthenon 94, 102, 176
Parthenon Marbles 94, 102, 170
Patagonian Sampson (see Belzoni, G.)
Patrick, Saint 128
Pausanius 99
Pazyryk 39
Peabody Museum 154
Peking Man 77
Peloponnesian War 105
Peloponnesus 170

Pendlebury, J. D. S. 101
Pennsylvania Museum, University of 170
Pergau Dam 67
Persepolis 47
Persia 45, 85
Persians 106
Perthes, Jacques Boucher de Crévecoeur de 14–15
Perticarari, Luigi 114–115
Peru 144, 150, 161, 163
"Pete Marsh" 38, *39*
Peter the Great 178
Petra 9, 112
Petrie, Flinders 73
Pharaohs 56, 62, 68–69, 71–72, 133, 138, 174
Pharisees 53
Pharos Lighthouse 175, *175*
Philadelphia, Museum of 48
Philae, Island of 67
Philip of Macedonia 73, 175, 180
Philistines 53
Phnom Penh 91
Phoenicians 133, 157
Picts 124
Pidoplichko, Ivan 22
Piranesi 116–117, *117*
Pitt-Rivers, Gen. Sir Augustus 94, 180
Pius, Antonmus 124
Plagues of Egypt 69
Plancus, L. Munatius 117
Plato 105
Plimer, Prof. Ian 141
Pliny, The Elder & Younger 118
Pocahontas 152
Poidebard, Père André 170
Pol Pot 90
Poland 22, 176
Pollux 116
Polo, Marco 85, *85*
Polosmak, Natalya 39
Pompeii 6, 118, 183
Pompey 116
Portland Vase 110, 111
Portsmouth 172
Portuguese 133
Potassium argon dating 20
Powell, John Wesley 151
Powhatan Indiams 152
Pozo, Cassiano dal 117
P.P.N.A. people 131
Prag, John 73, 180
Prehistoric artwork 17–18
Preseli Mountams 28
Priam's palace 96
Ptolemies 174
Public baths 105, 120, *121*, 123

Pudens, Gaius Flavis 123
Pueblo Bonito 155
Pueblo Indian villages 184
Punt, Queen of 71
Pushkin State Museum 97
Pyramids 6, 156–161, 177
Pythia 106–107, *107*

Qilakitsoq 40
Qin 77
Quechua language 163
Qumran cave *52*

Ramses 68, *68*
Ramses II 8, 66, *67*, 68, *69*
Raphael *104*, 105, 117
Rashid 58
Rathje, Prof Wm 169
Rawlinson, Col. Sir Henry 44, 45, 46, 48
Reck, Hans 20
Regent, Prince 103
Reinhard, Johan 164
Renaissance, The 11, 73, 77, 107, 110, 116–117, 161
Rescue archaeology 183
Resurrection, The 139
Rhodes, Cecil 133
Rich, Claudius James 47
Roberts, Dr Allen 141
Roberts, Paul 73
Robien, Marquis de 32
Röchling, Carl 177
Rock art 8, 16, 18, *18*
Roman Africa *123*
Roman archaeology 110
Roman artefacts 30, 176
Roman citizens 72
Roman Empire 72
Roman forts *52*, 53
Roman Forum 1 16
Roman temples 29, 37, 120
Romans 37, 102, 1 14, 133
Rome 6, 103, *109*
Rosetta Stone 45, 58, 59, 60, 103, 138
Rouzie, Zacharie le 33
Royal Crescent, Bath 29
Rubbish dumps 166
Rudenko, Sergei 39
Rufus, Annobal 123

Russia 22
Saarland 177
Sabratha 123
Sahara Desert 124
Saint Cosmo's Big Toe festival 111
Salisbury Plain 28–29

Samarkand 85
Santa Cecilia Acatitlan *159*
Sarajevo 60
"Saritya" 164
Saturn, Temple of 117
Sautuola, Don Marcel Sanz de 17
Saxon sites 94
Saxons 37, 81
Scandinavia 14, 38
Scara Brae 8, 34, *34*, *35*, 145
Schliemann, Heinrich 18, *94*, *96*, *97*, *98*, *99*, *100*, 133
Sennacherib, King *44*. 46–47
Severin, Tim 137
Severus, Septimus 123
Shaman *16*
Shang bronzes 78
Shang Dynasty 6, 78
Sheba, Queen of 132–133, *133*, 140
Shelley, Percy 68, *69*
Sheng, Prince Liu 83
Shipwrecks *166*, 170
Shona people 133
Shrine of the Book 52
Siberia 39
Silk Road 55, 84, *85*
Simpson, Lt James Hervey 154
"Simultaneous Evolution" 181
Sinai *126*, 137
Sipan 9, 160
Sipan, Lord of 161
Skeletons 37, 149, 180
Skraelings 147
Skulls 14, 21, *21*, 131, 159
Smith, Capt. John 152, *153*
Smithsonian Institution 60, 144, 151, 154
Smoke Jaguar 157
Society of Antiquaries 60
Society of Antiquaries of London 117
Solomon 128, 132, 134
South Africa 17, 133
South America 144
Space Age 169
Spain 16
Spanish missionaries 156
Sphinx 60, 70, 107
Spon, Jacob 6, 184
Squire, Ephraim 151
St Julien fort 58
Standing stones 32, *33*, 183
Stanton Drew 8, *182*, 183
Stara Ironworks 176
Stephens, John Lloyd 144, 157
Stirling, Dr M. W. 144
Stockholm 172
Stone Ages 6, 11, 13, 16, 29, 34,

120
Stone tools *34*, 36
Stonehenge 6, 8, 11, *24*, 26, *28*, *29*, 31, 32, 133, 148, 183
*Stonehenge Restored* 26
Strabo 113
Stuccoes, Tomb of the 115
Stukeley, Wm 27, 29, *29*, 148
Suetonius 37
Suleiman the Magnificent 134
Sumer 47
Sumerians 6, 48, 77
Sutton Hoo ship *166*, 169
Sydney University 141
Syria 45, 51, *51*, 124, 171

Tacitus 118, 124
Tahuantinsuyu 163
Taipei 78
Taiwan 78
Taj Mahal 28, 177
Takla Makan Desert 85
Tang pottery 85
Tanzania *16*, 20
Tara 128
Tattoos 39, *40*, 41, 138
Tello, Julio C. 145
Temple Mound 134
Temple of the Sun 163
Templo Mayor *159*
Tenochtitlan 9, 158, *159*
Terracotta soldiers 7, 8, 75, 77, 80–81, *81*, 86, *86*
Texier, Charles Felix-Marie 50
Thailand 91
Theodosius, Emperor 107
Theoes 65
Tholos temple 107
Thom, Alexander 33
Thomas, Cyrus 151
Thomesen, Christian J. 11, 185
Thompson, Meredith 73
Throckmorton, Peter 170
Tigris river 46
*Times, The* 102
Titus 134
Titus, Arch of 116
Tiwanaku 145
Tlaloc 159
Tollund Man 8, 38, *39*, 165
Toltecs 145, 151, 159, 163
Tourists, problems of *101*, 113, 119
Trajan's Column 6, 117
Trajan, Temple of 67
Treaty of Versailles 177
Trevithick, Richard 179
Trinity College, Dublin 14
Trojan War 96

Troy 9, 18, 94, 96, 96, 98
Tullius, Flavius 123
Turkana Boy 21
Turkana, Lake 21
Turkey 50, 51, 96–97, 102, *131*, 170
Turner J. M. W. 29
Turner, Maj. Gen. Tomkyn 60
Tutankhamen 8, 38, 62, 63, 71, 161, 170
Tyrol 39

Ukok 39
Ukraine 22
Ulu Burun shipwreck 7, 170
Underwater archaeology 167, 170, 1 71
U.N.E.S.C.O. 30, 66–67, 177
Ur 8, 48, *48*, 128
Ussher, Archbishop James 11, *14*

Valley of the Kings 62, 65, 69, 71
*Vasa* 9, 172, *172*
Vatican *104*, 115, 117
Veii 115
Venerable Bede 124
Venice 85
Ventris, Michael 101
*Venus de Medici* 103
Vereluis, Olof 6
Vergina 73, 175
Vesuvius, Mount 6, 118
Vikings 6, 34, 145, 146, *146*, 147, 151, 157
Villacamba 163
Vinci, Leonardo da 105
Vindolanda 125
Vinland 146, 147
Virginia Archaeology Service 153
Virgin Mary 135
Volcanal, Altar of 117
Volklingen Ironworks 9, *177*

Wainwright, Geoffrey 183
Wallace, Birgitta 147
Wan, Princess Dou 83, 83
Warren, Capt. Charles 128, 134
Wedgwood, Josiah 110, *111*
Weeks, Prof Kent 68
Wei, Emperor 87
Wetherill, Richard 154
Wheeler, Mortimer 36–37, 39, 48, 54–55, 94, 116, 185
Wilcox A. R. 17
Wilde, Oscar 30
Wilde, Sir Wm 30
William of Orange 128
Williamsburg 152
Williamsburg, Col. 152

Winchester Cathedral 110
Wincklemann J. J. 6, 111, 119
Winckler, Hugo 50
Wolvcscy, palace of 110
Wood henge *182*
Wooley, Leonard 7, 48, 48
World Heritage Council 67
World Heritage Sites 30, 67, 90, 133, 146, 157, 177, 178, 183
World War I 29, 48, *48*, 177
World War II 16, 33, 97
Wright, Wm 51
Written language 16, 43–45, 47–50, 55
Wudi, Emperor 85

Xerxes, King 106
Xianyang 81, 85

Yamato 86
Yangtze river 84
Yellow River Dam 66
Yn, Prince Liu 83
Young, Thomas 58

Zhou kingdom 81
Zimbabwe 132
Zinjanthropus Boisei *21*
Zoe, Marcia 117
Zurich, Lake 170

# PHOTOGRAPHIC ACKNOWLEDGEMENTS

The publishers would like to thank the following organizations and individuals for their kind permission to reproduce the photographs in this book:

**Robert Aberman** 132
**AKG, London** 6 right, 12-13, 17, 47, 60, 107, 117, 133, 138, 141, 153/Henning Bock 19, 91/British Museum 59/Erich Lessing 36, 126-127, 131/Musee du Louvre, Paris/Erich Lessing 114/Museo Archeologico Nazionale, Tarquinia 115/National Archaeological Museum, Athens 98/National Museum of Peking/Erich Lessing 79, 83
**Ancient Art and Architecture Collection**/Leslie Ellison 38/Ronald Sheridan 39, 61
**Muzeum Archeologiczne, Krakow, Poland**/Kazimierz Bielenin 176
**Bridgeman Art Library**/Bibliotheque Nationale, Paris/Giraudon 130/British Library, London 84, 135/British Museum, London 7 left, 44, 49, 72, 102, 111, 168/Chateau Ecouen, Paris/Giraudon 140 /City of Bristol Museum & Art Gallery, Avon 149/Bernard Cox 68/Corpus Christi College, Oxford 15 /Egyptian National Museum, Cairo/Giraudon 69 /Leptis Magna, Libya 123/The Marsden Archive, UK 27/Antony Miles, Ltd., Salisbury, Wiltshire 28/National Museum of India, New Delhi 54 /Private Collection 129/Stapleton Collection, UK 29, 139/Vatican Museums & Galleries, Vatican City, Rome 104 /Villa dei Misteri, Pompeii 119
**The Trustees of The British Museum**/The Sutton Hoo Archive 169
**Corbis UK Ltd**/Yann Arthus-Bertrand 96/Bettman 11, 124 147/Jonathan Blair 166, 171/Jan Butchofsky 121/Macduff Everton 172/Richard Hamilton Smith 145/Historical Picture Archive 174-175/Dave G. Houser 136/Hulton-Getty Collection 37, 48, 94, 100 left, 173/Library of Congress 117/Richard T. Nowitz 52 /Diego Lezama Orezzoli 55/Gianni Dagli Orti 2, 3-4, 30, 42, 50, 51, 64, 100 right, 101, 174/Greg Probst 146/Carmen Redondo 177/Sakamoto Photo Research Laboratory 86/Kevin Schafer 92-93, 160 /Roman Soumar 152/UPI 20, 21 right, 144/Adam Woolfitt 6 left, 31, 34, 120/Roger Wood 122
**Duchas/The Heritage Service, Ireland**/Con Brogan 10
**English Heritage** 178/Artist: Peter Dunn 182-183
**Hulton Getty Picture Collection** 14, 26, 33, 45, 46, 53, 62, 66, 95, 97, 99, 110, 170
**Phyllis Jackson** 181 top, 181 bottom left, 181 bottom right
**N.J. Saunders** 156, 158, 163
**Frank Spooner Pictures**/Gamma 82
**Tony Stone Images**/Glen Allison 74, 90/Christopher Arnesen 7 right/David Austen 70-71/Oliver Benn 125/Michael Braid 56-57/Andy Chadwick title, 112/Joe Cornish 32-33/D.E. Cox 76/Jeremy Horner 162/John Lamb 67/Mike McQueen 70 /David Paterson 113 /Jean Pragen 116/Ed Simpson 142-143/A & L Sinibaldi 108/Hugh Sitton 24-25/Keren Su 80-81 /Charlie Waite 106
**Telegraph Colour Library**/Masterfile/Courtney Milne 150
**Topham Picturepoint** 22-23 /Associated Press 165
**Werner Forman Archive** 35, 85, 88, 89, 118, 154, 155, 159/Henning Bock endpapers/British Museum, London 103/Egyptian Museum, Cairo 63/Field Museum of Natural History, Chicago 151 /The Greenland Museum 40, 41/Collection: Edward H. Merrin Gallery, New York half title/Museum fur Volkerkunde, Berlin 157/Ono Collection, Osaka 87/ Tanzania National Museum Dar es Salaam arlin, 16, 21 left

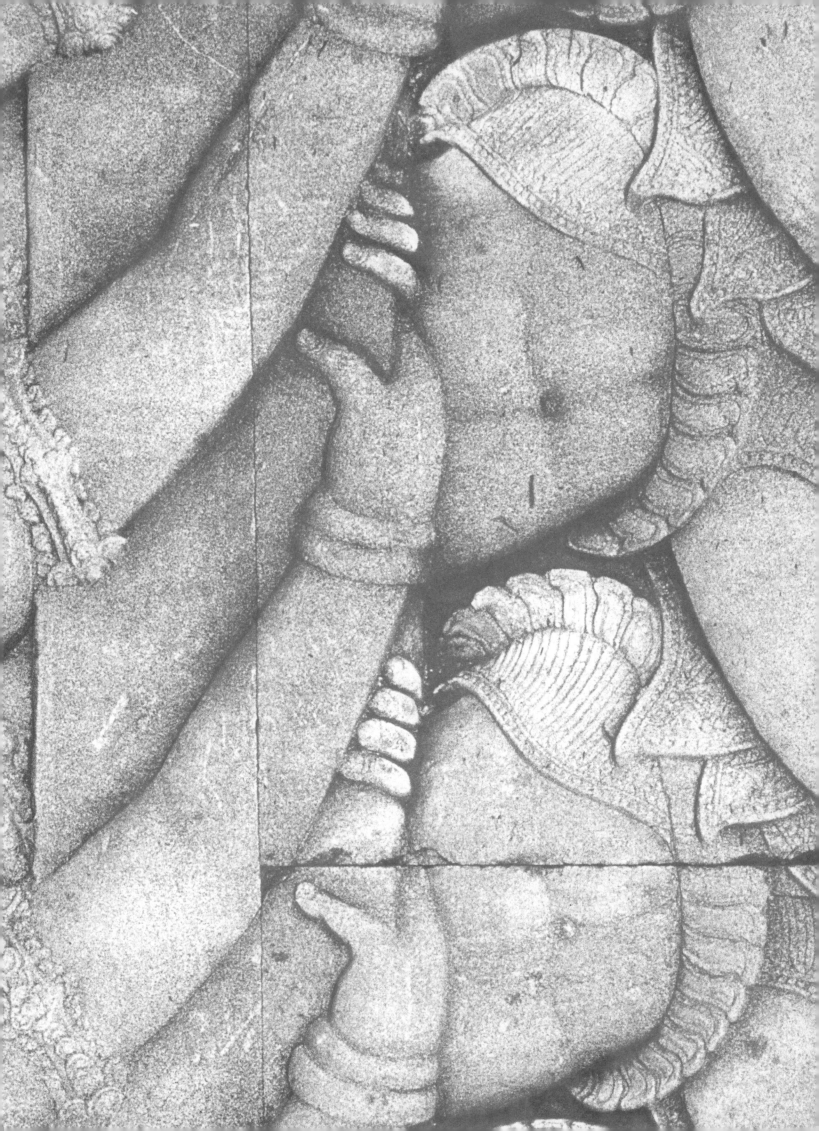